"This concise yet profound dive into the world of digital disruptions reveals how glitches echo deeper meanings, challenging our perceptions of digital flaws as artistic expressions. A compelling read for artists and digital enthusiasts alike."
—Dawnia Darkstone, Glitch Artist and Curator

◎

"What we see as mistakes or errors are much more than that, they can be a way to express something unique. Betancourt's writing is an exquisite tour de force. By delving into the complexities, uncertainties, past, and future of glitches and their relationship with semiotics and media, this book offers artists, enthusiasts, and academics new perspectives and insights. Whether you're after an ontological perspective or the in-depth analysis of glitches through the lens of semiotics, this is a book you should dip into. Its rich reference packed pages provide an in-depth and current exploration of the aesthetic, technical, and philosophical dimensions of Glitch Art, while emphasizing its significance in contemporary visual culture. It's the book I wish I had 20 years ago."
—Shay Moradi, Glitch Theorist and Curator

◎

"Glitch Theory is an essential text for understanding the exciting art movement widely practiced online, and increasingly offline, known as Glitch Art. This book documents the ideas behind these beautiful digital manipulations, and their evolving dance with encoded annihilation. What the reader will encounter is a dynamic and in-depth study of visual noise, electronically hallucinated with intentional/accidental malfunctions."
—Michael Jacobson, Publisher at the *Post-Asemic Press*

"As one of the pioneers of this niche medium, Betancourt
goes through the deeply buried history from analog to digital
of Glitch Art with precision. The alchemy of turning as-error
into as-not/error: embracing the ephemeral, glitch artists are
exposing the artifice of a polished house of cards, putting into
question and creating a metaphysics from our relationship
with electronic devices. He ushers mythology, literature and
linguistics while peeling the paradoxical relation of how
glitches turn into intentional methodologies of creation. The
essential connection of the ghost in the machine inevitably
will keep accompanying us long into the future."
—Uğur Engin Deniz, Glitch Artist

◎

"Assuming that art would disappear from the Earth
and would have to be decoded from the luckily surviving
Glitch Art, Michael Betancourt's glitch semiosis would be
the theoretical manual with which this reconstruction could
succeed. Betancourt once again presents a new standard work,
exciting to read for anyone who wants to seriously engage
with the theory development within Glitch Art.

As an artist, critical theorist researcher, and cultural historian,
Betancourt has been closely associated with the Glitch Movement
since the 1990s. In the area of tension between Digital Theory and
Criticism of Capitalism, Betancourt created a Theory of Discursive
Digitality in 2016 with the text *The Critique of Digital Capitalism:
An Analysis of Political Economy of Digital Culture and Technology*.
The new publication can be understood as an attempt at Digital
Aesthetics in the Post–NFT Era. It implements itself as a subversive
stabilizer: in the theoretical foundation of a Glitch Philosophy,
which also prepares the audience for an art historical
and curatorial reassessment of this art movement."
—Verena Voigt M.A., Art Historian, Investigative Curator, Potsdam

GLITCH THEORY:
ART AND SEMIOTICS

MICHAEL BETANCOURT

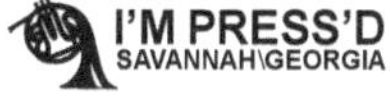

**Published by I'm Press'd
an imprint of Cinegraphic Media
www.impressd.net**

ISBN 978-0-9793215-5-9
FIRST PUBLISHED IN 2023
WITH PEER REVIEW

This analysis expands on previously published research:

Cinematic Articulation in Motion Graphics (New York: Routledge, 2022).

The Critique of Digital Capitalism (Brooklyn: Punctum Books, 2016).

"Discursive Aesthetics" *Research Art: glitches, poetics, typography and the aura of the digital* (I'm Press'd, 2021) pp. 41-53.

"Found Objects, Generative Footage, and Machinima: Peggy Ahwesh's *She Puppet* (2001)" *Found Footage Magazine*, no. 6 (2020) pp. 76-83.

Glitch Art in Theory and Practice: Critical Failures and Post-Digital Aesthetics (New York: Routledge, 2016).

"Glitched Media as Found / Transformed Footage: Post-Digitality in Takeshi Murata's *Monster Movie* (2005)" *Found Footage Magazine*, no. 3 (2017) pp. 48-57.

"The 'Intentional Function' in Still and Moving Photographic Images" *Semiotica: Journal of the International Association for Semiotic Studies*, vol. 246 (2022).

"The Invention of Glitch Video: *Digital TV Dinner* (1978)" *Millennium Film Journal*, no. 65 (Spring, 2017) pp. 54-63.

"The 'Material Function' in Cinema: Resolving the Paradox of the Glitch" *Semiotica: Journal of the International Association for Semiotic Studies*, no. 236-237, (2020) pp. 251-273.

"Stan VanDerBeek's Danse Macabre: Found sound, appropriated music, and rehearing" *Found Footage Magazine*, no. 8 (2022) pp. 64-72.

"Technesthesia and Synaesthesia" *Vague Terrain* (January, 2009), np.

"Visual Music and Abstraction: From Avant-Garde Synaesthesia to Digital Technesthesia" *Iconology of Abstraction: Non-Figurative Images and the Modern World (Advances in Art and Visual Studies)*, ed. Krešimir Purgar (Routledge, 2020) pp. 143-159.

CONTENTS

Glitches and Glitch Art provide insights into semiotics and interpretation by disrupting expectations, allowing a consideration of the initial sign formation process, while complicating binary oppositions and fixed interpretive schemas. Glitches reveal the contingency of meaning, and their use in Glitch Art is of interest to this examination because it challenges notions of authorial intent by problematizing distinctions between the symbolic meaning and diagnostic recognition of technical breakdowns. Their ambivalence defines liminal moments of unstable order. Shifts between these modes demonstrate mobile articulation. However, the apparent "paradox" of interpreting glitches as both errors and expressions reflects superposition between signal (meaning) and noise (irrelevance). Approaching glitches via semiotics highlights these ambivalences, allowing them to reveal interpretive processes through transitive shifts between distinct perceptual/interpretive modes.

Glitch Art reveals the role of the 'intentional function' in transforming perceptual cues into intentionality, expertise, and interpretation. Diagnostic and symbolic modes are parallel but incompatible. The paradox of Glitch Art exploits this shift between modes, revealing that the category assignment *as-expressive* starts with differentiating signal::noise. Imposing order on ambiguity is an autonomous, unconscious choice that determines and precedes the ordering of semiosis. The articulation of poesis exploits this initial ambiguity, unfixing meanings. The example of indistinguishable artworks is instructive in considering this modal shift since it demonstrates how past experience and established fluency mediate significance.

The 'material function' parallels lexical meaning, addressing the materiality of digital media as a semantic function that can shift into being expressive signification. Glitch Art arises from how this semiosis problematizes distinctions between actual technical failures, recordings of failures, and artificial simulations where shifts between diagnostic (*mal*function) and symbolic (*mis*function) modes depends on the viewer. The imposition of an 'intentional function' mediated by technical fluency demonstrates how digital and analog media have fundamentally different materialities due to a separation of media-object and media carrier in digital works that is impossible for traditional media. The aura of the digital descends from this technological difference to idealize the immaterial realm of digital code, devaluing the physical output in favor of a hypothetically perfect digital file (data): this emphasis on the immaterial data file renders its physical manifestations as merely flawed copies. Glitches foreground and disrupt this transcendence, revealing how the apparent paradox of "intentional glitches" highlights the entanglement of human agency with machine function, allowing Glitch Art to be both 'error' and the 'representation of error' simultaneously.

'Ontological exhaustion' critiques Modernist and transcendental ideologies for glitches by demonstrating how a semiotic, contextual approach to them challenges both medium specificity and Formalist "purity." This recognition unveils a 'diagnostic fallacy' in the conception, theorization, and interpretation of technical failures that treats glitches as indexicals linked to specifically proximate physical causes. However, because glitches also represent failure, their expressive articulation forces the diagnostic and symbolic modes to diverge. Glitch Art reveals semiotic and semantic processes rather than guaranteeing an inherent, interpretive criticality: their disruptiveness depends on context, not formal essence, returning questions of a political and engaged expression to issues of expressive content and audience expectation.

The avant-garde tradition of synaesthetic abstraction (whose iconography links sound, color, and spiritual ideas to the 'synaesthetic form constants' identified by German psychologist Heinrich Klüver in the 1930s) is apparent in visual glitches. These connections demonstrate the continuity of a specific aesthetic lineage whose morphology and structure links the embrace of errors, *mal*functions, and technical failures to broader cultural tendencies that shape the expressive uses and understanding of digital technology. Acknowledging this on-going concern with visualizing an unseen, transcendent reality transforms the alienating effects of digital, generative media into part of an established tradition.

Cultural fluency and past experience shape interpretation by displacing the immanent encounter through a 'pseudo-diagnostic' recognition, a doppelgänger, derived from past experience. Digital media enable this process of endless recombinancy that emerges through a 'discursive aesthetic' which mobilizes quotations and ideals of digital transcendence to displace direct experience because all recognitions of glitch implies an absent, unglitched source whose role in the semiosis of Glitch Art highlights the constructive role of culture and memory as determinants of apperception. The critical potential of glitches and Glitch Art are always already constrained by this implicit ideology.

Ramifications of the use of glitches and Glitch Art to examine the articulation of meaning from perception: semiotics provides a useful model for glitches and Glitch Art, but has limitations since these works are neither linguistic nor lexical. Glitches reveal the hidden perceptual processes of interpretation and meaning-making, and challenge dialectical oppositions by demonstrating the limitations of binary digital logic. Although Glitch Art continues the avant-garde lineage of using technology to express metaphysical or transcendent content, as glitch aesthetics become an increasingly familiar expressive element, they become a conventional gesture of 'authenticity' in digital art.

GLITCH THEORY:
ART AND SEMIOTICS

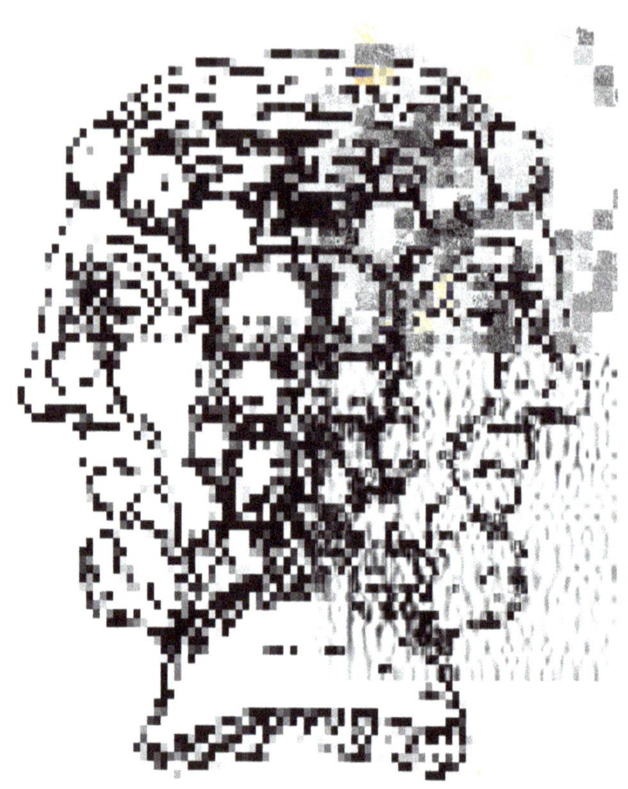

Frontis

Michael Betancourt, *Digital Janus* (2022).
Copyright © 2022 by Michael Betancourt / courtesy Artists' Rights Society (ARS).

1

INTRODUCTION

This book is not about human agency, intentions, movies, or art even if they all play a role in what follows. It is the direct product of more than thirty years of research into using, making, and engaging glitches in/as art. My first encounters with digital glitches were in popular media during the 1980s, so in 1990, when a NewTek *Video Toaster* glitched while I was processing an analogue video tape I immediately realized its flickering digital output (the glitches) was redolent with potential. The pursuit and tangential exploration around glitches has been a consistent background concern throughout all my work: interesting things happen at the margins, and glitches are one of the most self-evident liminal points confronting digital technology and its roles in art.

This book is a synthesis drawing together two very different strands of my theoretical work, but remains empirically informed by studio practice and considerations of existing art made by an international community of Glitch Artists who all employ these artifacts expressively. The first strand involves semiotic theory and is concerned with questions of mobile articulation in cinema; the second addresses interpretive questions that can only be asked at the margins, where what appear to be stable distinctions breakdown. This study uses semiotic theory—and although it is still concerned with the semiosphere, that realm of meaning—this choice was pragmatic because it provides a readymade jargon and scaffold for describing interpretive process and audience-dependent constructions. What liminal phenomena such as glitches offer to semic analysis are revelations of the sign formation process that imposes order and then recursively produces meaning. For experiential works, such as Glitch Art, syntagmatics are not a given, but a product of enculturation, expectation, and desire shaping engagement: familiar concepts such as 'intentionality' and 'signification' become contingent upon the audience's fluency and unintentional, autonomous apperceptions of the work—there is no such category as a "semiotic glitch"—glitches are all explainable through semiotics, or none are. This dynamic approach to semiosis provides the foundation for a discursive analysis whose premise is that perception and its initial evaluation of audio-visual sensory phenomena is determinative of all higher level interpretations, including the metaphysical claims around the *poesis* of Art. It is a view that renders articulation mobile and variable, rather than an *a priori* fact. The status and meaning of the liminal moments of articulation—such as glitches where the established and familiar become unstable—that bring these ambivalences into consciousness are the focus of this analysis.

At the same time, this semiotic model challenges assumptions about the ontology of media productions (as well as glitches) via any diagnostic consideration that treats the appearance of what seem to be errors, breakdowns, or *mal*functions as an indexical proof of the technical apparatus and/or its machinic operations ('the real'); this understanding of glitches as a reflexive materiality descends from the lineage of photography and has specific parallels in the realist film theories of André Bazin, Siegfried Kracauer, and Stanley Cavell.[1] In contrast, my analysis, following my earlier writing on this issue, conceives *all* ontological beliefs that shape, direct, or even constrain interpretations as cultural constructs, even though this ontological factor continually reappears as a reference point that requires clarification—it is the most evident aspect of Modernist aesthetics that continues to impact contemporary analyses (via vernacular beliefs).

These non-lexical (variable and perceptual) semiotics continue in the spirit of Eero Tarasti's earlier non-lexical musical semiotics, and borrow from the modal approach developed by A. J. Greimas,[2] to argue that any approach to glitches and Glitch Art can be addressed via a procedural semantics that converges on those of cinema and visual art in a larger continuum of signification, the semiosphere, apparent as the state of information.[3] Central to this approach is my earlier proposal of cinematic signs as instances of what Umberto Eco described as "independent signification," signs whose mobile articulations change identity and role at different levels of analysis, and that "are not parts of the content that the hyper-unit conveys."[4] Instead of fixed lexicality, informal "rules of engagement" guide audiences to determine *when* and *how* it is appropriate to interpret a glitch *as-if* it is encoded.[5] What is of particular interest in examining glitches semiotically is their reliance on non-signifying, semantic cues identifying "intentionality" in media. These non-signifiers are not directly chosen, but are instead technical features of the medium, predetermined aspects of the machine and its functioning; in the case of photography and the camera, they are all built-in to the system— immanent in the shape of the photograph, its color range, depth of field, sharpness of focus, etc.—while for digital systems these features become plastic and easily changed, they remain implicit reference points for evaluation. Their typical invisibility becomes apparent as the constants informing and enabling technical media articulations via the "plastic intelligence" gleaned from past experience that also allows the recognitions essential to the immanent identification of glitches.[6] This liminal status offers insights into the sign formation process and the role of the 'intentional function' in authorizing the expressive engagements that glitches render problematic: what would normally be an irreversible identification that produces the 'image seen' prior to any encoded meaning becomes a contingent assertion of a semic order that is always in doubt.[7]

Glitch Art creates a challenge to the teleological justification of interpretations by the "gignomenological law of identity"[8] through this unstable assertion of semic order. Where traditional semiotics concerns those enunciations and articulations whose interpretations are encoded *a priori* to their arrangement and modulation, the instability created by glitches forces a reckoning with those initial apperceptions that guide addressing it diagnostically or symbolically, throwing these foundations into superposition. The resolution of ambiguity requires a continual shifting between distinct (but related) modes of interpretation that organize the subjective transformation of a phenomenal encounter into coherence.

No technical media requires special skills, knowledge, or expertise to become coherent, but they do offer the potential for unexpected and unanticipated results that bring the audience's existing knowledge, expectations, and desires into the sign formation process. Eco's "mobile articulation" is essential to this semiosis of transient and unstable apperceptions precisely because it separates the sign from the 'sign function.'[9] Glitches reveal the mediating effect of the 'intentional function' for transiting between modes by bringing the role of assumed intentions in the identification of encoding into consciousness as an imposed order that is distinct from the semiosis it enables. The cultural entanglement that defines even the diagnostic consideration of media's denoted contents begins with assumptions about interpretation, production, and expression based on an intent to communicate (i.e. encoding) whose degrees of freedom are revealed by the autonomous operations invoked by identifying something *as-glitched*. Any "encoded meaning" begins with an examination for these empirically present semantic cues which are evidence for a residue of past intentional actions—the 'intentional function'—that justifies the *as-if* consideration and begins the sign formation process, expressive articulation, and interpretation of encoding. The 'intentional function' identifies those assumptions by the audience that organize specific formal, but individually non-signifying cues in the media work that together act to signify it is 'intentionally encoded.'[10]

Glitch Art, and even glitches in general, problematize and reveal the contingencies of this process. This disruptive potential remains apparent, even when their expressive role in a work is unquestionable or immediately obvious. Because they require a constant shifting between a diagnostic mode where the glitch acts to identify the machine's autonomous operations, and a parallel, converging, and coincident symbolic articulation where that autonomous action becomes a source of expressive meaning (thus cultural encoding), this redoubling of apperception creates superficial paradoxes since all these semic orderings are typically held as separate, independent modes—a separation that glitches reveal is a fallacy.

The discursive approach employed in this book is equally historically structured and theoretically focused. It provides a clarifying consolidation of my previously published theoretical work with glitches and Glitch Art that falls tangentially across a range of subject areas and fields, but is neither a general survey of disparate approaches to "glitch theory," nor is it attempting to be one. While it adopts a conceptual foundation in semiotics, it is empirically biased to propositions that are directly observable in an attempt to illuminate and produce generalized principles to consider a semiotics that is neither Peircian nor Saussurean, but instead engages glitches through the mobile articulation suggested by Umberto Eco in *A Theory of Semiotics*.[11] His analysis prompted the conceit that the audience's active engagement with their perceptions is a moving foundation where the nuances of what are commonly called "errors" and their capacity to inform our interpretations of technical media depends on the act that understands them *as-if* they were vehicles of symbolic meaning.[12] A post-structural critical and historical substructure shapes the new aesthetics made possible by digital technology, manifest in the emergence of a genre of digital art known as "Glitch Art"[13] that develops from artists embracing the flaws and unexpected artifacts generated by digital machines.[14] The protean expansion of glitch aesthetics into liminal, marginal, and conflicted domains beyond its technical origins within computer systems is a reflection of /glitch/ and Glitch Art's capacity to trouble nominally stable and fixed positions. This analysis explores the semic ramifications attached to that categorical and interpretive instability.

1.1 Definitions

Glitches and Glitch Art belong to a lineage of technical media[15] that emerged in the nineteenth century to reveal that questions which might seem obvious about art and aesthetics are instead problematic, transient expressions of a conflicted and paradoxical order. The development of digital computers has returned the role and acceptance of machines in art making to prominence as technical innovations such as AI bring the role of human agency back to the fore. These same problematics of authorial intent were

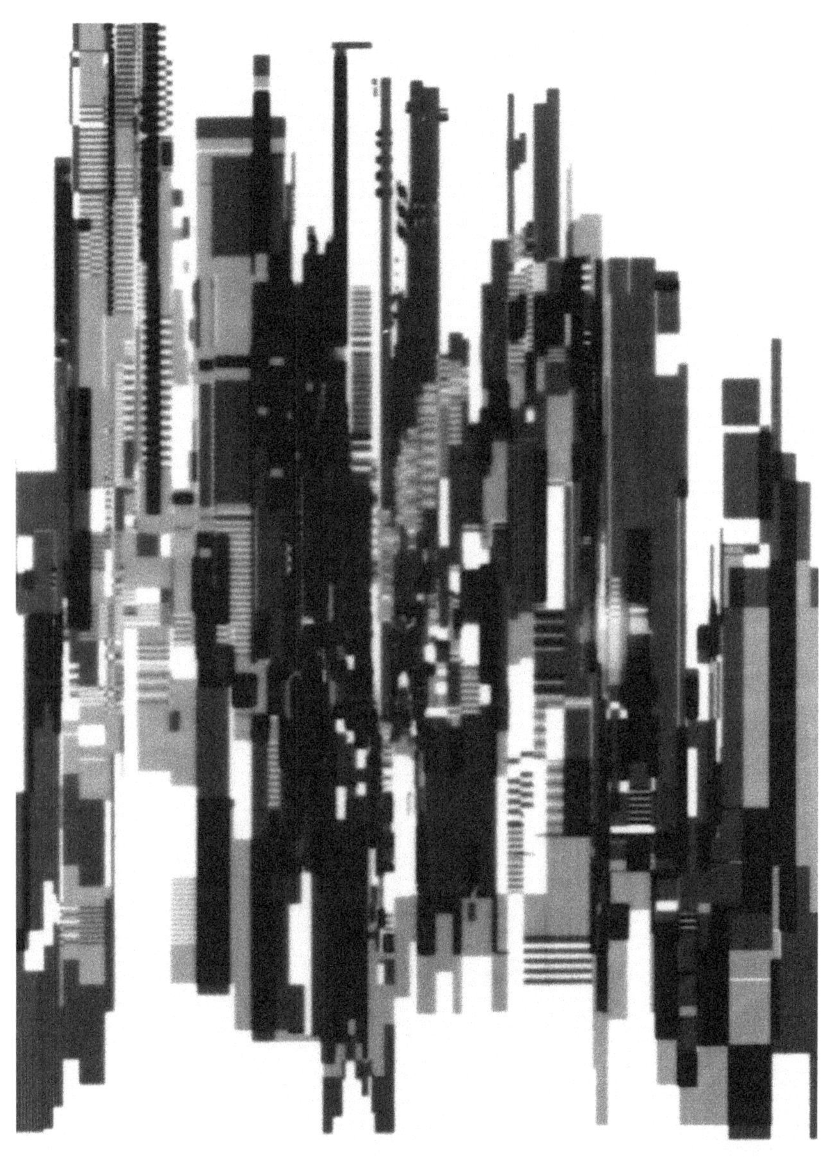

1.1a   Glitch Art: Ant Scott, *Skyscrapers Redux* (2021), photogram on Ilford RC
       paper created with a digital computer monitor, 7x5 inches,
       used with permission.

a critical-theoretical focus in the 1950s and 1960s, evident in both the readerly aesthetics of the "open text" movement,[16] and the "institutional theory" of art,[17] each of which shifted the *locus vivendi* of analysis from artistic/authorial intentions (and innate meanings) to the metastable realm of enculturation, interpretation, and context. This analysis is *not* an argument either for or against Formalist, Modernist, or Object-Oriented Ontological formations in discussions of glitch: the role of these established and now historical proposals is to provide reference points for making distinctions more explicit and clarifying the analytic.

1.2 Transitive Media

The first discursive question is precisely categorical: is it appropriate to understand Glitch Art as a movement, a specific aesthetic protocol, or the recuperation of technical flaws, failures, and breakdowns—*and to what extent is it all three?* [Figure 1.1a] This issue is closely related to definitions of /glitch/ since Glitch Art and glitches are often conflated, equated, confused. While Glitch Art can correspond to all of these things, it is both *less* and *more* than what each of these descriptions implies, as its historical development does not provide concise answers: the first artistic uses of digital glitches appeared in the 1970s in the context of synaesthetic video art performances in Chicago [Figure 1.1b],[18] but this origin does not constrain or delimit later developments[19] with the expressive use of computational errors rendered as the machine translates coded instructions into a human-readable presentation.[20] Accepting electronic and digital "errors" as materialist expressions of the digital medium[21] defined Glitch Art[22] during the 1990s as an aesthetic response to the encoding errors common to digital playback and sampling in music, static imagery, and motion pictures that became commonplace features of new technology.[23] These multifaceted and complex ancestries mediate between the folk and vernacular familiarity of digital glitches, their aesthetic incorporation into actual artworks, and the legacy of the Modernist avant-garde, apparent in contemporary works [Figure 1.1c].[24]

However, recognizing glitches *as-expressive* immediately poses a problem for their conception *as-error*. The glitched datastream or digital file is not an example of *invalid* code—the "halt" in the expression "halt and catch fire" vividly explains the results of technical failure in early computers—but a demonstration of how mismatches and deviations from the expected norms of machine function are transitive, a relational matter of perception and cultural iconologies, *not* mechanical operations.[25] These disparate and contradictory tendencies converge in the ambiguity and ambivalence of the designation "glitch," whose problematics challenge precise

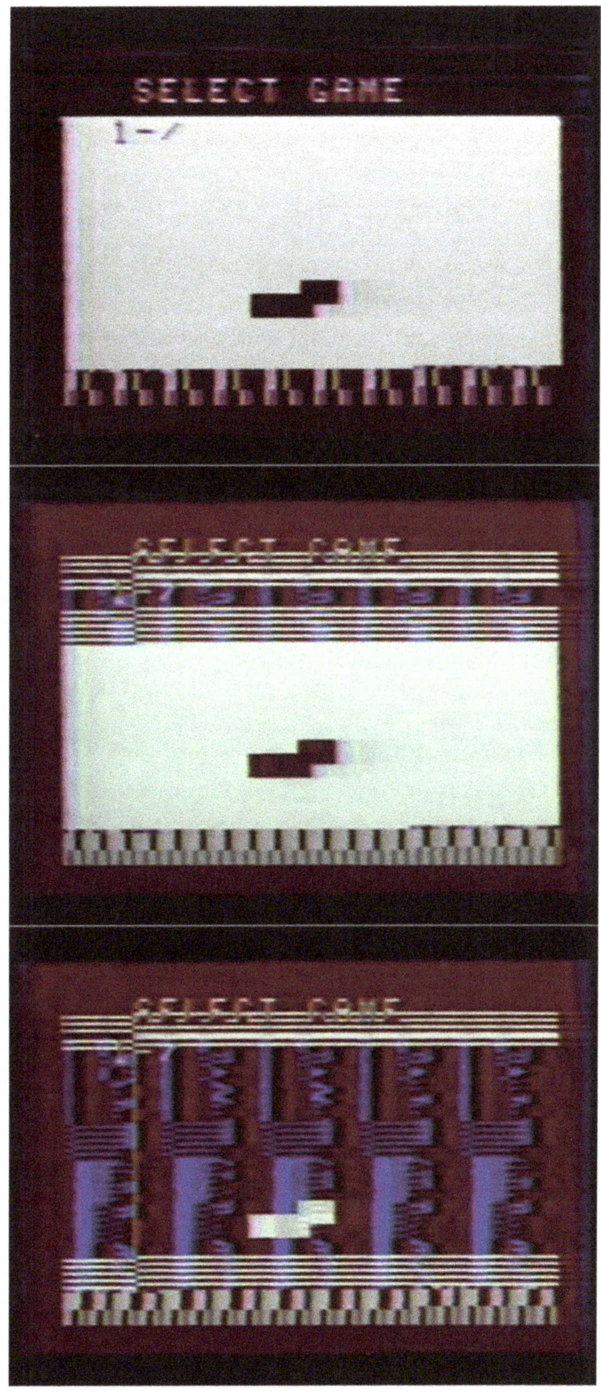

1.1b Glitch Art: Jamie Fenton, selected stills from the first digital glitch video, *Digital TV Dinner* (1978); produced by punching the video game console for the *Bally Astrocade: The Professional Arcade Expandable Computer System* so the game cartridge would pop out.

definitions, and which leads to its expansive and expanding application as a metaphor for all deviations and disruptions of expected or familiar interpretations and established orders.[26] This range of uses makes a semiotic consideration of glitches relevant and of general interest.

1.3 Technical Foundations

Glitches typically arise in digital facture performed by software whose instructions (the digital file) create an abundance of new works on demand, but the aura of the digital simultaneously hides the operations of the device which the emergence of a glitch can/may foreground, even if only momentarily,[27] because the glitch is often invisible: when viewing media that glitches the proximate assumption is that the problem is *local*—a transitory problem with the display, not a feature of the work—thus defining these disruptions as a *mal*function, an externality to ignore.[28] This relationship of physical presentation to the instrumental systems of its production creates an aura of information that elides how everything "inside" the computer exists as numerically encoded, fragmented (sampled) data, allowing the aura of the digital to define a fantasy where the digital system is a generative instrumentality divorced from the mechanisms of its operations.[29] Aside from "code poems," computer coding is typically instrumental, a foundation that enables diagnostic claims for the indexicality of glitches, and affirms the aura of information which asserts the data contained in the digital file (computer code) is interchangeable with the objects it renders for a human interpreter (i.e. reader/viewer/spectator/listener/audience). The impositions of normative 'transparency' concern the content communicated[30] and either erase the glitch as so much unintentional "noise" to ignore, or turn it into a symbolic 'material function' without the relationship to 'the real' that concerns diagnostic claims to indexicality. The technology of display establishes the apparently "natural" presentation of data as image, text, or sound. Simultaneously, Glitch Art is an aesthetic exploit incorporating these "errors" into signification protocols that do not necessarily develop the traditional model of art as a self-conscious production based on relationships to other art,[31] but relies instead on the audience's technical fluency with technology to shift from recognized breakdown into aesthetic apprehension.[32] However, the disruptions of function posed by the glitch are a reflection of the interpreter's own encultured ideologies,[33] always subject to ambivalence and paralogy.[34] Any symptomatic analysis of glitches as "technical failure" is a diagnosic re-articulation that tautologically justifies treating them as problems to eliminate. It highlights the elliptical role of the aura of the digital, evident in how the "average reader" ignores glitches as "noise"—an abyssal of non-signification.

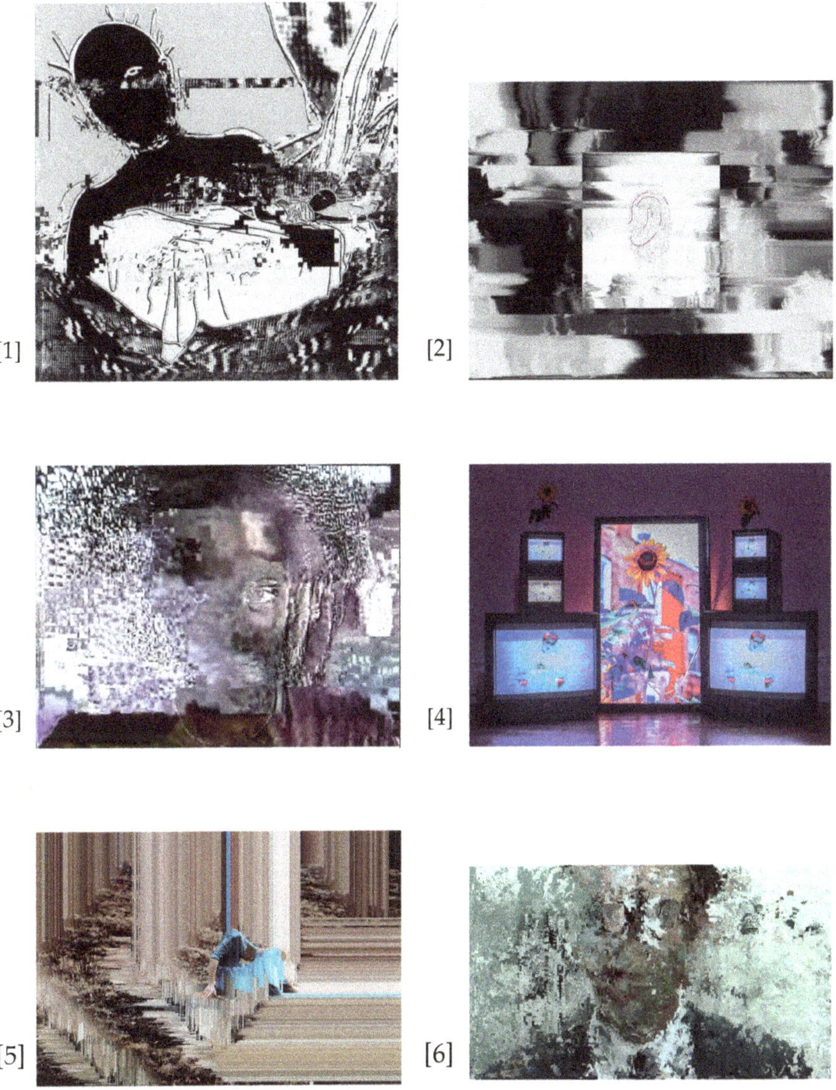

1.1c Glitch Art, works by Contemporary Glitch Artists:
[1] Suture Blue, *trying to find a pattern* (2020);
[2] Aleksandra Pieńkosz ale.png, *fingerprint_1.png* (2022);
[3] Nick Briz, video still from *Binary Quotes* (2008);
[4] Shrine (Sky Goodman and Jim Jam), untitled installation (2018);
[5] Sabato Visconti, *#20 Images Adrift* (2014), photograph of model Hale Hagen, processed with the Pixel Drifter pixel-sorting script by Dmitriy Krotevich;
[6] Kaspar Ravel, *Never Send A Human To Do A Machine's Job* (2017); Used with permission of the artists.

Relegation to this 'external realm' that neither requires nor demands attention demonstrates the entanglement between the diagnostic functions of glitches as computational products of machine operations and the symbolic uses of those artifacts—both are distinct modalities of interpretation that are interdependent, correlated through the consideration of glitches as "requiring attention."

The historically avant-garde precedent for treating glitches *as-art* descends from a Modernist aesthetic ekphrasis concerned with materiality-as-process that attempts to resolve the issues posed by technical systems,[35] and historically apparent in the lineage of Formalist aesthetics that defined each medium in/by restricting expression to its own specific features. It conceived the experiential "presence" created by materiality transcendentally, as an 'ontological aesthetic' grounded in the physicality of each medium.[36] The contemporary issues of reception transform this lineage by introducing the social role of encultured knowledge as a corrective that ties interpretation to context. The question of /intent/ posed by /glitch/ and its role in Glitch Art is at the same art articulated through the internalized, aesthetic "codes of representation"[37] known by an abstract and anonymous "average reader." What this hypothetical audience knows *a priori* to their encounter acts to reconfigure existing models of what and how the technical presentation *should* be understood to accommodate the immanent encounter.[38]

The purpose of this examination is not to clarify this history, neither to resolve any ambivalences in use, nor to provide a final, singular answer to either the problems of "glitch" or to the ambiguities and overlaps in its definitions. The resulting instabilities are "a feature, not a bug." Acknowledging that both glitches and Glitch Art are linked (their relationship is not merely a coincidental conjunction of formal description and expressive use) via /glitch/ defines the beginning for these problematics, rather than their conclusion. Categorial resolutions that define what falls within the scope of Glitch Art are beyond the scope of this study, which concerns the theoretical and interpretive significance of /glitch/ rather than debates on the relative merits of any specific claims, organization, or configuration of glitches or "Glitch Art" as such—even if these questions do appear in, overlap with, and converge on the discussion herein.

1.4 Radical Empiricism

This discursive theorizes /glitch/ as a refusal of dialectical thought, a non-binary conception describable by a semiotic approach to the interrelationships of diagnostic recognition (glitches) and symbolic expression (Glitch Art) as convergent, connected, and mutually influencing, but incompatible interpretations deployed by audience *desires* to assess and engage their perceptions of the world. This approach, while using semiotics as a reference point, is grounded in a radical empiricism where what is encountered in perception provides semantic cues for *all* interpretations, including those of metaphysics. The semiotic framework was selected for its utility, rather than as a final or totalizing model. In place of fixed and immobile signs, this analysis conceives them as mobile and unstable, contingent upon how *desire* shapes and guides apperception. While the illocutionary force[39] of internalized technical fluency[40] establishes the parameters of any interpretations producing glitches, understanding them as more than merely a technical recognition of *mal*function—i.e. via a specific aesthetic lineage or avant-garde tradition (*mis*function) that renders them expressive—reveals a constantly shifting and recursive type of mobile articulation whose transitive semiotics relies on the viewers' established expertise with parsing empirical cues.

Glitch Art emerges while the ideological apparatus of *the digital* rises into dominance: it is enveloped in the aura of information that abandons the vicissitudes of the immanent presentation for the hypothetical and idealized perfection of the digital file. Interpreting the digital media that technology renders as text, sound, image, or even objects invokes an absent 'original' (or hypothetical 'source') which the audience's technical fluency identifies with the immaterial data file suggested by, but not actually shown in, the computer's output. At the same time it is subject to the aura of the digital, which describes the tendency to ignore these physical dimensions of digital technology, considering the digital as a magical, immaterial realm beyond the physical limitations of cost, scarcity, and labor.[41] These cultural factors are emergent in the art historical emphasis on coding in critical appraisals of "computer art"[42] and the role of digital systems in generative processes controlled by programming; the emergence of Glitch Art (and its relatives "Post-Digital Art" and "New Aesthetic") was likely inevitable due to the patrimony of this Modernist aesthetic heritage, however unfashionable that association may be.[43]

By insisting on the empirical encounter with the glitch and the role of that encounter in/as the starting point for the emergent edifice of interpretation embraces the variability and instability of shifting identifications that are at the heart of the /glitch/. This process demonstrates the identification of intentions, materiality, and error all depend on the same internalized codes that make articulation possible. [It thus converges on Jacques Derrida's concept of *différance*, a term born in misspelling (glitch), that excavates the codes of communication for philosophical consideration.[44]] The semic approach is not an argument against the role of "ontology" in analysis, merely a recognition that it is a product of the same interpretations it enables.

1.5 Everyday Experiences

Our vernacular familiarity with glitches is a commonplace
part of our experiences with digital media because they circulate
freely via protocols that offer manifold potentials[45] for the data
corruption that produces the characteristic affects of streaks,
flows, and fragmentation apparent in visual glitches.[46] Slight
variances in either the data file or the decoding codec[47] create
dramatic differences in the rendered work displayed for the human
audience.[48] Recognitions of any digital artifact as *being-glitched*
identifies it as a liminal phenomenon that can provide opportunities
to consider the otherwise hidden and masked dimensions of semio-
perception at their moment of coming into existence: unanticipated
results arise because digital files do not simply store data, but are
instead products of algorithms that compress and decompress data
(instrumental instructions) in a determinate process that renders
them human-readable,[49] even if the result appears aberrant.[50]

The use of the aesthetic qualities of these 'technical failures'
presents an extensive aesthetic lineage[51] beginning with avant-
garde artists working in analogue audible and/or visual media.[52]
Expanded access to the tools of production has made these
dimensions of digital technology a commonplace part of everyday
life,[53] allowing the recoding of 'technical failures' as markers of
authenticity and cultural value.[54] Yet this recognition of glitches
is not a given, but precisely a specific violation of the normative,
refractive separation of *signal* from *noise* which acts to banish
all deviations from expectation, whether transitory, minimally
disruptive, or even extensive and integrally transformative.
This essential interpretative differentiation always begins as an
imposition of familiar order in which the designation "noise" is
nothing less than a labeling of those elements that are *not relevant*
for interpretation and can then be ignored.[55] Philosopher Jacques
Attali explained this role in *Noise: The Political Economy of Music*, a
foundational text for the theorization of digital glitches:

> With noise is born disorder and its opposite: the world. With
> music is born power and its opposite: subversion. In noise can
> be read the codes of life, the relations among them. Clamor,
> Melody, Dissonance, harmony; when it is fashioned by man
> with specific tools, when it invades man's time, when it
> becomes sound, noise is the source of purpose and power, of
> the dream—music.[56]

The model that informs Attali's analysis is "music," but conceived in
an expansive fashion as the 'signal' that conveys signification. The
materiality of "noise" presents a specific collection of artifacts and

forms that circumscribes the physical exhibition of all digital media, whether textual, audible, or visual. The aesthetic value of aliasing, crashes, distortion, and errors[57] in the semantics of digital culture is not simply a product of their material nature, as media historians Christiane Paul and Malcom Levy explain:

> The terms "glitch" and "corruption artifacts" in the broadest sense refer to images and objects that have been tampered with; their creation relates to the core of the media apparatuses used to store, produce and relay information. These corrupted images can be created by adjusting or manipulating the normal physical or virtual composition of the machine or software itself, or by using machines or digital tools in methods different from their normative modalities.[58]

What defines all the digital products termed "glitches" is their difference from the interpreter's internalized model of what a typical (normative) result *should* be, from a mismatch between expectation and immanent encounter. This recognition is not formal, but a product of encultured knowledge intersecting with technical operations and their typical ouputs. It reflects the audience's established expertise in parsing media, rather than a reflection of an innate ontology. These apperceptions and affects are immediate and invisible demonstrations of the essential refraction apparent in the capacity to impose order— the interpretive "bet" about what in perception is ready-to-signify.[59] Each identification or recognition occurs as an immanent dimension of how attention is parsed; human perceptions are the very "material" that provides the foundations for all interpretations. /Glitch/ offers a rare opportunity to analyze the sign formation process as it emerges, before questions of intention or past experience impose order and develop signification within the domain of *signal*.

1.6 Questions of Intentionality

All those technical phenomena that the viewer is inclined to spontaneously identify as "glitches," whether intentional or unintentional, reflective of a *mal*function, or crafted for expressive purposes, are of concern to this analysis. Treating glitches as exclusively a failure in the technical operations makes any question of meaning not only irrelevant but also nonsensical since they are products of purely autonomous operations proceeding in error. Diagnostic understandings of glitches as evidence for *mal*function—a mechanical deviation without expressive significance—dismisses any potential for meaning because once the *thing–in–itself*[60] has been recognized there is nothing more to consider; the intrusion into consciousness of errors is capricious, easily ignored, and quickly

forgotten because "broken" things are not engaged semiotically—
they are ignored, repaired, or replaced. This fundamental category
mistake—a type of expression that identifies "broken" being mistaken
for 'the real'—mystifies the symptomatic analysis as an "empirical"
perception (thus an ontological claim), fostering the assumption
that what is identified *as-indexical* in technical media is an encounter
with 'the real' apart from the cultural beliefs and internalized past
experiences with media that shape how it presents 'the real,' and the
more basic questions of enculturation that direct what *in* perception
receives attention and what is ignored as proof for 'the real.' This
belief precludes all other entangled complexities since to identify
anything *as-error* blocks all other encoding and intentionality required
for expressive communication; identifications of *error* are tautological,
foreclosing on any potential semiosis before it begins. Thus the
problem posed by identifying glitches as proofs or evidence for a
breakdown is a simple axiom:

> **Where there can be no intent, there can also be no
> signification because there is no encoding of meaning
> for the audience to decode (interpret).**

Thus a diagnostic appraisal conceives glitches as an interruption
in the otherwise normative progression of encoding. However,
audiences do make shifts in function and use, and this transitive
nature—**mobile articulation**—is precisely what makes glitches
of critical interest. The semic actions that change diagnostic into
symbolic (and back again) are illuminated by considerations of
/glitch/. They are changes of category, decisions that establish
modal distinctions between ontology, materiality, and the episteme
that intersect and entangle all symbolic appraisals; /glitch/ is an
instructive protocol for distinguishing incompatible, mutually
supporting modalities (the diagnostic and the symbolic).

The abstraction created by mobile articulation provides a series of
nested and interconnected semiotic modes (much like Matryoshka
dolls) where the lowest level initial decisions about the nature
of perceptions shape and direct the highest levels of interpretive
comprehension. But they are metastable, a fractal recursion that can
never escape its initial constraints and choices about signal::noise,
but which is always ready for the complete re-appraisal demanded
shifts in attention or consideration. The axiomatic nature of this
initial sorting of perception into apperception distinguishes what
needs attention (signal) from what can be ignored (noise), enabling
the clear separation of diagnostic phenomena (and questions
of depiction) from those symbolic expressions (and issues of
denotation) that are more commonly of concern to semic, historical,

and theoretical analyses. Glitch Art has the potential to place these comfortable distinctions in disarray, and it is this capacity that makes the intersectional ambivalence that is /glitch/ of broad critical and theoretical interest since it describes limina, margins, points of contact where mutually exclusive potentials converge and collide. Their conception is demonstrative of superposition, and emblematic of concerns with paradoxes that began during the twentieth century—an unstable and mobile articulation that evokes an epistemology not based on certainty—where contingency and variability dominate interpretations that embrace these ambiguities.[61]

In the second decade of the twenty-first century the concept /glitch/ has come to identify this event horizon as a quantified point of transition, enabling its discussion and consideration, yet not its precise isolation as a fixed or determinate value. This convergence with the liminal problematics posed by the paradox is obvious. Both present a special case for interpretation, one where a simple selection from within the array of potential interpretations poses a type of interpretive contradiction that undermines easy resolution or simple definition: if /glitch/ were equivalent to the anti-signal, *noise*, then it would simply be a synonym for the uncoded and unmodulated realm outside and apart from interpretive significance, yet this is not what the /glitch/ describes, nor how the various aesthetics for digital media emergent around it employ its disruptive operations.

The paradox emerges immediately when confronting Glitch Art: the /glitch/ describes an *error* which at the same time is *not/error*. It is transformative as well as transient, an alteration in perception and recognition that is particular to digital technology despite its analogue heritage in earlier media, but it does not tip over into the realm of inchoate chaos—a relativist disruption in the 'signal' being communicated—even as it glides across the surface of such dissolutions of coherence, courting disaster. This unresolvable, ambivalent complexity reflects the paradox *all* limina pose for interpretation: /glitch/ confuses definitional separations by lying exactly between them, superposed as the moment of contact that defines a change between categories, belonging to neither, yet incorporating aspects of both. Its emergence and adoption as a designation for the marginal and marginalized in art, culture, and society originates with this precise, conceptual locus as the interface between mutually exclusive states; it is also the source of its complications for discursive and dialectical reasoning. Moments of contact are critically important to understanding and conceiving the features that define differences, but must forever remain as the threshold between them.

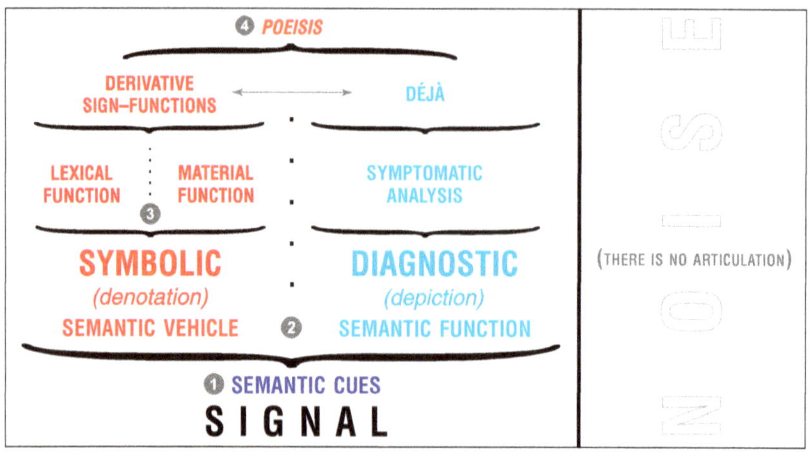

1.2   The separation of signal::noise initiates a repeating process of refraction, identifying [1] signifiers, then further articulating them into the lowest level signs: [2] the *diagnostic* (depiction) and *symbolic* (denotation) modes; which enable [3] the infinitely recursive, fractal layering of signifieds into increasingly complex types of semiosis as the primary ('lexical function' and 'material function') and secondary articulations (the derivative sign functions that include *narrative, naturalism, realism,* and *abstraction*); then finally as [4] a transformative *poeisis* (the 'poetic function' that re-articulates *all* the other articulations).

1.7 Problematics of 'the real'

To conceive of glitches as a "correspondence in fact"[62] to a technical breakdown or other error conflates Peirce's categories of *indices* and *icons* to convert the digital representation that is the human-readable form of the digital file into the object being represented: *those features that suggest the error are not actually the error.* The conventionality of this indexical association between the denoted content of the work and the processes that may have produced it is the cultural heritage of analogue media, that while no longer applicable to digital media, nevertheless continues to inform its apprehension. This lineage defines the diagnostic functions of *glitches-as-failures.* Understanding glitches as the *thing–in–itself* (as demonstrations of 'the real' or *actual* errors and breakdowns) produces a refusal of signification that is essential to the construction, operation, and maintenance of machines of all types. This issue lurks around every evaluation of glitches, but their symptomatic analysis identifies them exclusively with technical breakdowns: there is no development of semiosis when employing the glitch as an indication of 'what has gone wrong.' When considered in relation to symbolic elaboration, the indexical role for these artifacts of machinic operations acts against the expressive evaluations and considerations of Glitch Art, even when those symbolic functions dominate.

In defining /glitch/ for critical analysis, separating the functions of denotation (indexicality) and depiction (semiosis) demands a clear division of diagnostic from symbolic modalities. Their estrangement becomes an essential stage for apperception that avoids ontological and intentional fallacies,[63] a refraction that makes the necessity of these categorical divisions obvious [Figure 1.2]. The decision to attend to any glitch, rather than ignore it as irrelevant, proceeds from the initial separation of signal::noise producing the diagnostic and symbolic modes whose semiosis spirals into an infinite, fractal recursion [Figure 3.3, page 63]. All levels in these engagements are created by the interpreter using past experience and the 'intentional function' as guides for different but converging fields of interpretation: the physical presentation (i.e. the recognition of semantic cues) is the foundation for the identification/recognition that produces the first dimension of diagnostic articulation; the symbolic content, including its connection to traditions, similarity or difference with other objects, and the audience's relationship to the particular object, and all the entangled significances produced through reinterpretation of those same cues forms a second, parallel dimension that continuously intersects the initial diagnosis of what is present. While the second, symbolic order requires the physical presentation, it transforms the diagnostic since interpreted content exists as an excess to recognitions of the initial assessment of these cues. The flaws of the physical rendering typically disappear from both levels of consideration, rejected by the aura of the digital as unimportant noise.[64]

Deciding something is what it appears to be (i.e. a diagnosis of its identity) precludes its intentional encoding or expressive significance—unless the diagnosis recognizes it *as-language,* thus demanding symbolic consideration—the choice to interpret something *as-if* it was encoded describes the transformation from an identification of things to the recognition of encoding that semiotician Umberto Eco identifies as a challenge to conceptions of *indexicality*:

> Recognition occurs when a given object or event, produced by nature or human action (intentionally or unintentionally), and existing in a world of facts as a fact among facts, comes to be viewed by an addressee as the expression of a given content, either through a pre-existing and coded correlation or through the positing of a possible correlation by its addressee.[65]

Diagnostic and symbolic interpretations, however closely linked they appear to be, are and remain incompatible types of assessment: the diagnostic is always a terminal evaluation of what *is* present, beyond which no further consideration is warranted or necessary.[66] The change from diagnostic to symbolic modes is always already

an autonomous decision by the viewer made before they identify
any signs in apperception. The choice to interpret something
encountered in perception *as-if* it is encoded (including the
recognition of language) changes the diagnostic recognition (via the
'intentional function') into an engagement with symbolic form that is
inherent to any semiosis. This action distinguishes all the expressive
productions of Glitch Art from the non-coded, diagnostic functions
of glitches *as-errors* and other breakdowns. It separates meaning
from the apperceptions (semantic cues identified from perception)
that enable it. This transitive re-assessment proceeds without end
or limitation, and since the symbolic realm parallels the diagnostic
assessment as an entirely different modality of engagement, there
is always the potential for glitches to return to a simple diagnosis
of *mal*function, undercutting any stability or resolution within
the symbolic realm precisely because the diagnostic approach to
depiction has been conflated with a phenomenal proof of reality (its
role as indexicality) self-evident in the history of photography.[67]

1.8 Material Markers

Technical fluency assesses and interprets glitches, often placing
these 'material markers' in the domain of "noise" that identifies
irrelevancy for interpretation. However, the utility of diagnosing
them *as–failure* for the construction and maintenance of these systems
cannot be denied, even as that utility creates misconceptions for
hermeneutic analysis: a belief that ontology, the *source* producing
the glitch, determines or constrains its interpretation. The Modernist
demand for an ontological (indexical) distinction between 'real'
or 'fake' (what Glitch Artist Rosa Menkman critiqued as the
difference between "glitch" and "glitch-alike"[68]) seeks to contain the
ambivalence of /glitch/ as a threat to coherence, or conversely, to
transform that ambivalence into a transitive relationship between
idealized and innate states, rather than rest in its uncertainty as an
uncanny space in which mutually exclusive, superposed potentials
preclude any resolution, a realm of paradox that threatens to infect
both signal and noise with its shifting and contingent reordering
of knowledge. This /glitch/ is uncomfortable, a disruptive force
that shatters familiar and accepted heuristics as simply one model
accompanied and challenged by a panoply of alternatives.[69] These
unstable, paradoxical identifications highlight the audience's role
in mediating aesthetic significance[70] that ironically begins with
the diagnostic recognition of /glitch/, but also counteracts that
proposition of "*mal*function" by making an assumption that the
digital machine is functioning *properly* (either at the level of hardware
or software). Glitch Art renders the 'material markers' anomalous
precisely because the system is producing what it is *designed* to create;

these "aberrations" describe the illusory and superficial paradox of an *error-which-is-not-error* arising between the recognition of a digital artifact and the technical expertise that identifies the materiality of digitally generative imagery. Sheldon Brown, Director of the Center for Research in Computing and the Arts at the University of California, San Diego noted the prominent lineage of glitches as a revelation of the 'substance' of electronic, generative media for the avant-garde:

> Bit-depth, gamma range, object edges and noise were some of the new compositional elements that analog and digital signal processing made apparent. Over the following decades this new semantics permeated image culture at large, becoming the *de facto* material basis by which media is produced.[71]

The formal elements that Brown identifies are immediately apparent in how errors have been employed historically as symptoms for diagnosing breakdowns,[72] granting these 'material markers' of the technical medium a symbolic role in which features such as bit-depth, gamma range, object edges, and noise[73] become expressive, linking the materiality of digital media to the analogue materiality of processes such as optical printing[74] and video synthesis.[75] Multiplicity and replication dominate the designation of these generative products as "materiality," reflecting how technical fluency conceals the instrumental nature of media and computer code as isomorphic but discrete expressions converging in the generative outputs they produce, despite their categorical differences. The "unexpected" or "random" results of glitches are predictable in advance and necessarily determinate—encoded instructions are always uniform in what they render, *provided the decoding system remains constant.*

1.9 The Indexicality of Error

The traditional assumption that technical images and media are comprehensible as indexicals for 'the real' begins in the nineteenth century with photography's invention, yielding a long held "indexical fallacy"[76] about their utility as demonstrations of reality apart from the interpretations that render them coherent.[77] This belief is apparent from the history of 'spirit photographs,' those technical images showing "ghosts" that were produced with either in-camera processes or dark room manipulations,[78] and offered as proofs demonstrating an unseen, metaphysical realm; they have a long association with glitches and other types of technical malfunctions.[79] These exemplars of the entanglement between symbolic interpretation and the diagnostic reinforce the assertion of indexicality; without this claim their "demonstration" of the existence of spirits becomes untenable[80]—spirit photography prompted cultural and ultimately legal battles over fraud [Figure 1.3].[81] This duality of address in the lineage of technical media, via the entanglement of diagnostic and symbolic modes, is the source of ambiguity for Glitch Art.

The differentiation of these modes does not resolve the superficially paradoxical nature of identifying a technical failure as also being an expressive gesture. This fallacy arises from a demand for a fixed positioning, rather than the shifting ambivalence of a mobile articulation, even though that demand clarifies how these interpretive operations lie within entirely different domains. The tendency for diagnostic recognition to conflate the assessments of the actual source or nature (ontology) with its interpreted significance (epistemology) is a category error which converges on the fallacy apparent in earlier indexical claims for photography. Higher level interpretations such as *naturalism* (in which the depiction is correlated with everyday experiences) is typically assumed as the default nature of photography,[82] leading to the documentary claims of "spirit photography." But these claims are not products of ontology (being an *index* or *icon*), but of enculturation whose mnemonic recognitions and contingent identifications shift within a fixed teleological and tautological order.[83] The "problem" lies in the apperception of the output: any deviation from what the average audience anticipates (i.e. questions of enculturation) creates a mismatch between any indexical claim and the suggestion that glitches are expressive.

Interpretive problems posed by glitches thus compound and expand exponentially because the human viewer's identification of glitches *as-error* (via their variance from both the anticipated imperfections of the immanent work *and* the hypothetically perfect, ideal source assumed to be immanent in the digital file[84]) also requires an identification of Glitch Art *as-error* and *as-not/error*. The multiplicity of these symbolic interpretations creates a paralogy that recodes glitches into the 'material function' paralleling the more familiar textual semiosis of the 'lexical function'[85] that addresses writing and language, and which entails the ascription of expressive significance to the glitch, even if it does not produce a singular or coherent meaning.

The use and production of these artifacts and their potential relationships to technical breakdowns and other types of *mal*function[86] does not alter the essential distinction between the *source* of what is encountered, the audience's *interpretation and assessment of what that source might be,* and *the appropriateness of engaging what they encounter via symbolic interpretation.* Art exploiting the capacity of apperception to identify products of autonomous digital systems as both instances of a *diagnostic* addressing *mal*function as well as an *expressive* feature of articulation (*mis*function) defines a lineage and convergence of

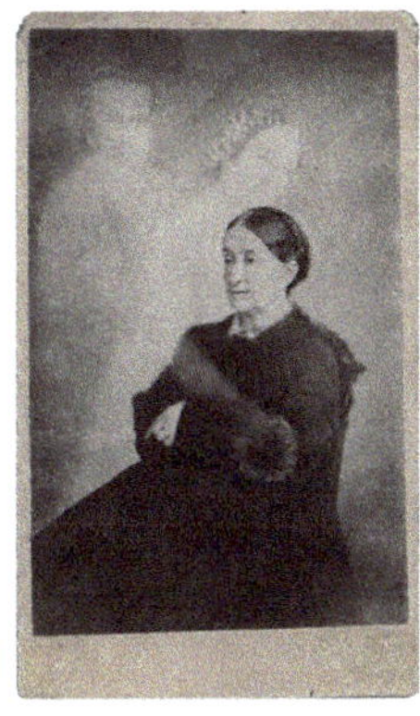
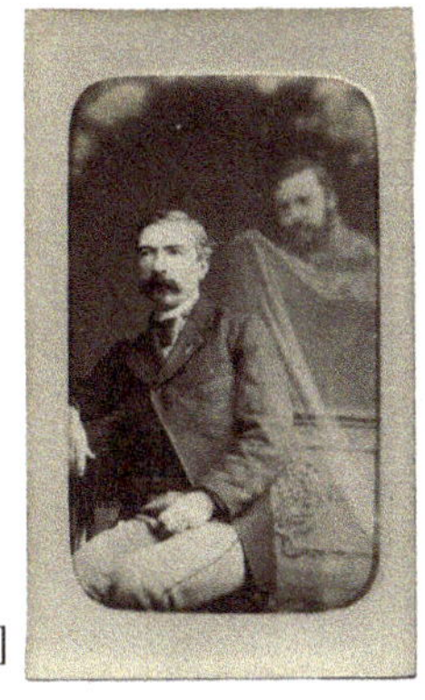
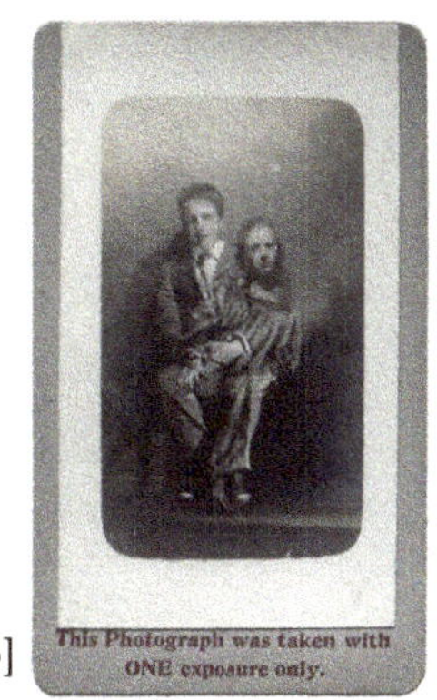

1.3   Three nineteenth century "spirit photographs" whose identification
as depicting a phantasmal apparition advances a metaphysical claim
to document an unseen spiritual realm that is contradicted by how
all three images were actually created using double exposures:

[1] William Mumler, *Mrs Ollsan of Boston, her spirit daughter
    and husband* (c. 1865-1875);

[2] Édouard Isidore Buguet, *'man with spirit'* (1874);

[3] circle of William Hope & William Walker, *The ghost of Margery
    Walker with her brother* (c. 1910).

use that makes the emergence of a "glitch aesthetic" in digital media
(and Glitch Art) inevitable.[87] While the diagnostic link of any glitch
to the technical operations of the machine is an artifact of a learned
technical fluency, the "bet" that it is appropriate to interpret the glitch
as-if it was intentionally encoded *as-expressive* does not depend on any
ontological basis *as-failure*. This distinction changes the concern with
glitches from an ontology of the technical system revealed through
its operations to the semiotics of apperception and their limiting
role in interpretative evaluations whose foundational principle is
the ambiguity of perception. The identification of signs begins with
objects encountered in life, and semiosis is therefore necessarily
subject to the same instabilities and caprices as any other category of
interpretation based on experience. What prompts the shift from a
diagnostic recognition of 'what is present' to a symbolic 'articulation
of meaning' depends on an autonomous pre-semic decision by
the audience. This 'intentional function' cues an imposition which
justifies their choice to distinguish and organize their encounter
as-if communicating an expressive coherence. Semiotician Floyd
Merrell noted this transformation of perceptions is implicit in Charles
Saunders Peirce's proposal of semiotics:

The inevitability of incompleteness in all signs of general
nature allows for the entrance of unexpected thirds without

conceivable end. Yet, Peirce writes in so many ways that the collusion of possibility, actuality, and potentiality makes up our 'semiotically real world' as we perceive and conceive it, which, if we are fortunate, stands a chance of approximating some portion of the 'real.' Any and all 'semiotic worlds,' in this light, must remain radically uncertain.[88]

Merrell's analysis of indeterminately vague signs (such as glitches) concerns the tendency to propose an infinite and unbounded proliferation of interpretations, but does not develop this argument to its logical conclusion: the audience's *desire* for order within their apperceptions leads to their use of the 'intentional function' which provides the necessary and sufficient justification for the encoding of significance onto the mute matter of experience, creating the inflected order of signs.[89] The 'intentional function' avoids the problems posed by assertions of indexicality as an ontological property of the work because its ascription of /intent/ is neither obvious nor inherent in something encountered, but must be cued by non-signifying aspects of perception defined by enculturation. In shifting the organizing capacities of /intent/ from the artist/author to the interpreter, the vernacular proposition of an innate and inherent quality of "broken" that separates 'real' and 'simulated' glitches[90] becomes nonsensical, rendering the question of their indexicality as merely a product of *how* the glitches are being interpreted, rather than an innate ontological feature of their existence apparent to their audience.

1.10 Autonomous Generation

Digital technology interposes layers of implementation between the "medium of code" (data file) and the work encountered by viewers, a distancing that offers the series of material sources shown by Figure 1.4 a utility in conceptualizing the relationship between diagnostic identification and the rendering of glitches,[91] simultaneously providing both a mechanical explanation for them as a symptomatic analysis of *mal*functions, as well as enabling their transformation into semiotic expressions, *mis*functions, that arise from the mismatch between expectation and immanent encounter. Unlike the physical 'carrier'[92] that was a singular dimension of technical relations in analogue media, the digital is bifurcated between the 'display' and the 'instrumental instructions' of the data. This separation distinguishes the machine-generated file from its human-readable presentation and informs how /glitch/ complicates interpretation: unlike a motion picture (film) where the screen is simply a reflective surface, or the analogue television receiver whose screen is a direct, isomorphic display of voltages in the electronic signal, the images produced by a computer are distinct from the

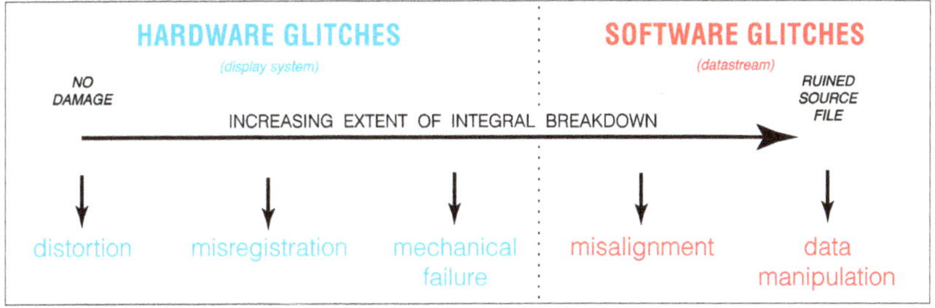

1.4   The empirical referents for the 'material function' in Glitch Art
derive from glitches' capability to serve as diagnostics for technical
breakdowns. These 'material markers' provide observable cues
whose articulation reveals their diagnostic recognition (and any
indexical claim about technology *as-broken*) also depends on the
same encultured knowledge that defines technical expertise itself.

codes and data generating them. The digital file's independence from
its display is inherent to digital technology. Constraining glitches
to the taxonomic framework derived from empirical phenomena in
Figure 1.4 [see *Appendix*] defines their 'material markers' without
altering or challenging their role in symbolic interpretation. What
this range of effects identify is not just the increasingly reproducible
glitch, but also the relational nature between the glitch and the
systems that produce it as an artifact. Both hardware and software
glitches arise from mismatches between two distinct elements: the
system providing *a priori* order and the /object/ passing through
that system: glitches emerge from an incomplete and imperfect
alignment of elements in both halves that are being joined. It is
within this liminal space of encounter that the relationship of
technical display system to technical media being displayed creates
the human-readable phenomena most commonly called glitches.
These surface appearances and the relational processes they suggest
are both examples of the same phenomenon—correlated interpretive
affects whose material and immaterial dimensions are parallel,
conceptually linked, yet remain independent.

   Glitch Art thus always "flirts" with disaster without actually
becoming real failure.[93] These aesthetic relationships begin with the
internalized technical fluency that parses the 'material markers'
that are both a signifier *of* and *for* technical failure in all technical
media into their expressive roles via the 'intentional function.'
These distinctions are the heritage of an avant-garde synthesis
that restrains the ambiguity of articulation.[94] For the digital, it
manifests as the aura of information's tendency to conflate the
physical and immaterial as equivalents in a transformation of

objects to semiotic data, suggesting the specific basis of Glitch Art is the series of electrical signals within the machine, and offering both the instrumental code and its rendering into a human-readable object as identical, interchangeable expressions. The digital object is composed from both the physical media that transmit, store and present the work to an audience, and the binary code processed by machines: all 'digital art' is a combination of code and a human-readable work created by the computer from a digital file. The aura of the digital arises from how that human audience ignores/devalues the physical output, authorizing a Modernist emphasis on the hypothetical instrumental perfection of the digital file (code). The Formalist approach is doomed to fallacy because technical fluency parses the distinction between glitched and *unglitched*, rather than an autonomous and essential nature. Although technical "glitches" *can be* errors, at the same time, they also *represent* errors,[95] a superficial contradiction resolved through the clearly different levels of interpretation involved.[96] The Post-Modern aesthetic heritage resolves this paradox of materiality by embracing semiotics (post-structuralism) and those dimensions of subjectivity and variation whose significance was explicitly denied by Modernist Formalism.[97] Maintaining the separation of diagnostic and symbolic is essential to avoiding this fallacy; it understands digital technology is instrumental, and acknowledges its coded instructions are specifically determinate, but also recognizes how the diagnostic recognition renders glitches as irrelevant problems that signification must ignore, removing them from direct consideration as candidates for expressive articulation.

1.11 Ambivalences

Acknowledging the interpretive instabilities and ambivalences of /glitch/ phenomena unites the technologically distinct glitches of analogue and digital media to address the interface between autonomous machine operations and the realm of human significances: understanding: /glitch/ is a 'material marker' *of* and *for* technical failure, a consequence of its technical basis in sampling and reproduction, but unlike human language (which is discursive), and physical objects (which are always unique instances of specific classes—books, recordings, photographs, etc.), all digital objects are basically the same, a series of instrumental instructions, whatever their appearance once they are rendered as human-readable forms. Errors and breakdowns are commonplace in digital media, and when confronting either simple *mal*functions or disruptions in the smooth and proper operations of the machine, their problematics for interpretation are not necessarily evident because all 'digital objects' have the same underlying form—binary code—whose operations and implementation are purely descriptive. The semiotic nature of the digital, although related to the semiosis of human languages, remains distinct; unlike human communications which depend on and articulate ambiguities, machine code is completely constrained and delimited, concerning only those tasks which can be fragmented into discrete steps and performed without intelligent oversight.

The ambivalence of /glitch/ developed in this study belongs to a lineage concerned with the limits of knowledge and logic that came to dominate discourse in the twentieth century. These earlier concerns with paradox challenge the instrumentalist desire to render all potentials immanent, and critique that radical relativism where nothing is true and all things are allowed because everything is equivalent, while rejecting the nihilism that obstructs any political, social, cultural act in advance. The /glitch/ is not a harbinger of this alienated and nihilistic relativism precisely because it demands the existing frameworks of signal::noise for its existence and identification. The /glitch/ arises from these *a priori* frameworks—it can neither supplant them nor replace them since to do so would result in its own disappearance and irrelevance. This interstitial relationship belongs to the critique of the deterministic, "clockwork" universe created by nineteenth century science and philosophy that emerged from the probabilistic reality described by modern physics: the superficial appearance of paradoxes is precisely an illusion created by a misunderstanding of what superposed potentials are (combined with expectations for singular or determinate proofs). The contemporary embrace of an indeterminate range bounded by poles of mutual exclusion posits a replacement of Manichean absolutes, marking a radical shift in thinking about the physical world, and also in how it is modeled, conceptualized, or interpreted. Concerns with marginality and liminal encounters changes the familiar and traditional singular "truth" into one truth among many whose relationships and points of transition become the point of critical concern for an epistemology not based on certainty but mutually assured validity.[98]

1.12 Liminal Moments

/Glitch/ is one descriptor for the interfaces between incompatible interpretations such as the diagnostic and symbolic modes; however, all these interpretive relationships are recursive—once created, every new iteration is a *further* elaboration of the information space and the relationships it contains. This expansion and incorporation into semiosis creates an infinite recursion, but rather than being a fallacy, the emergence of this excess is a necessary and essential feature of an epistemological framework based in ambivalence and inconsistency, distinct from the closure and containment of classical analysis. The superficial paradox is an illusion created by a superposition between signal::noise, an interface addressed via its collapse into a definite resolution identified by /glitch/ as the transitive realm marking the limits within this system: it is both and neither signal and noise, a disruptive mediating concept that is commonly mistaken for noise in its impacts on signal, but which equally disrupts the designation *as-noise*. A glitch within noise becomes signal—creates coherence and order that invokes the structure of signal, but this disruption is reversible, creating the opposite within signal. Contingency defines this momentary resolution as an unresolvable ambivalence whose coherent recognition as signifying or non-signifying is only one temporary moment within an on-going sequence where each and every formative element is subject to radical revision and reassessment.

The fallacy of an autonomously critical art derives from how /glitch/ transforms semic function: the critical 'unmasking' it appears to perform depends on the interpreter's acknowledgment of this relational and contextual dimension of apperception that refracts into those elements of significance (signal) and those elements to ignore (noise). But glitches pervert this process through the uncertainty of their recognitions: *when to engage* and *when to ignore* are neither fixed nor predetermined, but are instead reflections of the audience's *desire* for coherence that directs their interpretations via the 'intentional function,' coupled with their interpretive fluency. /Glitch/ describes the boundaries within this unstable and shifting assertion of order. This expansive conception of /glitch/ as a relational interpretation enables its application to more than merely the technical failings that define glitches' commonplace appearance in music and Glitch Art. While glitches can interrupt the flow of interpretations, these flows do not exist in actuality—the spectator responds to and assimilates them into their engagement, either understanding them as signal to consider, or rejecting them as noise; this ambivalence offers the potential for these eruptions to become a redirection of meaning, and demonstrates the relational instability of /glitch/ as a designation. Its liminality is an always receding horizon that cannot be occupied, merely identified and acknowledged in a cycle of return and reconsideration that precisely demonstrates the recursive and interdependent roles of the diagnostic and symbolic modes that are forced into superposition by /glitch/.

1.13 Glitch, itself

'To be expressive' is a product of symbolic interpretation.

Glitches reveal the instability of the superficial stability of the systems they address, and the expressiveness attributed to glitches brings this function into consciousness. To say that something is expressive and broken is not a contradiction, but like any paradox, it depends on the interpretive fluency of its audience to adapt to the chimera it creates. In the discursive approach to glitches employed in this book there is no singular, linear argument being advanced—to do so would be at odds with the subject of its inquiry. Instead, it proceeds through a series of overlapping and convergent discussions where any superficial repetitions are actually serial iterations that collectively illuminate its focus. To try and impose linearity on glitching with the finality of determinative logic would create an imaginary closure to the glitch, one that conflicts with its interdisciplinary and transgressive nature. In place of that structure is the circulation, mirrorical return, doubling and repetition created by revisiting a shifting and meta-stable object of inquiry that continuously verges on disappearance and escapes from descriptive capture.

A discursive mode of presentation and analysis allows these dimensions to emerge, but their unstable definition precisely depends on the clarity of the terms being challenged. For this analysis they are the distinctions between a diagnostic recognition of the glitch that apprehends it as an error, a symptom of *mal*function or failure, and the symbolic articulation whose expressiveness is not limited to language, but includes any meaning or value distinct from the attempts to describe 'the real' as a distinct entity apart from human intentions that always motivates the diagnostic. These twin modes are entangled in all interpretations, a comingling and overlap that glitches bring into consciousness. This study explores the indeterminacies that the convergence of intentional construction with the unintentional identifications of things enables.

2

EXPERTISE AND EXPRESSION

Questions of intentionality have haunted art made by / with machines since the invention of photography in the nineteenth century. Glitch Art belongs within this lineage of aesthetic machines, a contemporary exploit of digital technology where the 'intentional function' that transforms apperceptions into expressions becomes an unstable mediator of significance. The autonomous operations of technical media such as photography, digital art, and glitches are produced by machines that all reveal the issue of human agency is essential to justifying semiosis. Without the justifications for *as-if* engagement created by the 'intentional function,' apperceptions must remain within a diagnostic realm, mere symptoms of physical processes understood in indexical terms: the 'intentional function' describes how the interpreter autonomously employs empirically present but non-signifying semantic cues in perception during sign formation[99]—a refractive choice preceding the articulation of meaning because when the semiotic process confronts perception, it depends on this initial refraction that interprets *as-if* there is symbolic encoding (i.e. intentionally encoded).[100] The separation of action, ideation, and production apparent in contemporary artistic uses of machinery illuminates the ways that digital systems have continued the historical distancing of direct human agency that began with the invention of photography, making the role that assumptive "intentions" play in sign formation and semiosis increasingly obvious.[101]

How Glitch Art poses a question of / intent / via its aesthetic uses of glitches accentuates the audience's imposition of "intention." This interpretive choice to recategorize a glitch as a symbolic expression incorporates the glitch as a diagnostic feature of the work, but doing so compounds how semiosis derives from implicit expectations for human agency as the *prima causa* of the foundational cues essential to communication and expression. However, this concern is masked throughout semiotic theory, which addresses the results of that assumption,[102] rather than its problematics.[103] Glitches bring this omission into consciousness via the vernacular understanding of glitches as demonstrating the *reality* of the machinic processes themselves, rather than being an ambiguous result of a stoppage that demands human intervention.[104] The entangled familiarity of glitches *as-expressions* and *as-errors* elevates the importance of / intent / in

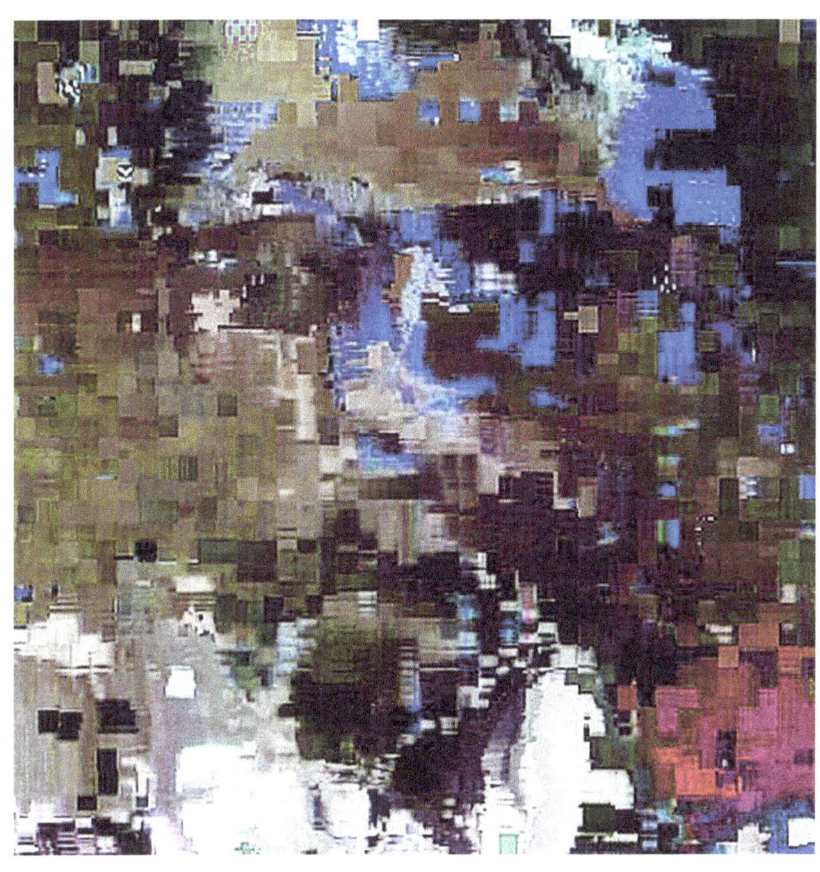

2.1   Michael Betancourt, *The Face of Glitch* (2016) a databent and datamoshed
      still from the movie serial *Going Somewhere.*
      Copyright © 2016 by Michael Betancourt / courtesy Artists' Rights Society (ARS).

the interpreter's apprehension of symbolic meaning, demonstrating changes to *what* and *how* they engage apperception creates radically different types of interpretation.

2.1 The Lineage of Recognition in Technical Media

The emergence of Glitch Art and its exploits of glitches in technical systems of all types foregrounds the necessity of the 'intentional function' for art generally because /intent/ is linked to the questions of expertise, perception, interpretation, and technical fluency that determine aesthetic significance: the audience's essential category shift from diagnostic recognition into the parallel and convergent mode of symbolic denotation resolves this ambivalence. It demonstrates the fluency and the expertise assumed by semiotics. There is no diagnostic recognition of denoted content that does not also recognize the *in*stability of this identification. The face that may or may not exist in Figure 2.1 draws attention to the recognition "face," revealing the act of recognition begins with *how* the audience separates abstraction and represnetation to identify what they encounter through their past knowledge and established expertise. Even if the identification of human faces is something that happens so easily and autonomously that mistaken recognitions have created a class of optical illusions known as *pareidolia* where people "see" faces in things that are neither human nor faces: diagnostic recognition is a discursive turn that decides something has "come from somewhere else." It is a semantic assessment of identity whose significance recalls Ludwig Wittgenstein's observations about "recognition" being the essential starting point for all interpretation:

> The very expression which is also a report of what is seen, is here a cry of recognition.
>
> What is the criterion of the visual experience?—The criterion? What do you suppose?
>
> The representation of 'what is seen.'
>
> The concept of a representation of what is seen, like that of a copy, is very elastic, and so *together with it* is the concept of what is seen. The two are intimately connected. (Which is *not* to say that they are alike.)[105]

The recognition of 'what is seen' initiates an unending process of apperception that converts ambivalent visual experience into coherence by imposing order. Semiosis normally *begins* with this recognition that prompts the 'intentional function' to attempt to derive meaning from those things encountered in life, transforming experience into communication. It is an identification that links the known quotation to other kinds of mnemonic familiarity, including both lexical form and the iconography of visual art. The designation /quotational/ is not *only* a generic suggestion of anterior production—the audience must also identify the particular source, that the work is sampled from—that specific earlier production which the audience also already knows. This use of established media fluency informs the immanent encounter by recognizing how the new immanent use relies on that established expertise: any recognition of a sign is *not* an empirical feature of the environment, but a product of how audiences interpret their perceptual encounter. Addressing anything in perception as containing encoded statements assumes the role of human agency in their creation: to establish them *as-expressive* requires an implicit belief in a productive 'intent to communicate' responsible for the work, and cued by/in the contextual presentation of the work itself. However, these ambivalent liminal phenomena are revelatory not of the object being examined, but of the examination. The essential role for interpretive expertise displaces any transcendent, or essentially metaphysical basis for semiosis in art—or in any other form of communication—disputing all claims for an ontological essence defined by expressive encoding. Thus errors by the interpreter in creating an interpretation are distinct from identifications of glitches because every example of /glitch/ announces itself by disrupting the semic process; unlike logical fallacies which designate mistakes hidden from normative analysis, but that undermine the validity of the result. In contrast, /glitch/ does not undermine the results of semiosis—it alters, exploits, and redirects them, belonging to an entirely different category than logical fallacies: they are a deflection of the semic process towards unfamiliar and unexpected outcomes, rather than an undermining of its operations. Glitch Art brings these problematics into prominence.

The question of syntagmatics[106]—that 'statements' are structured by established codes—posed by technical media such as photography which lacks any *a priori* codes[107] can be resolved through recourse to understanding their "encoding" as both an emergent product *and* object of the same primary articulations of signal::noise that also allow its identification as an encoded phenomenon.[108] The "coding" of technical media is a tautological invention of the viewer, rather than a feature of the work; "finding" meaning is actually imposing order. The autonomy of perception is the precondition for its refractive sorting into apperception by the 'intentional function' that demarcates the moment of this transformation from mute experience into expressive significance as an autonomous, uncontrolled, and invisible process, a linkage that gives the assumption of /intent/ for semiosis its apparent independence from thought as a "reality" or phenomenon identified in the world. By transforming ambivalence into order, the 'intentional function' endows perceptions with human agency, a special valence that transforms mere matter into vehicles for expression. The /glitch/ unmasks the uncertainty of this designation implicit in confronting the autonomous products of art-making machines—photographic, reproductive, digital, and AI. Thus, unbidden, an elemental uncertainty about the appropriateness of identifying semiotic encoding "in" apperception in general (and in glitches specifically) returns to questions of semiosis confronting technical media precisely because the 'intentional function' lies at the foundation of semiosis. The implicit and autonomous decision that something was /intended/ provides the first justification for choosing to interpret it *as-if* encoded—but this choice depends on there being 'intentions to communicate,'[109] otherwise any recognized encoding or appearance of a "message" is only an hallucination,[110] an invention of the audience confronting an uncoded artifact.[111] Any mistakes in this foundational "intentional apprehension" beget a great variety of logical fallacies, (including the pathetic fallacy, reification, even animism), by impugning agency where there is none—transcendence is always contingent.

2.2 Unstable Signification

Mechanical production enables the reflexive capacity of glitches to draw attention to the protocols of sign formation, semiotic apperception, and interpretive category assignment. It instrumentalizes the axiom common to information theory that 'noise' is a disruption of communication,[112] but depends on the positivist assumption that there can be a clear *a priori* differentiation of signal from noise. /Glitch/ reveals this belief as a solipsism defined in the universe of binary dialectics whose certainty was instrumentalized in the clockwork universe of the nineteenth century.[113] The shift to a paradigm described by relativity, superposition, and the meta-stabilities of ambivalence in the twentieth century replaces what were assumed to be fixed foundations with a realm of constantly shifting potentials, mobile articulation, and contingency. Glitch Art invokes this realm where diagnostic functions (unintentional) and symbolic enunciations (intentional) are superposed.

The paths which lead to the "ontological" identification of glitches as a diagnostic recognition of *mal*function thus collide with the correlation fallacy because understanding *glitches–as–failures* is guided by a learned 'technical fluency' that is a form of cultural knowledge. The *a priori* of assumption that something is a 'communication' prioritizes and masks the refractions created by the 'intentional function' allowing those aspirations to be an indexical demonstration of 'the real' that is the diagnostic claim to identify *things–in–themselves*. However, the expertise that defines articulation for Glitch Art converges the semiotics of *mis*function with the initial diagnosis of *mal*function to confound any claims derived from indexicality as an unstable and conventional product of enculturation—a demonstration of how the distinction of signal::noise is not a given, but must be produced through the *a priori* assumptions about form, intention, and communication—the *desires* that create "noise."

2.3 Category Assignment and Semic Ordering

Initial apperceptions define each recognition: this axiomatic, semic ordering enables all higher level interpretations to proceed. Without this initial assessment, nothing else happens. This foundation chooses what is important to attend to and potentially employ in signification, and what can be ignored, but this instantaneous judgment is never final. It is constantly subject to reconsiderations, renovations, and reassessments. The initial diagnosis comes prior to any decisions about meaning—it is a choice about *what* is present in perception, a definitional moment that separates *language* from *image,* and creates the distinctions of perceptual and lexical semiosis. But this immanent and unconscious choice is also unstable—even for such seemingly fixed expressions as written language [Figure 2.2].[114] When a reader looks at a collection of marks and decides they *are* letters,[115] this decision comes in advance of an appraisal of which letters, in what order, forming particular words,[116] as the genre of asemic poetry[117] called "Typoetry" demonstrates. Deciding a series of marks are language is a modal shift to consider their syntagmatic order—not the *belief* that they signify, but as the proposition that they signify *at all*—enabling a symbolic interpretation of lexia that defines signs as vehicles of thought and / or mechanisms of communication.[118] But communicating meanings elaborated through encoded form requires that the ascription of / intent / justified by the 'intentional function' cannot only be personal, subjective, essential. This autonomous decision about what is present in / for perception is the moment of individuation whose specific choices are as tentative as they appear to be inevitable and fixed: maximal legibility denies expressive *visuality,*[119] separating a text's 'palpability of signs' from its consideration as a visual object.[120] The identifications that enable reading to happen are not simply a "mechanical skill"[121] but a function of enculturation—the reader must be able to both recognize signs in perception and then link them to their signifieds, actions produced by / from enculturation and established expertise. Since ambiguity is inherent in perception, it also affects this process of sign formation via that imposition of / intent / that defines *language* and without which there is no signification, no communication, no semiosis.[122] The commonplace capacity of an artwork to support multiple, even contradictory, interpretations first depends on the ascription of an intelligent (intentional) ordering to their construction, as Eco described in "The Poetics of the Open Work":

> We see it as the end product of an author's effort to arrange a sequence of communicative effects in such a way that each individual addressee can refashion the original composition devised by the author. [...] The addressee is bound to enter into an interplay of stimulus and response which depends on their unique capacity for sensitive reception of the piece. In this sense the author presents a finished product with the intention that this particular composition should be appreciated and received in the same form as they devised it. [...] From the Baroque to modern Symbolist poetics, there has been an ever-sharpening awareness of the concept of the work susceptible to many different interpretations.[123]

What Eco termed an "open work" is an object whose availability and multivalent stability for interpretation is unconstrained from claims of *intentionalism*,[124] i.e. authorial privilege.[125] His refusal of authorial intentions is not simply an epistemological argument over the reliability and verifiability of sources.[126] What matters is not the 'intention to communicate,' but the audience's capacities via their established expertise, past experience, and fluency to impose the 'intentional function,' identify familiar signs, and then interpret the work—factors external to the Formalist concern with an *experiential* aesthetic[127] whose "purity" separates significance from the material vehicle of its presentation.[128] Eco's proposal displaces the critical framework of *intentionalism* where an imaginary relationship between the audience and the author, created via the work, depends on an 'intent' that is then located via biography or its hypostases in society, history, liberty, psyche. The kaleidoscopic multiplicity created by interpretive expertise addressing ambivalence demonstrates the interpreter's skill with managing the impacts of context, presentation, and expectation—but must still be immanently imposed following an encultured recognition (the 'intentional function') by addressing the semantic cues contained in the work: the fleeting emergence of letters in Figure 2.2 that disappear on examination make this imposition process evident. In resolutely directing attention to the reader's central role for interpretation,[129] the theory of the "open work" developed by Eco,[130] Barthes,[131] and Foucault[132] directs attention to the intertextual constraints of past experience on interpretation, and proposes that communication becomes a traumatized and uncomfortable conclusion unable to rest comfortably in either certainty or finality. Expertise and past experience become central to these ambivalent semiotic

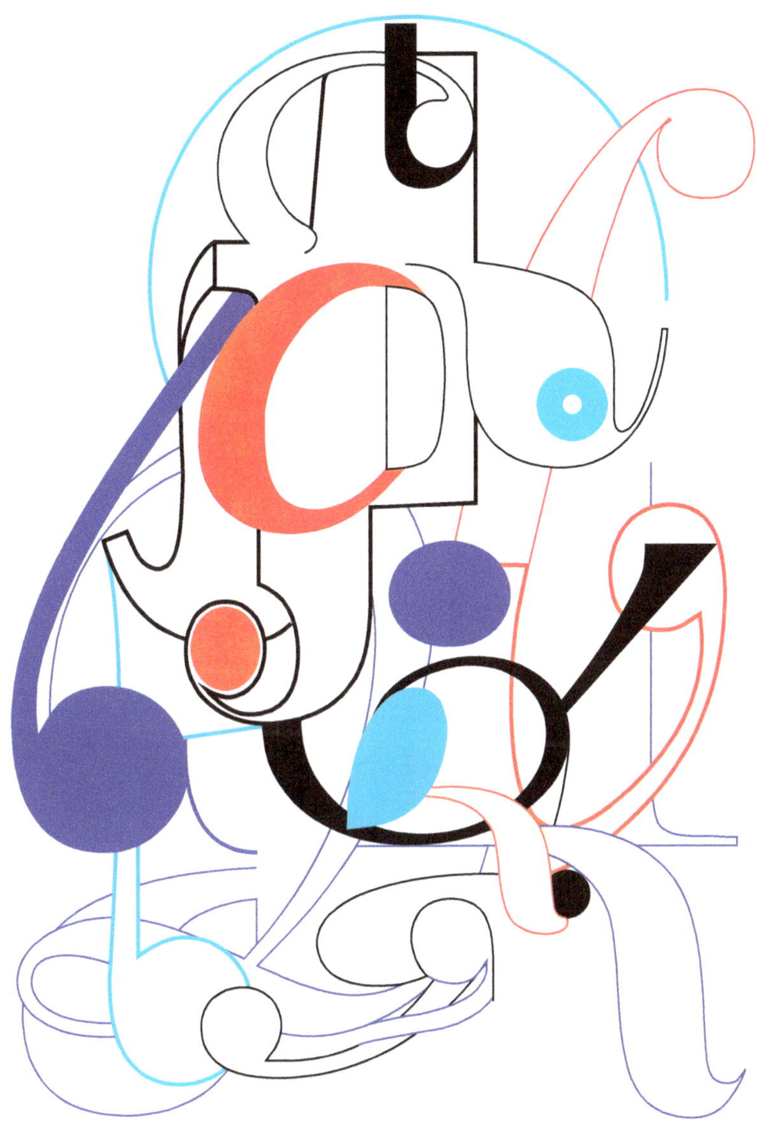

2.2   Michael Betancourt, *Typoem #2022–37* (2022). Typoetry exploits how the process of linguistic apperception is subject to the same perceptual ambiguities as any other sensory experience: there are no letters in this example — the appearance of any letterforms is fundamentally an imposition by the reader. Originally published in *Type Faces* (RedFox Press, C'est mon Dada no. 184, March 2023, ed. 150).
Copyright © 2022 by Michael Betancourt / courtesy Artists' Rights Society (ARS).

engagements, indicating the change in methodology that brings liminal encounters such as /glitch/ into prominence.

2.4 Intentionality and Poeisis

The viewer's autonomous decision to interpret glitches aesthetically produces Glitch Art, and thus reveals the vicissitudes implicit in the problematics of an "intentional glitch" are linked to the intentional fallacy[133] that philosophers William K. Wimsatt, Jr. and Monroe C. Beardsley proposed as a means to separate interpretive claims about the work from the work itself. They distinguished claims that engage with the actual words, lines, images, and sounds by separating that analysis from claims for significance that concern *why* the artist made the work—those external statements made privately or published in journals, in conversations, etc. that are independent of the empirical contents of the work. The poetic utterance is a paralogy that reflects a challenge to the basic, unconscious, even autonomous decisions shaping semiosis and communication; however, poetic expressions unmask the /glitch/ emerging between enunciation and its signification, revealing how the peculiar dynamics of apperception and interpretation of *poeisis* create different aesthetic and interpretive problems from vernacular speech. Understanding the role of these shifting and subjective redirections that change the identification of *lexical* signs parallels the perceptual ambivalences of their counterparts in visual perception. This convergence makes the function of encultured fluency and expertise apparent.

Decipherment and articulation are specific problems posed by Glitch Art, but their convergence with *lexia* reveals that all articulations are mobile: they depend on the same categorical expertise to produce *as-if* interpretations from the mere recognitions that identify what is present in/to perception. These problematics accompanying /glitch/ are hardly new, or novel, but have an extended presence in literary fictions, such as the struggles Alice encounters when conversing with Humpty Dumpty in Lewis Carroll's *Through The Looking-Glass* [Figure 2.3]. Their conversation parodies the theory of *intentionalism* where authorial claims determine meaning, a discussion that clarifies the differential between encoded meaning and imposed significance:

> "I don't know what you mean by 'glory,'" Alice said.
>
> Humpty Dumpty smiled contemptuously. "Of course you don't — till I tell you. I meant 'there's a nice knock-down argument for you!'"
>
> "But 'glory' doesn't mean 'a nice knock-down argument,'" Alice objected.

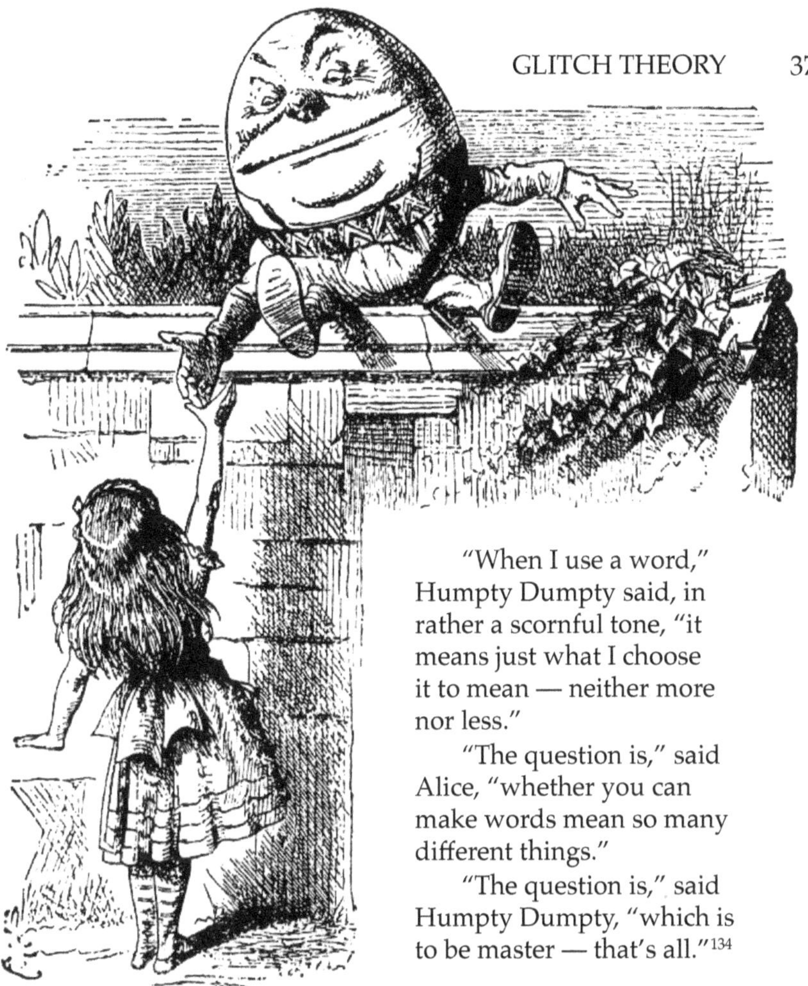

Humpty Dumpty's statements announce the problem of expertise where the imposition of order can appear predetermined and unquestionable, but is not. His demand for the primacy of his /intent/ in the articulation of meaning is a fundamentally Modernist silencing of his audience, Alice, and her role in their dialogue. Humpty Dumpty is an avatar for the theory of *intentionalism*,[135] which conceives its audiences as passive, taking no part in the interpretive process. His perverse relationship to Glitch Art is self-evident: he demonstrates how past experience and established expectations are unreliable. This paralogy is semiotician Roman Jakobson's 'poetic function' where *expressive* dynamics alter meaning on phonic, grammatical, and lexical levels, but simultaneously depend on a tacit agreement between author and reader for coherence.[136] The shifting signification that cues/is cued by the identification of *poeisis* recursively transforms

2.3   John Tenniel, illustration of "Humpty Dumpty" (1871), from *Through the Looking-Glass* by Lewis Carrol.

expected and typical meanings into idiosyncratic and unique utterances that may not be predicable from past experience, since without his explanation, the word "glory" does not mean what he says it does—in fact, the peculiarity of his use is precisely the point of poetics. It substitutes one meaning for another, a circulation of significance that may leave the reader bewildered, as with Alice. This literal derangement (glitching) of meaning is an opening of significance to other potential uses that cannot be anticipated, and whose instability is the essential dimension of paralogical constructions in general, *poesis* specifically, and it demarcates how /glitch/ is liminal.

But articulation depends on *context*—not just on actual usage—and this immanent constraint will always have primacy over any past experience to fully and completely constrain meaning *a priori* to shape the particularities of *utterance*: what it illuminates are the complex, mediating impacts of culture and enculturation on the proposition of any poetics, which develop from both intrinsic and extrinsic modalities.[137] Distancing the essential and inescapable link to the subjective knowledge that enables Humpty Dumpty to become coherent demonstrates how the 'intentional function' mediates the role of enculturation and past experience ironically because his claims to dictate signification demonstrate the essential role of the disgnostic recognition he rejects: it constrains and modulates the utterance with the identity of the terms themselves, a factor that displaces his stated authorial intent as a capricious, idiosyncratic redefinition (a symbolic articulation). These intersections of the objective and subjective aspects of semiosis become explicit with /glitch/ and its role in Glitch Art. The instabilities of Humpty Dumpty's argument refusing diagnostic recognition extends to the symbolic approach to glitches: *poeisis* can also intersect with diagnostic recognitions, but actually addresses the symbolic mode by replacing mundane interpretations with an expressive doppelgänger.

The assumptive transparency of interpretation is an illusion challenged by /glitch/ revealing the extent to which signification can not proceed without considering the impacts of ambiguity. Glitch Art reveals how the interpretive expertise that parses expressions develops from shifting relationships between immanent encounter and past experience: these instabilities inform Humpty Dumpty's claims about "glory" as "a nice knock-down argument," but at the same time his claims for this poetic meaning are contrasted by the everyday, vernacular significance of the term "glory." The *poesis* this mismatch creates becomes a precisely expressive statement about his quarrelsome character, and an ironic comment on his (literal) fragility. While the first aspect of this *poesis* might be certain for his use *as-author*, the second, ironic dimension is only apparent to the spectator who knows the children's rhyme—yet both dimensions of significance are superposed, articulated without either of them being correct, incorrect, or even stated. These expressive potentials exist within the same ambivalent range as Alice's own comments that refuse Humpty Dumpty's assertion of authorial intent: *all* interpretations—even if disproved empirically—have 'validity' within the range of potential interpretations *as* interpretations—the state of information is a description of "all possible interpretations."[138] Wimsatt and Beardsley's intentional fallacy directs attention to the same empirical features that are the reference point for the 'intentional function,' but they describe an epistemological collapse whose glitching clarifies the claims advanced by Humpty Dumpty, and the challenge posed by Alice's diagnostic confusion: the meaning of words is not defined by their enunciator or use alone, but interactively with/by the intertextual knowledge of the audience, and the role of context in prompting an appropriate response. Accommodating this vast range draws attention to the coexistence of each potential within a conceptual space where emergent, equally valid, yet mutually exclusive options all lie within a delimited framework manipulated by subjective expertise. The ambiguity this multiplicity contains corresponds to superposition. Thus separations between diagnostic and symbolic are identical to the discrepancy between the machine operator's intentions and the machine's operations themselves: what the artist may have *intended to do* is independent of the work, and creates a model for interpretation where /glitch/ is the privileged moment of distinction within an expansive and expanding field. Embracing these spectral potentials corresponds to a radical shift in thinking about how the physical world is modeled, interpreted, conceptualized, and communicated.

Poeisis depends on both parties to the communication recognizing the allusive play of language; the cryptographic analogy for metaphor and allegory makes this alternative process of decoding apparent.[139] Considering the subjectivity Humpty Dumpty asserts for "glory" as an instance of *poeisis* without relying upon the theory of *intentionalism* requires a reconsideration of this 'intrinsic contextuality' for the term's role in their discussion. That *he* means "glory" is "a nice knock-down argument" is a specific personal (poetic) use whose apparent capriciousness may also be an interpretive error Alice made by failing to recognize the poetic nature of their conversation: her misunderstanding renders the poetic claims Humpty Dumpty makes as a rhetorical glitch which instrumentally disrupts her ability to interpret his statements due to her expectations for the normative function of *language-as-information*.[140] This failing demonstrates how the 'poetic function' requires a self-conscious and tacit agreement between both author and interpreter in which the multiplicity and idiosyncratic meaning of terms is embraced, maximizing their ambiguity as an expressive dimensions of semiosis.[141] Thus Alice and

Humpty Dumpty are speaking different languages, but using the same terms—hence the /glitch/ that emerges from their dialogue as the *a priori* constraints of lexical signifieds become unfixed in his shift to poetic statements. Alice/Humpty Dumpty's dialogue emphasizes words and meanings are not fixed, but relative and negotiated, opening semiosis to potentials beyond the limits of everyday speech that cannot be anticipated from the established codex of meanings.

Abandoning *intentionalism* resolves the epistemological problem of verifiable sources,[142] but it highlights the problems of context and enunciation that Humpty Dumpty demonstrates, while simultaneously eliminating his claims for the centrality of authorial /intent/ to direct signification. Navigating this expended field of interpretation whose liminal overlap connects the instabilities of 'poetic function' to the potentials exploited in Glitch Art indicates the roles of ambivalence and expertise in parsing any *utterance*; however, these problematics are central to how all expressive *poeisis* structures mobilize and undermine familiar systems of semic order.[143] This shift to the 'poetic function' illuminates the problematics of considering glitches as *noise*, a 'failure to communicate.' This instability is a function of the audience having to acknowledge their interpretations as unstable and ambivalent.

The /intent/ to communicate is one half of the semiotic process, the other half being the active participation of the interpreter who engages via a set of mutually shared techniques that either converge on a similar set of significances or diverge radically, as in the conversation between Alice and Humpty Dumpty. The poetic identification about when to consider glitches *as-encoded* (expressive) requires both author and audience to mark the separation of established intertextual knowledge from the immanent significance of signs provided by their usage. *Poesis*, in contrast, emphasizes the gaps between signs and how their signifieds enter into the same type of mutually recognized and contested relations that defines the /glitch/ as a liminal moment in semiosis. The expertise and fluency required to parse Glitch Art draws attention to this potential for redefinition contained in every utterance, and demonstrates this relational activity is precisely unstable and ambivalent for both sides of the interpretive process: thus the openness of a text remains constrained by the semantic cues that define the text, even when the 'poetic function' acts to recode and alter what terms are present.

2.5 Expressive Ambivalence

Audiences confronting digital errors must literally answer the question ***to what extent should they engage the work as-encoded?*** Glitches demonstrate an uncertain relationship to human agency, and Glitch Art exacerbates this difficulty with its emphasis on disruptions to normal machine processes and operations by claiming potentially inchoate breakdowns of the digital system *as-expressive*. The question posed for human agency (/intent/) by the autonomous and generative production of all digital works is highlighted by the interpretive ambiguity that glitches bring to the fore: they undermine the appropriateness of engaging them *as-encoded*. While it is always possible to engage *as-if* something is expressive; the issue is the justification for that symbolic engagement. The reality of "actual" breakdown is irrelevant to symbolic interpretation, only the identification *as-glitched* matters, thus unifying their conventionalized use in commercial media generally with the 'materiality' of avant-garde film and video art. The foundational identification that all /glitch/ rests upon develops from a paradoxical role for expertise, demonstrating the difference in the modal actions of 'diagnostic' and 'symbolic' interpretation. While a glitch identifies an immanent deviation from the audience's expectations/anticipations for machine operations—an error or other fault in the system that emerges precisely at a moment of machine function—it becomes Glitch Art when the interpreter does more than merely identify the output as an error but allows it to become an *utterance*.

Vernacular understandings assume that if a glitch is a result of an autonomous process, then it should not be considered *as-encoded*, even when the 'intentional function' invites that recognition. This everday belief is the problem because Glitch Art obfuscates all these distinctions through its embrace and exploit of aleoric, autonomous and happenstance glitches—*mis*functions—within the finished work, without addressing their *causes*. Neither technical nor lexical expertise can resolve these ambiguities around the validity of *any* encoding or its role in semiosis. Conceptualizing them as evidence of a multivalent boundary that asserts the distinction between identifying glitches diagnostically as 'the real' and their role as a 'material function' does not resolve these problematics. The empirical and cultural values for glitches are connected, yet must also remain apart.[144] They are not in opposition, but are instead contingent, mutually emergent (superposed) interpretations recognized in the circulation of the potentials they enable through multiple and discrete category identifications. What happens with /glitch/ is not a state of incompatibility, as with classical assumptions about semiosis, but a pattern of relations defining a space of polyvalent meanings and recognitions where ambivalence dominates all signification.

2.6 Paradoxical Glitching

The superficial circularity apparent in the expressive use of glitches is demonstrative of their interconnected and mutually dependent articulation by the diagnostic and symbolic modes. The reflexive semiosis self-evident in Glitch Art has an avatar in the mythical entity named *Titivillus*, the "patron demon of scribes," who is responsible for the insertion and creation of those *unauthored* errors that disrupt meaning, but do not destroy semiosis [Figure 2.4].[145] This animistic figure resolves the uncomfortable ambiguities and unstable relations between the intended and unintended dimensions of glitched semiosis by proffering an answer to the question *who is responsible?* by identifying all glitches as demonic interventions posed as disruptions of meaning: *Titivillus* is a pathetic fallacy who reveals a deep seated awareness of the uncanniness these transformations between signal::noise have always posed for questions of intention. This justification for the presence of glitches is not just an escape from responsibility for producing errors, but a recognition of their potential to signify despite their being unintentional "noise." While these are not new problems for interpretation, this superstitious and folkloric animism brings the autonomous decision that something was /intended/ into consciousness as the first justification for understanding some aspect of apperception *as-being* an encoded, expressive act. In ascribing /glitch/ to a mythical figure, its transgressive power and destabilizing force are neutralized.

Titivillus masks another problem: assuming the recognition of glitches should be understood as critical interventions or violations of the normative 'transparency' of media derives from a fallacy that confuses the disruptions of 'noise' for an expressive, formal use of the medium. It is a category mistake. The conversion of a disruption into an expressive "signal" requires that the interpreter not consider it diagnostically, but syntagmatically—as an utterance—with encoded significance revealed through its use. However, because *mal*functions are unintended, autonomous products, when they converge on symbolic form, their duplicity distinguishes them as the *mis*functions *Titivillus* creates. The conventional stability of signification leads to the circularity of Glitch Art whose expressive poetics are *intended*, but whose identification *as-glitched* depends on a diagnostic recognition of the glitches as an *unintentional* disruption of normal function. What would normally be a stable change of address in semiotic form becomes an unstable and shifting set of identifications: to proceed *as-if* a glitch is signifying, the error must first be admitted to the realm of signification via an assumed author—such as *Titivillus*— who makes it subject to expressive modulation justifying semiosis; however it superposes this recognition of expressiveness with the

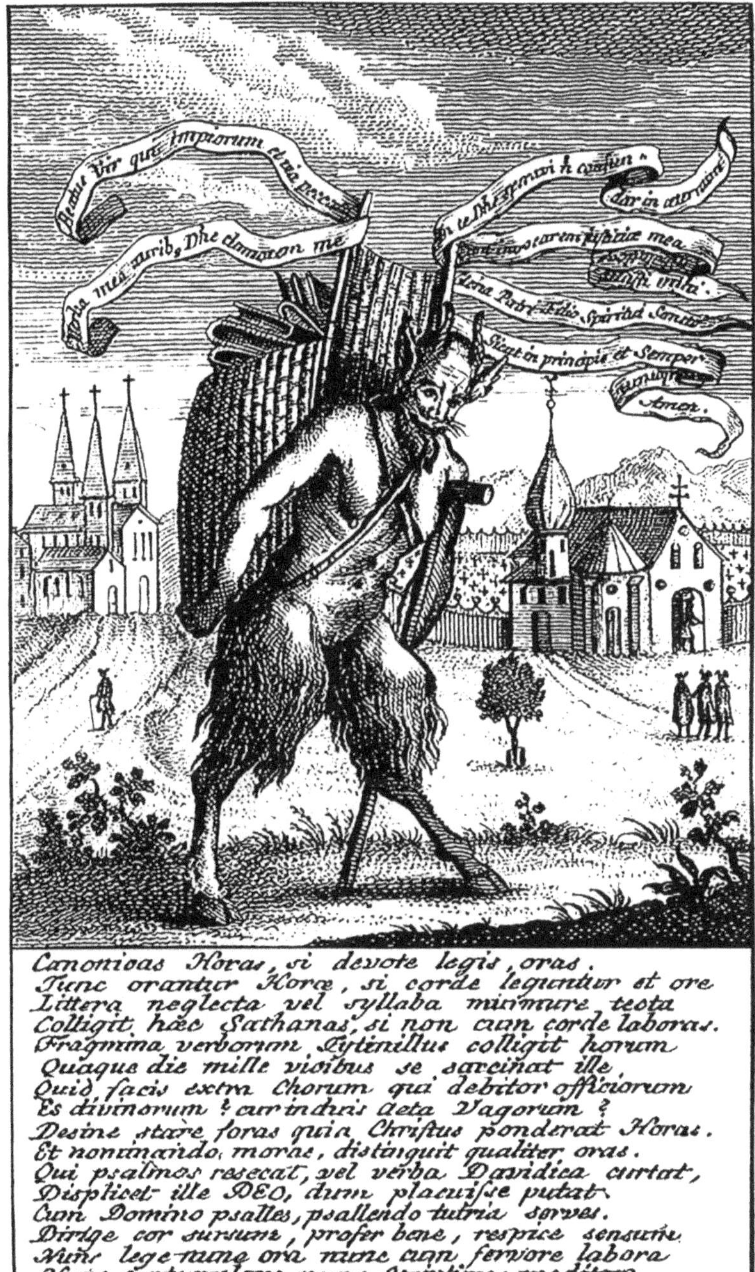

2.4   The demon tasked with collecting typos and other errors, "Tytinillus,"
also known as "Titivillus," as it appeared in a seventeenth century
German woodcut by an uncredited artist;
published as "Figure 6" in Montañés, J. *Titivillus: Il Demone
dei refusi* (Perugia: Graphe.it Edizione, 2018) p. 58.

diagnostic recognition of their identity *as-error,* thereby enabling the belief in a prior signification that *should* have occurred, but which was blocked—an ambivalence of diagnostic recognitions that produces a slippage at the threshold between signifying and insignificance. Although the 'material markers' that desigate these forms originate with the medium (the range of technical failures identified by Figure 1.4), their symbolic articulations are identified by a transformation into the 'material function' that depends on abandoning without rejecting the diagnostic identifications provided by technical fluency to reconsider them as *expressively* or *intentionally* produced. This decision is the moment of differentiation where the choice to engage the glitch as *mis*function becomes a reciprocal demonstration of the act that views it *as-if* it was encoded. The decision to recegorize a *mal*function *as-expressive* defines the shift from a diagnostic to symbolic interpretation no matter what their ontological source might be.

The tautological expressiveness of Glitch Art raises familiar questions about agency and intent for technical media in general, but its problematics arise precisely and exactly because the semic role of glitches depends on an instability in how audiences act to separate the operations of the machine from the human agency (/intent/) of the operator. This transitive instability illuminates /glitch/ in relation to the longer history of ludic play that is interpretation. As engagement changes address from a diagnostic of error to the *as-if* considerations of expressive encoding, it separates the 'intentional function' as a qualitatively different value than the vernacular concerns with 'intention' that identify assumptions about the metaphysical and subjective desires or beliefs of the presumptive encoder. What is apparent in the agency granted to *Titivillus* is a resolution to the problematics of un/intentionality that have been extensively theorized,[146] but must remain distinct from the 'intentional function.' Glitch Art exploits this ambivalent shift into the symbolic mode that brings these superficially unintended artifacts within the realm of objects and forms identified by the 'intentional function' and subject to consideration *as-if* encoded—a specifically meta-stable exemplar of how perception and apperception are entangled via enculturation and its role in semosis.

2.7 Past Expertise Mediating Experience

Distinguishing the diagnosic recognitions of glitches and the symbolic articulations of Glitch Art are neither obvious nor certain. The intertextual constraints of past experience and social context shape semic considerations of otherwise immanently similar (empirically identical) objects. Indistinguishable objects have a particular importance for thought experiments, providing opportunities to consider differences that are not apparent from a consideration of the work—raising anew the probematics of the intentional fallacy—as in the writings of "Pierre Menard, Author of the Quixote."[147] Glitch Art makes indistinguishables immanent. This idea is central to *The Transfiguration of the Commonplace*, where aesthetic philosopher Arthur Danto argues that their distinction depends on the interpretive expertise and cultural fluency of the audience encountering them:

> Two artists, one of whom is J and the other his arch rival K are commissioned and because of their mutual contempt, great efforts are taken on the part of either not to reveal the work in execution to the other; it is all carried out with the greatest secrecy. When all veils fall on the day of revelation, the works of J and K [are identical: each has painted a pair of monochrome squares, arranged vertically.] ... How extraordinary, were one to hear [the artists' claimed intentions in the form of] explanations, to discover the indiscernibility of the works. And at the level of visual discrimination, they cannot relevantly be told apart.[148]

J and K intended very different things, and yet the works are indistinguishable. As with glitches and Glitch Art, the two paintings in Danto's discussion are in fact identical. Nevertheless, their interpretation presents a fundamental problem, since for us to understand these two identical works as having completely different meanings superficially requires a falling-back onto the intentions claimed by the artists in an example of the intentional fallacy; the 'induced glitch' also appears to create an intentional fallacy, but this is a category error because this claim confuses the *intentions* of the machine operator with the *operations* of the machine.[149] Danto resolves the intentional fallacy by showing it is an illusion: neither painting exists in a vacuum, but are instead /objects/ made within an historical context and belong to particular lineages shaping significance without necessarily determining their form, as Jorge Luis Borges argues about Menard. This reframing of "intentionality" as a contextual lineage reconceives materiality as an affect of the shift to *as-if* encoding, thus emphasizing interpretive fluency (past experience) as the crucial mediator that renders one work meaningful while removing significance from the other. While these paintings by J and K may be empirically identical monochromes, that does not mean their individuation is only an issue of a metaphysics of intentions; if placed within the context of other objects by each artist—J and K respectively—another intertextual dimension emerges that is connected to enculturation and past experience, not the artist's claims of intent. What matters is precisely the lineage: distinctions are a matter of past production informing expectations. It is a distinction *by* the audience, rather than innate to the work. These two identical paintings mean radically different, incompatible things because the audience chooses to address them semiotically *as-if* they do. Any artistic deviation from their contextual history creates an interpretive mismatch that reveals significance is function of both personal and encultured iconography. Parsing the symbolic mode depends on individual, subjective expertise and fluency.

The separation of action, ideation, and production apparent in artistic uses of machinery illuminates the ways that glitches establish the intentional function in sign formation lies at the foundation of semiosis and leads inexorably to the margins of linguistic and artistic practice where the interface between intended and unintended becomes palpable: glitches and Glitch Art describe and exploit this ambivalent intentionality as unquestionably a product of the interpreter/reader/viewer/spectator/listener/audience continually shifting their attention between a diagnostic consideration of symptoms and the symbolic modulation of semiosis. This doubled identification *as-error* and *as-encoded* is a superposition of potentials; the entanglement between these modes is /glitch/. These questions about intention and agency arise for all technical systems; they derive from assumptions about human agency as the necessary and essential *prima causa* for art that embraces the irrelevance of /intent/ within Danto's contextual argument. The meaning of art alters over time and in relation to past experience and established fluency, thus implicating not /intent/ but the intentional function in all considerations of encoding and expressiveness.[150]

Danto avoids any return to the intentional fallacy by positing a social function for art[151] that enables materiality to become a product of past uses (i.e. the 'material function') coupled with how *poeisis* expands the realm of articulation to include new and hitherto rejected forms. His solution to the indiscernibility problem thus converges on how the 'intentional function' directs semiosis by showing distinctions arise not from materiality, but from fluency and apprehension, eliminating the problems posed by the intentional fallacy. Glitches being understood *as-error* and *as-expression* converges on the problem posed by Danto's thought experiment about two paintings whose identical appearance accompanies a paradoxically complete and utter distinction from each other in terms of significance—a tautology that produces a rhetorical (and illusory) conflict between *mal*function and *mis*function (apparent as the superficial paradox of an induced 'glitch' as 'technical failure'—i.e. a *desired* glitch whose production was the focus of the technique employed).[152] His argument assumes that materiality is a special category of symbolic encoding that addresses the media-carrier as a media-object, relying on the meaning it produces to justify its application. Glitch Art exploits these transitive functions as a differentiation between a vernacular technological failure (*mal*function) and the *encoded* "technological failure" (*mis*function) of an art object. This expansion ironically returns to the question of materiality, which does not diminish, but instead accentuates the role of the interpreter in addressing physical cues in the work via the same fluency and expertise that determines all signification.

Materialist recognitions require familiarity with the full range of how digital technology normally functions, including typical 'proper' functioning and the 'improper' functions identified as "glitches." Without that foundational fluency—if all outputs are fundamentally novel and unprecedented—then no recognitions of glitch or not-glitch are possible. This essential basis for semiosis autonomously, unconsciously invokes the 'intentional function' when audiences understand glitches as an expressive materiality and therefore encoded.

The relevance of Danto's argument for glitches and Glitch Art is obvious: subtle entanglements between diagnostics, fluency, contextuality, and past experience are precisely the point in this semiosis. Acknowledging the symbolic elaboration of glitches rearticulates their diagnostic presence as-if encoded demonstrates the transformation of *mal*function is a cultural construction in dialogue with concepts of 'the real' and indexicality distinct from the physical nature of the media-carrier: "materiality" emerges from the audience (implicitly, unconsciously) identifying the glitches as worthy of attention based on their past experience. This decision to shift interpretation revising the initial diagnostic recognition made at the foundational moment of interpretation, while simultaneously allowing the 'material markers' to suspend their other identification *as-encoded* by energizing the combination of the 'event' of perception with its representation. The role of glitches *as-error* and *as-expression* are not solely immanent qualia, but rely on context and past experience for their articulation. Decentering /intent/ establishes its identification as a tautological justification for the shift into symbolic modes while remaining concerned with diagnostic features empirically present in the work: "intentionality" is a semiotic product of unintentional and pre-semic semantic cues that shape and direct sign formation and semiosis: these elements define the 'intentional function' in action.

2.8 Diagnostic Problematics

Ontology exists as what Hegel described as an essential truth—a truth of the mind—that is not evident in natural perceptions of the world. Ironically this conceptual nature pushes the ontological out of immanent encounter into the realm of interpretations and beliefs, a contingent and emergent dimension of interpretations that are concerned with diagnostic recognitions, but which do not actually address or rely upon them, instead deriving from the role of diagnostics in/as symbolic forms. The conception of glitches via inferences about causation and generative source within the technical operations of the digital system make this diagnostic apparent: if *smoke* (the glitch), then *fire* (the particular technical breakdown).[153] This causal linkage assumes a connection to 'the real' which Danto explained as "to be real is simply to satisfy a semantic function, but not as a semantic vehicle."[154] Acknowledging this semantic function leads to a derealization of *failure–as–failure*, rupturing the ontological claim. It draws attention to how the identification of glitches *as-error* is one of multiple, but contingent, interpretations that connect them to known *cultural* referents and existing fluencies. To change from addressing glitches as a *mal*function symptomatic of 'the real' requires acknowledging they are always a semic interpretation indicative of experience and expertise.[155] This approach to aesthetics expands from the Formalist concern with empirical features to converge on the 'intentional function' and all the products of enculturation. Describing Glitch Art via contingent and variable social actions affirms /glitch/ as a product of these protocols/capacities to create paralogy.

The entanglement of symbolic and diagnostic modes of semiosis demonstrated by /glitch/ brings their supporting functions into consciousness as a series of tipping points between different kinds of understanding. These ways of addressing the glitches encountered in Glitch Art are not limited to the expressive or poetic construction of media. What the clarity of their interrelationship enables is the expansion of /glitch/ to include any liminal moment that emerges from the codependency of what appear to be mutually exclusive categories. Instead of distinctions and separations, what glitching produces is a spectrum that lies between distinctions, complicating them without necessarily replacing them.

3

TRANSCENDENCE, MATERIALITY, CAUSALITY

"Materiality" is the hobgoblin of all technical media, but digital media offer a categorically different quality of materiality than earlier analogue media precisely because digital technology attenuates the unification of 'presentation and signal' apparent in chemical photography, the electrical currents of video, or even the groove cut into a record. Because the vernacular engagement with the digital understands it as an immaterial medium produced from instrumental code, resolving distinctions between the semantic function of the **diagnostic recognition** identifying *mal*function via *spectacle* (claiming glitches are indexical to 'the real,' i.e. giving them a semantic function—*failure-as-failure*—without expressive encoding) and the **symbolic expression** posed by the semantic vehicle of *mis*function clarifies artists' expressive use of machines. This separation of the audience interpreting a glitch *as-if* it was encoded versus the symptomatic analysis is a distinction in modality and semic roles, but these engagements are not mutually exclusive. Distinctions of not/encoded for digital "materiality" are grounded in a narrow concern for the difference between the technical operations and mechanics of analogue recordings of all types distinguished from the computational basis of the digital medium. An insistence on physicality as the basis for materialist interpretation is a check on the tendency for digital analysis to ignore the technical system.

The differences between the materiality of digital and analogue media are absolute. Analogue media are literally analogous—they unite the 'media-carrier' and the 'media-object' as an inseparable unit where the source being recorded has a physical connection to what is present in/as the recording. When analogue media are played, this physicality is translated from one form into another, as with electrical impulses in videotape becoming the intensities of illumination on a phosphor screen: the values of the phosphor dots are directly expressing the impulses stored on tape. This empirical trace is foundationally distinct from the immanent 'media-object' generated by a computer for digital display: data is not the image being displayed but information describing that display—a set of instructions for its creation—and is often stored in a compressed form where the particular values of any specific pixel may not be directly contained in the data, but is instead invented by the algorithm that decompresses and then renders the file for its human audience. This technological difference creates all the other distinctions between analogue and digital media, but it also alters the nature of materiality for digital works, creating an emphasis on the encoded nature of the data rather than the physicality of its storage or presentation.

However, digitally encoded data is entirely invisible in the 'media-object' and remains inaccessible to its human audience. Unlike a film strip which can be held and inspected, digitally encoded data can only become accessible through an intermediary of some type, whether it is a media player or a system editing program that displays the data as hexadecimal code, there is always a software interface between the data and any human encounter with it. This distancing of the 'media-carrier' produces a commonplace idealization of the source file apparent in the technical fluency that shapes how audiences engage digital works. The data encoded in the file becomes a transcendent, but absent, referent in a demonstration of the *aura of the digital's* refusal of physicality. This denial of the physical features of the presentation (media-carrier) to focus on the interpreted contents of the media-object converges on the isolated aesthetic object shown in the gallery/exhibition context or "white cube" of Modernist aesthetics.[156] This twentieth century heritage informs how contemporary digital presentations disappear from consideration because their audience understands them as an imperfect "copy" of an absent original: the source is reified, paradoxically, in the glitches which are a disruption and effacement of this anticipated ideal—a perverse reversal where materiality comes to serve as an immanent cue for a transcendent expression dependent on technical fluency for its emergence—a symbolic reordering of apperception that transforms the diagnostic.

Glitch Art exploits the reception of any glitch as a *transitory* failure to indicate this transcendent conception of the 'source file' as incorruptible: deferral to an absent perfection that would otherwise appear—the *un*glitched work—is precisely a discursive relationship that reconsiders the 'iconography of error,' which might otherwise serve as a demonstration of digital materiality, but instead functions as a denial of that same materiality. Understanding these inversions as *"discursive"* is apt: the Latin noun *discursus* means "running about,"[157] a replication of works and energies that sometimes match and other times diverge from expectations. It suggests a circulation whose reappearance happens in a variety of locations and guises, precisely matching the protean display of digital media that prioritizes their variability in relation to an ideal form that never appears and may not actually exist. Glitch haunts all questions of digital media via this aspect of transcendent a/materiality, mirroring how the aura of the digital renders the physicality of perception and the enconter or presentation 'invisible.'

3.1 Post-Digital Expressions

Avant-garde art and music equally define the lineage of materialist engagements from Impressionism's visible brush strokes to the fragmentation of Cubism, no less than the lineage from Luigi Russolo's Futurist intonamuri through to music concrete, and the Structural film's incorporation of light flares, scratches, dust, and all the physical detritus that can adhere to celluloid. This lineage emerges with the belief that programing the computer code/data is the essential medium of 'the digital,' apparent in how artist David Temkin describes the protocol known as "databending" to directly transform the internal instructions (encoded data) the computer uses to make a human readable form, thus generating glitches:

> We can replace all the "DF"s with "1A"s. The result is an image which becomes glitchy in appearance as the image data is altered. The exposure of the code-behind-the-image is part of what helps us recognize this as Glitch Art. The raw data is exposed for us to hack — this is how many of us began in Glitch Art, messing with an image data directly in a hex editor, working blindly or referencing glitch tutorials or ancient white papers for file formats. [...] What gives JPEG corruption its signature look is the way that data for each pixel is not mapped one-to-one to a place in memory but distributed within a matrix, along with the changes we introduce (the "error"). We have not actually "broken" the image in any meaningful sense; we've introduced no structural damage.[158]

Changing data within a hexadecimal digital file—altering the file's internal code—may result in an anomalous (for the audience) but technically valid rendering[159] [Figure 3.1, Top]. This protocol reprograms individual files to create interventions in their rendering. The avant-garde tradition restricting artistic agency to a directorial role in making art reveals a trajectory that began with the photograph in the nineteenth century and continues through Conceptual Art into Computer Art and on to Glitch Art. The artist sets parameters and direct/devises production, but they are not required to themselves physically produce the work. This lineage was apparent in works produced by computer scientists working at Bell Labs in Murray Hill, New Jersey[160] and shown at the first exhibition of Computer Art at the Howard Wise Gallery in 1965.[161] This show established the parallel between the role of information/instructions in Conceptual Art and the instrumental function of computer software.[162] Emphasizing coding rather than output identifies the artistic act with programming rather than production.[163] It dissociates human agency from the created work and attempts to distinguish between the activities performed by the human artist and machine operations. Situating Glitch Art within this lineage makes *aesthetic* concerns with manipulations of computer programming (coding) essential to the conception of materiality for digital works since if 'code' is the *medium* of digital art, then the specific technique of 'databending' is the prototypical instance of its artistic manipulation—a direct handling of that material.

The historical emphasis on the aesthetic role of coding and computer programming continues the dissociation between the artist's actions and the resulting work begun with photography. The artist creating the software (code) emphasizes the role of human agency in determining the outcome (the art), but places the CGI work at a greater distance from the artist's agency than even the photograph, which was still constrained by the photographer's manual operations of the machine and the activities they performed in the darkroom. Ant Scott's use of the photogram process in pieces such as *Repetitive Beats no. 8* (2008) that record glitches displayed on a computer monitor with photographic paper in a mediated photogram process makes this continuity explicit [Figure 3.1, Bottom].

In the 1980s, the emergence of general purpose software shifted concerns from *coding-reliant art* where every digital work required the creation of a unique computer program, to *software-reliant art* in which most digital works were created using a pre-existing software tool. The change to software-based production fundamentally altered the role and place of coding in the production of digital artworks, but this initial model that enshrined computer programming as the essential dimension of artistic engagement remains a powerful challenge to what is now the dominant mode of working with digital tools; the transition from the coding-reliant to software-reliant approach remains a point of debate, reflecting the importance of how aesthetics conceives materiality for digital art, however, the processes of interpretation that registers materiality remains constant, producing the 'material function' as an excess that refers to the physical substance of the technical presentation through the 'iconography of error.'

3.2 Illusions of "Intentionality"

Symbolic recognitions in Glitch Art depend on dimensions of apperception that prevent a singular or final signified because the 'media-object' is the result of semiotic protocols happening twice, first by the machine autonomously rendering the data for viewing, then again as the audience engages the work. Autonomous technical systems invite denials of /intent/ as a determinative factor in

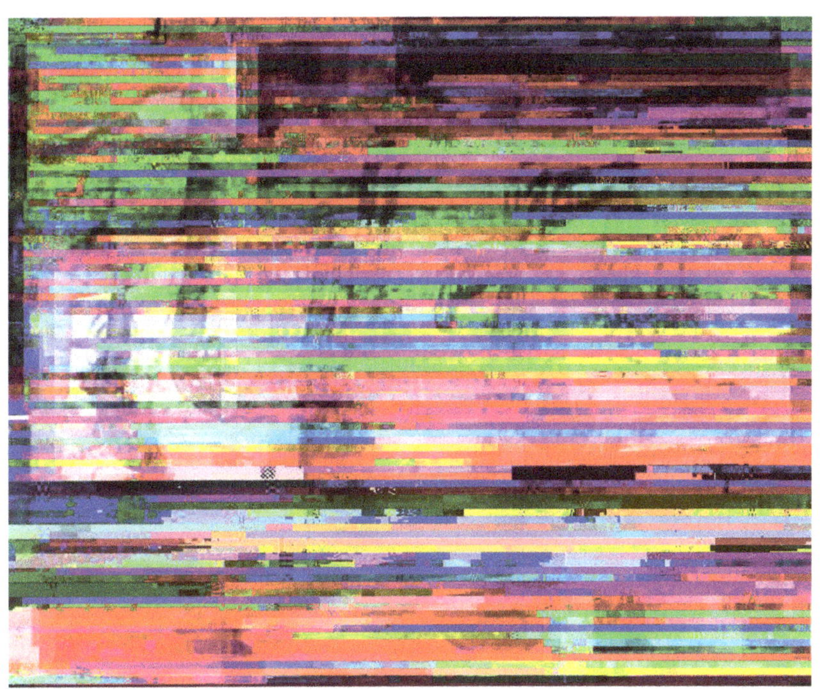

3.1   [TOP] Michael Betancourt, *The Gunz* (1996), a databent JPEG image.
Copyright © 1996 by Michael Betancourt / courtesy Artists' Rights Society.

[BOTTOM] Ant Scott, *Repetitive Beats no. 8* (2008) photogram on Ilford
RC paper created with a digital computer monitor, 7x5 inches;
used with permission.

their creation,[164] an argument that connects historical photography to contemporary Glitch Art. When glitches seem irrelevant or 'unintentional,' they may be ignored as "noise" and vanish from apperception, or be addressed symptomatically as errors to eliminate, but *never* as an expressive articulation, a semantic vehicle. The semic connections between a glitch, its role as an expression, and its expressive capacity define the necessary and sufficient conditions for 'materialist' articulation: a reflexive engagement that is a refraction of diagnostic recognition into symbolic analysis which changes the 'material markers' and 'iconography of error' (*mal*function) into the 'material function' (*mis*function). Deciding to consider a glitch *as-if* encoded is the crucial moment of differentiation between diagnostic and symbolic modes, making Danto's solution to the indiscernibility problem a seemingly inescapable dimension of articulation when confronting Glitch Art: it tautologically asserts that the glitches were produced "intentionally" when it confronts them as-expressive.[165]

3.3 Error Messages

Because glitches do not automatically produce a symbolic meaning, the same glitch may be recognized as significant or insignificant depending on the audience engagement with contextual cues, past experiences, and expectations for semiosis that direct their desires when apprehending the work. Diagnostically identifying *glitches as being what they appear to be* (a technical failure) addresses them as empirical signs of 'what has gone wrong.' By assuming they are random and erratic truncations/deviations, the *failure-as-failure* designation (unintentional and thus unencoded) is obvious, inevitable, even natural: this diagnostic recognition of glitches is precisely the point in maintaining and repairing technical systems. A solely semantic function correlates the 'iconography of error' (the symptom) with the ontological reality of technical breakdown (the cause) as a terminus for their consideration—a designation foundational to the 'transparent' articulation of these expressions as a *spectacle* symptomatic of *failure-as-failure*.[166] The superficial and fallacious entanglement of indexicality with materiality, and their convergent role for 'transparency' confuses these simple category distinctions to produce a reductive fallacy immanent in the indexical claim that glitches are necessarily and only instances of *failure-as-failure*, semantic functions that cannot also become vehicles for signification.

Glitches are always already mechanically arbitrated, a cultural product whose self-referentiality undermines indexical separations because all digital media are simultaneously a presentation, a product of, and a vehicle for representational systems—and their interpretations depend on the same technical fluency that is neither exclusively, nor merely an *en passant* problem in the theorizations of glitch. *Failure-as-failure* demonstrates the separation of signal::noise is contextual, limited by apperceptions of materiality, and determined by the desires of the audience engaging the work. Yet what matters for the shift into symbolic interpretation is how past experience informs both *mal*function and *mis*function.

3.4 Indexing 'The Real'

Presentations of 'the real' in the vernacular approach to digital media demands the diagnostic recognition of a "glitch" conceive it as an anti-representation that is the 'ontological fallacy' created by ignoring the generative and procedural nature of digital media. This attempt to reclaim an immanent concern with its physical/material nature as the *thing–in–itself* connects the productive operation to its reproductive status (derived from code). It understands glitches as singular, unified expressions whose indexicality, objectivity, and claims to *being-factual* are articulated by aspirations to being a proof of 'the real' that dominates their articulation as *spectacle* in the absence of other explanatory desires; thus, encultured knowledge disappears from the apprehension of *spectacle* in a denial of any other dimensions of articulation, leaving the perception of the *thing–in–itself.* This desire to engage the contents without mediation corresponds to the audience's desire to "see through" media to consider the depiction and those significations derived from it. This mode renders anything that impedes or confuses that process *as-noise*, thus creating a cul-de-sac for the perception-interpretation of materiality—*a glitch!*—because it establishes the digital medium by understanding glitches as only being symptoms of technical failure.[167] These semiotics are demonstrations not of an essential meaning, but the contextual dimensions of culture imposing limits and guiding interpretations. The transcendent refusal of materiality renders the digital file both source and ideal work by denying the physicality of glitches as an expression. This rhetorical substitution of an ontological claim about their nature unveils the heritage of Modernism shaping contemporary interpretations of glitches, glitching, and Glitch Art.

Aesthetic uses of *glitches-as-materiality* to assert an indexical claim to 'the real' creates a discursive articulation that complicates the diagnostic and symbolic modes. Their convergence on the question of materiality combines technical fluency and the audience's 'transparent' concerns for depiction to transform glitches into a *spectacle* (familiar from "sports" or "pornography") where the interpreter's concerns are not with a semantic vehicle (symbolic form), but in the apparent details of their perception (denoted content) that might indicate *mal*function.[168] This designation *as-noise* renders glitches as evidence for autonomous processes that are easily confused with 'the real' by superficially deflecting the artifice of technology by turning the interpretation—*indexicality*—into a proof[169] that fuses the representation and the represented, and which conflates the model with the reality being modeled.[170]

3.5 Entanglements of Indexicality and Materiality

The role of materiality in digital media derives from earlier conceptions attached to analogue *photography*, whose dynamics continue to shape the semiosis of technical media. While the production process for analogue media such as photography implies an indexical connection to a physical source in reality—the necessary and sufficient condition to its analogue nature—their semiosis also requires a different type of 'transparency' than traditional hand-made art which cannot be separated from the direct productive actions of the artist. Digital media marks the difference from analogue media explicitly in vernacular approaches to glitches. 'Transparency,' indexicality, and materiality all converge in the diagnostic recognition (*spectacle*) of technical failure which assumes the 'iconography of error' is always a symptom, but ignores the fact that this identification depends on iconography which is a semiotic identification, and thus can be produced by any number of processes. Its refusal of semiosis compounds the challenges created by the aesthetic lineage of the avant-garde that persist beyond the end of Modernism. These beliefs continue to pose endemic concerns for the physicality of technical media, apparent in assertions that materiality and indexicality are empirically present features of the work, as artist and critic Brian O'Doherty explains in his study *Inside the White Cube*:

> Much of our experience can only be brought home through mediation. The vernacular example is the snapshot. You can only see what a good time you had from the summer snapshots. Experience can then be adjusted to certain norms of "having a good time." These Kodachrome icons are used to convince friends you did have a good time—if they believe it, you believe it. Everyone wants to have photographs not only to prove but to invent their experience.[171]

O'Doherty's example of "having a good time" demonstrates how indexical beliefs both mask and are shaped by enculturation. This historical approach apprehends all diagnostic recognitions via past experience and social convention. Those interactions imbue technical media with authenticty, yet tells us little about the reality of the experience in "looking at snapshots," which is separate from those images' representation of "having a good time." This *spectacle* mobilizes familiar cultural codes which might suggest narcissism, insecurity, or even pathos (implicitly condemning the "holiday snapshots" as a trite expression of a naïf cultural belonging). His rejection of interpretive 'transparency' allows him to describe the cultural basis of 'having a good time' by identifying the relational and contingent aesthetics that rely heavily on the audience's technical fluency and past experiences.[172] His observations about memory and perception are a critical rejection of 'transparency' as an explicit concern with content (depiction) that is problematic because it understands these pictures as *spectacle*: the snapshot is evidence for what they depict—an indexical directly describing 'the real'—but this designation relies on the social relations between people *around* the object being considered. His refusal to acknowledge the *spectacle* allows O'Doherty to identify the active engagement required by 'transparency' that makes the convergence of "having a good time" with those linked to the "symptomatic analysis of glitches" obvious: if the depictions seem credible (indexical),[173] it is because they correspond to those pre-existing values that conceive media as demonstrations of 'the real,'[174] short-circuiting the difference between reality and model.[175] Yet if they aren't convincing, then their indexicality also disappears.[176] For glitches this indexicality is their vernacular identity *as-error*, just as in the "holiday snapshots" it concerns "having a good time." This Modernist paradigm assumes there is no need to separate materiality from indexicality, but to treat any technical media as a symptom of 'the real' depends on a social context that permits this assertion. Therein lies the difficulty with the confrontation between semiosis and materiality. The same set of recognitions and fluencies apply to all cultural distinctions, but unlike the hypothetical snapshots O'Doherty considers which necessitate his distanciation, the ambivalences of Glitch Art unmask the instructive role of enculturation by forcing engagement with *errors* that are *not/errors* in a superposition that hesitates between being a semantic function or semantic vehicle.

3.6 Errors into Expressions

The relationship between the paradigms of technological development[177] and their aesthetic expression in Glitch Art reflect category errors that mistake the audience's interpretive transfers between symbolic form, technical fluency, and diagnostic recognition for paradoxes.[178] The 'intentional function' centers the role of the audience whose initial category assignments serve to bind the cultural to the perceptual and the empirical by imposing a percepto-semic order at the lowest levels of encounter.[179] This intersection allows Glitch Artists to conventionally indicate their medium by exploiting the physical faults and failings of display (the 'iconography of error'). The materiality of Glitch Art depends on predefined codes of representation for interpretive coherence, thus conflating *mal*function (diagnostic of technical breakdown) with *mis*function (symbolic articulation of meaning), and masking their distinctions as a "natural" consequence of signification.[180] This heritage links the 'material markers' of digital and electronic media[181] to the analogue features film historian P. Adams Sitney identified for the avant-garde genre of "Structural Film" that attend to the physicality of photography / cinema / celluloid: loop printing, the flicker effect, rephotography off the screen, and a fixed frame from the viewer's perspective (fixed camera position).[182] Although the range of 'material markers' in film extends from the superficial (surface scratch) to the foundational (structural breakdown), the aesthetic roles for both physical damage and the digital glitch equally invoke their status as 'material markers' to engage with the "substance" of the medium. The digital 'iconography of error' is aligned with the generative artifacts of computational operations: the aliasing, crashes, distortions, disruptions, repetitions, and other types of errors that circumscribe the exhibition of digital media.[183] However, while these immanent features are commonly associated with technical breakdowns and faults, the 'iconography of error' is actually produced by the normal operations of the system.

Emphasizing "artistic programming" in an attempt to avoid these issues masks how cultural, economic, and political expressions of 'the digital' are affected by the fact that digital media are performative: the file that generates the human-readable form always creates it anew, "live," at the moment of encounter, justifying the traditional concern in digital art with the act of computer programming and control over information processing.[184] Reliance on this technical knowledge does not resolve these issues because that action is not apparent in the actual work encountered; instead, any insistence on programming reproduces the intentional fallacy. It attempts to transform the role of programming (code) into a *materialization* of authorial intent. There is no escape from these problematics: the performative, generative basis of digital media means its 'material markers' are artifacts whose diagnostic value as a proof of the code's functions is an illusion. The digital's indeterminate experiential nature comes into focus because all three potential identifications of "technical failure" can have the same morphology and structure within a given work:

[x]   as an actual *technical failure* that was produced by a breakdown

[y]   as a *recorded* version of an actual breakdown

[z]   as an *artificial design* containing something resembling a glitch produced by an actual breakdown

The paralogical[185] nature of glitches and Glitch Art unites all three identifications. 'The real' demonstrated by glitches is a product of contingent factors and *a priori* beliefs—the 'material markers' are themselves products of enculturation whose semantic function without expression is diagnostic recognition. The designation of *glitch-as-materiality* is explicitly problematic since there is no meaningful difference between an actual error and a non-error merely displaying the 'iconography of error.' This is the same problem Danto considers for his hypothetical artists J and K: viewers cannot distinguish between "real" [**x**] and "unreal" [**y**/**z**] glitches—what they employ for diagnostic identifications, the 'iconography of error,' is distinct from 'the real.' These are semantic cues whose self-similarity renders the apprehension of a 'real glitch' and a 'simulated glitch' (domesticated or glitch-alike[186]) perceptually equivalent and semantically indistinguishable. *All* glitches are products of the audience's established fluencies (lexical, perceptual, intertextual) that enable the decipherment of the work; the audience's designation of Glitch Art thus identifies and invokes unanticipated divergences from the expected outcome—especially when the original is unknown— that are changes to the "organic" structure of the machine-generated presentation in ways that may draw attention to its generative basis (i.e. its materiality), but is always a discursive product of the audience's contingent engagement with the human-readable form generated by the machine. Acknowledging glitches are neither indexicals nor ontological proofs whose materiality neither affirms nor challenges digital immateriality renders their semantic functions self-evident as an endless process of shifting accommodations.

3.7 Discursive Operations

Glitching is a discursive reflection of the audience's technical fluency that reveals the continuity of 'material function' between historical media (such as film or video) and digital media. Their differences reveal that although the same morphology extends from the superficial (surface scratch) to the foundational (structural breakdown), the indexical claims made about these interventions in the *media-carrier* remain constant. Selectively altering the data does not necessarily corrupt the datastream as a whole, because there is nothing *technically* wrong with the file. It continues to function properly, but the results dramatically distort and destroy the coherence of what is displayed. The contents of the digital file being rendered become questionable; it may be unclear *what* the contents were originally. Only fragments come through, visualizing a dis-integration where recognition and comprehension are in doubt, but whose recognition *as-glitched* depends on the interpreter's assumptive recognition of the immanent work as derived from the technical operations of the digital system, a mechanically arbitrated, cultural product whose self-referentiality via materiality undermines the separations of diagnostic and symbolic interpretations, allowing them to be simultaneously a presentation of Eco's *thing-in-itself* and a product of representation.

The glitch techniques used by artists Nick Briz and Aleksandra Pieńkosz [Figure 3.2] both correspond to the role of the artist in manipulating digital code, and both works converge on earlier interventions in physical media. Their approaches reveal the belief in coding as the Formal *qua* of digital art, but instead of addressing the artist's role in programming the machine, glitching develops this engagement as a tactical intervention in the machine's operations that does not "break" it in any important sense[187] because the alteration of data is *not* structural damage.[188] The visual artifacts employed by Glitch Art parallel the audible artifacts embraced in music composition identified as "post-digital" by composer Kim Cascone:

> The "post-digital" aesthetic was developed in part as [...] the "failure" of digital technology that this new work has emerged: glitches, bugs, application errors, system crashes, clipping, aliasing, distortion, quantization noise, and even the noise floor of computer sound cards are the raw materials composers seek to incorporate into their music.[189]

This "post-digital" aesthetic embraces elements that are commonly considered "noise," a designation which justifies either ignoring them or regarding them as barriers to the clear and coherent expressive contents of the work—an invisibility to attention that explicitly effaces those empirically present properties that help to produce meaning. These "material" eruptions are familiar from Glitch Art as cascades of blocks, as bars/bands of variable length, or as "holes" in the image where nothing appears. Glitching distorts and abstracts *any* encoded imagery, but the areas around these glitches often maintain their 'original' (unglitched) appearance with minimal transformation [Figure 3.2, Bottom].[190] Selectively altering data does not necessarily corrupt the file as a whole, but the results of the changed data do propagate into unglitched areas as the machine renders the instructions, transforming the 'iconography of error' into content of the work.[191] But the final form of the human-readable object is irrelevant to this materialist protocol, although changes to encoding in the human-readable output are more pronounced when alterations change compressed rather than raw data.[192] This use of interruptive structures creates aesthetic gestures towards the substance of media that have become familiar, even conventional. Ironically the primacy of digital code/programming asserts a particular immaterial fantasy where the data becomes the 'real' form of the work and the human-readable (or physical) is thus simply an epiphenomenon, inconsequential. It justifies claiming the discursive aesthetic posed by

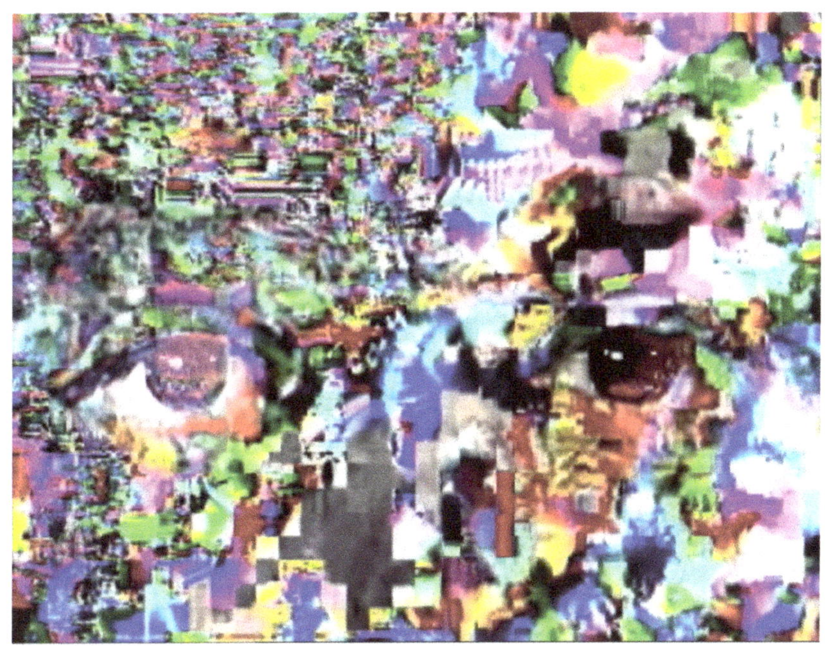

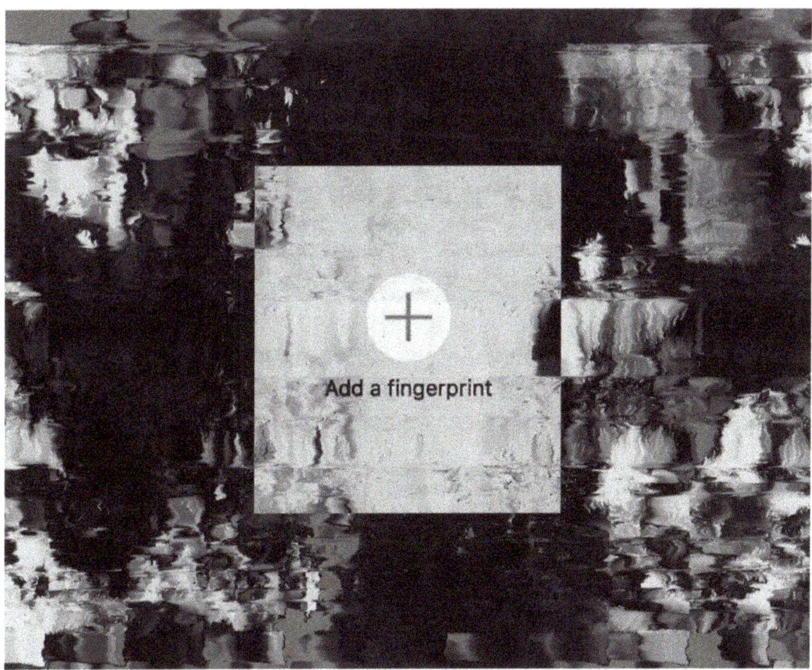

3.2   [TOP] Nick Briz, video still from *A New Ecology for the Citizen of a Digital Age* (2009); [BOTTOM] Aleksandra Pieńkosz ale.png, *fingerprint_2.png* (2022). Both used with permission.

digital glitching is transcendent. Materiality's semiotic role depends on the identification of glitch *qua* glitch—as 'technical failure'—even though it is a 'technical failure' transformed into a signifier: glitches are thus conceived as eruptions interfering with and blocking the messages' communication,[193] a role whose avant-garde pedigree informs their embrace as an aesthetic component, normalizing their disruptions.[194]

3.8 Relational Designations

Digital art no longer requires the specific programming expertise that defined Computer Art prior to the 1980s. The historical technical requirement to code meant the intentionality of the work was not always in question in the ways it is with Glitch Art and contemporary digital media whose emphasis on questions of materiality derives from the recognition that human perception conflates the presentation of a thing with the *thing–in–itself*, making the ambivalence of /glitch/ 'transparent' under normative circumstances because the spectator ignores both their perceptions and the presentation, considering only the denoted contents being displayed. Perceptions are immediate, irreversible identifications that produce 'what is encountered' prior to any encoded meaning.[195] The "post-digital" aesthetic exploits this ontological exhaustion. When the 'material markers' become the aesthetic focus, the emphasis on coding that typically minimized *glitch-as-materiality* shifts to become a discursive awareness of the symbolic considerations of metaphor, semiosis, or *poeisis*: materiality is more than merely a selective focus on physical features foregrounded by a work's construction, operation, and content.

However, the heritage of Modernist Formalism continuously returns, unbidden, as an automatic question raised by medium specific aesthetics and the concept of "purity,"[196] as well as in the appearance of those technical elements normally hidden by the operation of the system.[197] These refusals of the physical object depend on an assumed isomorphy between what the code predicts will be made and what is actually produced: conceiving the output as a 'proof of function' denies its aesthetic qualia and the importance of those properties that emerge from the interplay between the artist, the apparatus, the art object, and the audience.[198] These dynamics reinforce /glitch/ as a relational designation within the unending process of *moble articulation* and subsequent re-articulation shown in Figure 1.2 (page 16): audience desire guides apprehension and comprehension to create a continual alternation between signal::noise and symbolic::diagnostic—limited by the empirical encounter (perception) and guided by past experiences, encultered knowledge, and discursive analysis re/shaping sign formation (semantic functions becoming expressive, semantic vehicles).

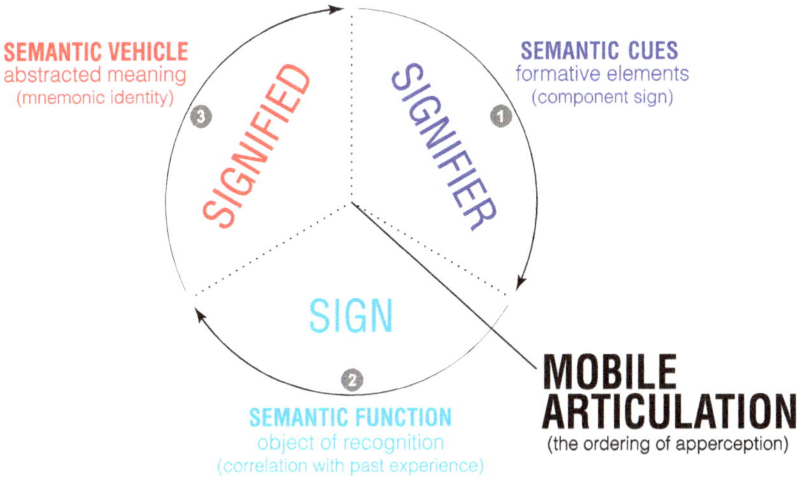

3.3   *Mobile articulation* is a spiraling process of reassigned roles where
      lower level functions become the formative elements of articulation
      employed at higher levels of semiosis, allowing the articulation from
      signs to signifieds at one level to become the signifiers employed by
      another, higher level. This recursive process creates the illusion
      that low level interpretations are identifications of 'the real.'

3.9 A Question of Agency

How the 'intentional function' distinguishes the diagnostic glitch
from its role in symbolic functions depends on identifying specific
semantic (but individually non-signifying) cues that together act to
signal the potential for conscious encoding. To say something was
"intentional" is to designate its diagnostic functions as products of
conscious agency, thereby justifying the shift to symbolic analysis
and the 'material function.' This ascription of 'intent' is an empirical
product of past experiences with other, similar objects of type that
have already been determined to have encoding; it is *not* a conscious or
rational act, but the recognition of structure that defines the sign.

The audience must make an initial choice that organizes *perception*
as articulation and enunciation to begin the semiosis of *materiality*.[199]
This foundation links the recognition of *glitches-as-materiality* and
their role in Glitch Art to aesthetic debates over agency since this
proximate enframing of experience enables those morphologies
and structures that determine the apperceptual order to be both a
technological presentation and a moment of discursive revelation via
encultured expectations and mnemonic recognitions [Figure 3.3].[200]
Cascone's "post-digital" aesthetic invokes the expressive reversal
of the conventional designations of signal::noise—what was taken
to be "noise" (materiality) becomes the expressive substance of the
work. This inversion entangles the 'intentional function' with the

'iconography of error,' understanding 'materiality' as an expressive dimension of articulation—thus indicating that it is appropriate to interpret glitches *as-if* it they are encoded. This fulcrum between diagnostic and symbolic interpretations defines the /glitch/ as a liminal identification. Semiosis must be imposed on glitches as a conscious interpretation via the 'intentional function,' but at the same time, it is subject to an automatic, and autonomous dismissal *as-noise*. Resolving /glitch/ with a semiotic identification of 'materiality' thus returns to the fundamental distinction of diagnostic and symbolic modalities, expanding and complicating their entanglements:

[a] **Diagnostic interpretations** of *mal*function (actual *failure-as-failure*) as a symptom aspires to being an ontological demonstration of technical failure, potentially requiring some response from the spectator, thus ending their interpretive engagement with the depiction as-being the *thing–in itself*. No further semiosis is possible since, in being reality, it precludes symbolic articulation.

[b] **Symbolic identifications** of *mis*function, a reflexive claim to being-factual, (i.e. as "historical testimony" or proof of 'authenticity'), articulates meaning through the encultured structures of realism as a naturalistic "veil of nature" that limits them to being a statement about the image's materiality, as with simulations of degraded footage that denotes malfunction, but requires no response—it is not a symptom of breakdown, but an element of découpage produced by symbolic articulation in two closely related forms.

[c] **Illustrative identification** of *failure-as-failure* is a special case of *misfunction* where the "error" is shown to *represent* a "breakdown." This role of a glitch serves as an illustration of something *being-glitched*, but is not understood as an actual breakdown or a causal product—for example, as an element of the diegesis incorporated and explained through the narrative functions of sujet and fabula as a result of events depicted, or in a different non-narrative fashion.

[d] **Failure-as-aesthetic** defines an artifact presented and used expressively as a method to cue and identify *poeisis*, which demands the 'iconography of error' receive consideration for its own specific properties and which incorporates the ambivalence of invoking a diagnostic recognition that then requires decoding *as-if* a symbolic object.

Technical failures happen invisibly; the cues to their reception are always immanent in perception. Audiences employ these cues to posit a difference between *being* failure [a] and the varied roles that *represent* failure [b/c/d] to produce all their interpretations, including the *poeisis* common to expressions of Glitch Art.[201] The unstable character of these interpretations, the paralogy that defines glitches, draws attention to the interpreter as the crucial mediator of meaning.[202] 'Transparent' demands for internal consistency are guided by the audience's desires for coherence that shape their apperceptions. Symbolic encoding comes into being because it is a product of the audience's choices about intentionality (the 'intentional function') that proceed as simultaneously conscious and autonomous "bets,"[203] a superposed–yet-collapsed ambiguity arising recursively from discursive reasoning modulating perception and re-articulating apperception. /Glitch/ identifies this site of entanglement between diagnostic and symbolic modes without resolving their superposition.

As semiotician Roy Harris noted, meaning is always and inevitably contingent because signs depend on context: their "activity or complex of activities is to be integrated with another in a particular set of circumstances."[204] The dynamics of materiality posed by glitches correspond to an immanent pairing of the audience's technical fluency with the operations performed by a network of physical, electronic, and communications protocols/technologies that returns once again to the problem of indexicality contained by the acknowledgment that all failures necessarily conceive of glitches as a demonstration of *being-factual*, which is obvious in the disparate connections between [a] *mal*function and [b] *mis*function, along with its implicit role in [c/d] aesthetic appraisals. The glitch diagnosed as [a] an artifact of *failure-as-failure* renders it a paradoxical instance of the materiality of the immaterial coding, a rhetorical demonstration of the underlying substance of computation and digital media. Expressiveness depends on the 'intentional function' to assign them an additional role *as-encoded*; it allows /glitch/ to be engaged *as-if* it was an intended creation while maintaining its diagnostic function. The difficulties in separating the diagnostic [a] from the symbolic approaches [b/c/d] that define the varied semiosis of glitches in Glitch Art and entertainment media derives from how the autonomous products of machines invoke a residual encoding by virtue of being produced by and for an audience. The machine is autonomously constrained by cultural orders in advance of any diagnostic or symbolic aspects the media-object might have, giving its productions the structure and organization of expressions, and thus facilitating /glitch/.

Within this framework of shifting apperceptions, enculturation, and semic modes, a glitch (technical failure) is never "only" a technical failure: it also always *signifies* "technical failure," even (or especially) when considered diagnostically as a symptom of 'the real'—a semantic function, but not a semantic vehicle for expressive encoding.

Simultaneous identifications of *mis*functions and *mal*functions as semic products of distinct modes clarifies how they are *not* mutually exclusive: the diagnostic [a] understands glitches as examples of technical failure, and is thus complicated by the secondary appraisals of "post-digital" aesthetics [b/c/d] that rely on understanding the 'iconography of error' as a symbolic representation of technical *mis*function whose identification *as-encoded* makes materiality into an intentional presentation of the medium, rather than a mere fact of its construction. The contextual change recodes the glitch as an artifact of human agency. This immanent potential when confronting any glitch is complicated when Glitch Art specifically challenges the viewer to consider the glitch within a particular work, inviting an acknowledgment of the varied fluencies that make its identification possible. This ironic play on agency and machine operations again exploits the same past experiences and technical fluency, allowing audiences to acknowledge the dynamic of diagnostic::symbolic and how their own expertise informs the work. Enjoying the interplay of recognitions and misrecognitions, inviting the viewer to reflect on their encyclopedic competence and interpretive skill defines Glitch Art as a specifically discursive engagement with the problems of materiality.

3.10 The 'Material Function'

The ambiguous and ambivalent semiotics of the 'material function' doubles the realm of encoded signification whose 'lexical function' concerns the clearly and unambiguously articulated encoding of language forms.[205] The 'material function' parallels these recognition of language, resolving the superficial problematic posed by the 'material markers' emergent through/hidden by the operations of the technical apparatus: *glitch-as-materiality* conflates /objects/ with signs and confuses perception for the refraction of apperception, bringing its role in digital media into consciousness as an imposition of meaning and form. The diagnostic rejection of glitches *as-noise* [a] is an illusion posed by the mismatch between the cultural designation of materiality as mute, unordered, autonomous and an ideological onanism that claims intentions (agency) are transcendent rather than immanent in how audiences engage their experiences. *Mis*function reconsiders these diagnostically recognized, semantic cues to produce an interpretation of the glitch as an encoded expression [b/c/d] that transforms what might otherwise be disruptive "noise" into a component of 'transparent' articulation—assigning a signifier to the sign. Any use of glitches beyond the diagnostic of the *thing–in–itself* thus activates the 'material function' as a vehicle which mediates the symbolic basis for claims of indexicality with other, ideological aspirations to encounter 'the real.' These dynamics inform the discursive aesthetics of Glitch Art.

The subtlety of this distinction is central to the hermeneutic problematics of 'transparency' that define semiosis: beginning with issues of sign formation (the 'intentional function') the refractive decision about what requires expressive consideration guides interpretive decisions about *which* rules to apply, and *when*. However, these guides are not determinative of the final or even the only possible interpretation—the audience is always able to shift into *poesis*, a meta-stable realm of shifting signification that redirects meaning following an alternative system of significances (a paralogy) distinct and apart from the 'transparency' implied by conventional approaches to all media. (The shift to materiality is one potential cue for this changed approach, although it is one of the most familiar.) The potential challenge to familiar semiosis comes from a disruption of the 'transparent' ordering process concerned with meaning; however, this potential to create disarray depends on glitches being acknowledged in the work—the audience must designate them *as-if* encoded before they can affect the semiotic protocols that produce meaning.

The 'material function' cannot be understood diagnostically as *mal*function; it arises as a product of the audience's *a priori* decision to engage perceptions through the 'intentional function' *as-if* encoded. However, the question this change in approach directly raises—*What are the features that promote the identification of encoding?*—creates a category error: understanding a glitch *as-if* encoded is not a formal feature of the work, but an autonomous product of the audience's desire for coherence shaping perception into apperception. There are no specific cues that can define this shift, while a change in context—situating the work in an art gallery for example—will prompt this form of address no matter what the formal appearance may be. While articulation is defined in past experiences—its also exceeds those foundations. The choice of *which* rules to apply, and *when* arises from an internal, autonomous decision by the viewer that is as often cued by *context* as by form alone: anything encountered at anytime may be subject to an aesthetic consideration (the historical embrace of glitches depends on this capacity), but the subjective appraisal of *as-if* encoded transforms the semantic cues into an 'iconography of error' whose reception and interpretation deploys the technical fluency that identifies the glitch for expressive ends. It is the 'fact of *being-glitched*' that becomes expressive and which distinguishes Glitch Art as a genre.

Separating signal::noise defines all aspects of this process that allows understanding the glitch as a type of "digital materiality," but derives precisely from a duplicitous and contradictory set of engagements both challenging and affirming the 'transparency' of encoded meaning, or more precisely, the assumption making features in perception *as-being* a residue of past intentional actions. The entangled dynamics of perception::signification reveals how distinctions between interrelated levels of signification create superficial paradoxes via how /glitch/ links enculturation to 'the real.' Eco explores these problematics for representation in *Kant and the Platypus*:

> We speak of perceptual semiosis not when *something stands for something else* but when from something, by an inferential process, we come to pronounce a perceptual judgment *on that same something* and not on anything else. [...] The fact that a perception may be successful precisely because we are guided by the notion that the phenomenon is hypothetically understood as a sign [...] does not eliminate the problem of how we perceive it.[206]

Considering perception as a type of semiosis superficially conflates perception and signification, a duality that is reduplicated by glitches and the generative nature of digital media. Thus it is sufficient that the audience has identified something in their perception *as-glitched* for the 'material function' to designate the medium in question. The shifting roles of glitches in both diagnostic recognitions of technical failure and their symbolic interpretation as meaningful expressions demonstrates these distinctions and demarcations between glitches-to-ignore (*noise*), glitches-as-symptoms (*failure-as-failure*), and glitches-as-expressions (*symbolic*) all derive from the degrees of human agency (via the 'intentional function') attributed to their organization. The same belief that glitches are autonomous effects (eliding human agency) unifies all diagnostic recognitions. Because the computer is a semiotic machine, producing media first as the machine-readable file, then through the encultured order that governs the human-readable form, the audience's capacity for 'transparent' engagement with content defines these implementations of code as communicative, while the aura of the digital masks their failings—any apparent breakdown is merely a transitory problem with the particular display that can and should be ignored.[207] The entanglement and superposition that is the range of diagnostic::symbolic effected by /glitch/ establishes the complexity of these articulations by parsing the bare sensations of perception into the ordered realm of *significances* and *insignificances*, but this separation is not yet an engagement with meaning or signification, although it lays the foundations for that semiosis. What appears *as-glitch* is an expression of this capacity for the expressive doppelgänger, a refractor of signal::noise, that informs how apperception attracts, deflects, and organizes *attention* into the varied scope of interpretations. Glitch Art is thus not a challenge to 'transparency'—it requires and exploits the condition that allows 'transparency' to exist.

4

'ONTOLOGICAL EXHAUSTION'

Glitch Art continues the Romantic tradition of 'transcendent art' despite the doctrine of medium specificity that dominated art in the twentieth century.[208] Disentangling the diagnostic and symbolic aspects of glitches clarifies how the heritage of Formalist aesthetics conflates the empirical features noted by perception with those interpreted via the refractive semiosis of apperception; however, interpreting glitches as an expressive part of the work, or a novel result of a transient technical failure, or a mixture of the two—there is no reason a recorded glitch cannot also be subject to a later technical breakdown.[209] These developments originated in the debate over abstraction versus representation[210]; however, the heritage of this Modernist concern for 'ontological essences' obfuscates the hidden complexity and ambivalence of /glitch/: the proposal of an aesthetic "purity" from Emile Zola to Clement Greenberg sought to escape the problematics of intention and resemblance via an 'aesthetic ontology'[211] that replaces the ambiguities and ambivalences of perception with a system of predetermined and established meanings that validates the autonomy of art.[212] Medium specificity descends from conflicts over depiction that developed from assumptions about the medium.[213] This Modernist "purity" is substantively different than the ontology of philosophical investigation.[214] It derives from *a priori* decisions dictating which features receive attention and which are ignored—an instrumental aesthetic that enables art production to be automated.[215] The claims addressed in theory and "demonstrated" in practice created a fixed and reified medium, specifically yielding fallacies because the nature of a thing is not a determinative given that can be realized in the fixed and instrumental protocols created by artists.[216]

The heritage of Formalism provides an implicit ground for Glitch Art because it remains a gravitational attractor for aesthetic production. Modern art critic/theorist Clement Greenberg argued for an 'aesthetic ontology' which he explained as the "acceptance of the limitations of the medium. The arts, then, have been hunted back to their mediums, and there they have been isolated, concentrated, and defined."[217] His Spenglerian vision of Modern art challenging then defeating cultural decay through a ritual cleansing and ascetic withdrawal makes its religious overtones apparent. This theory has cast a long shadow via its denial of the essential dimension of *poeisis*, "ambivalence." It denied context, aesthetics, and cultural significance—these problematics are familiar,[218] and its hazards for interpretation are obvious: in claiming an ontological status for the specific *a priori* features being emphasized, Greenberg collapses and negates symbolic interpretation into a Kabuki–performance of fixed roles and predetermined outcomes that moves through a sequence of stations, each with its own significance,[219] but produces neither additional, novel signification, nor modulated expression.[220] However, his claims for ontological aesthetics are idealist, and differ from a philosophical ontology oriented towards realism, such as Graham Harman's proposal of object-oriented ontology "OOO" (Tripple O) in which 'the real,' because it remains unknowable, must be approached indirectly. Reality is withdrawn from human access, but nevertheless constrains action and the potentials for interpretation.[221]

Unlike the mediated and contingent approach of OOO that builds on the discursive role of mediation inherent in semiotic approaches, Greenberg's ontology is an attempt to encounter reality directly, by erasing the distinction of empirical encounter and the mediation of past experience. The heritage of this Formalist aesthetic where seeing is believing that affirms the diagnostic encounter as 'the real' continues to shape *failure-as-failure*. The literalism posed by Formalist art attempts to defeat the ambiguity of semiosis and communication by identifying and focusing on the "significant form" ('iconograph of error') whose "purity" is guaranteed in advance of any encounter with the work. These demands create a power struggle over signification where the artist dominates the audience who are conceived as passive ("powerless") in the perverse dynamic art historian Donald Kuspit invokes for Modernist art:

> The power struggle—the struggle to be master rather than
> slave, to dominate rather than submit is inherent to theater,
> which is why it is the art which most explicitly shows
> what art is about. In theater the artist attempts to dominate
> the spectator by sadomasochistically "submitting" to—
> simultaneously dominating and enslaving—[the audience].[222]

Modernist thought has a long history of defining its audience as passive, immobile, and imbecilic, acted upon but unable to act for themselves: Formalism belongs to this lineage—its concerns for 'aesthetic ontology' enclose interpretations by restricting them to both offer and define an empirical reality apart from literal perception, conceiving them as a product of disinterested contemplation.[223] By proclaiming the convergence of (philosophical) ontology with 'aesthetic ontology'[224] Greenberg's Formalist aesthetic theory reveals the *sine qua non* of its evaluation: art becomes an expressive instance of 'the real,' a specific category of *object–in–the–world* with particular and precise characteristics that serve to define it through the innate features of each medium (thus subject to precise philosophical identification), rather than through the capricious and variable role of cultural designations and encultured experiences without inherent qualities (as in the "institutional theory of art"[225]).

The generative nature of all technical media asserts the necessity for a complete break from Modernist concerns with 'aesthetic ontology' by acknowledging the fallacies created by claiming glitches as the *thing–in–itself,* a mistake that takes the representation for the reality of actual breakdowns, confusing the recognition of *things–in–themselves* for their doppelgänger. The circularity of those relationships that justify the indexical claims about glitches at the heart of Formalism by the 'gignomenological law of identity' (which constrains signs *a priori* to their arrangement and modulation[226]) exhausts "purity" as a tautology: the indexical claims that justify how diagnostic recognitions autonomously identify glitches as 'technical failures' are also the same justification for their a simple and direct association with *mal*function (indexicality), a circular logic. The appeal of this tautology comes from the vernacular mistake confusing interpretations for perceptions—that what is encountered in technical media is entirely and only what it appears to be. This realization of fallacy requires these Modernist beliefs be rejected before any consideration of /glitch/ can proceed: 'aesthetic ontology' constrains digital glitches to considerations of their relationship to 'the real' via the assertion that the 'iconography of error' common to Glitch Art is only "pure" when it is a product of *actual error*, which precludes the symbolic functions, technical expertise, and past experiences required for either recognition *as-error* or *as-not/error.*

4.1 Active Engagement

Semiotic theory requires conceiving the audience as actively engaged, allowing them to become 'critical readers' at any moment through their own internal decision, allowing any object to be subject to discursive reasoning and critical analysis, no matter how banal it might appear to be.[227] Shifts between the appraisal of broken technology and the aesthetics of Glitch Art are always an immanent aspect of this genre of work, inviting the audience to embrace how their technical expertise and past experiences shape their encounters, since each glitch, no matter how superficially obvious, can only be an inference guided by technical expertise and past experience. Philosopher J. L. Austin describes how diagnostic meanings become possible because 'to look,' 'to see,' does not address the generative

actions of technical media, but confronts the audience's encounters
with their products:

> If there is to be communication at all, there must be a stock
> of symbols of some kind. [...] There must also be something
> other than words [symbols] which the words are used to
> communicate about: this may be called "the world." There
> is no reason why the world should not include the words,
> in every sense except the sense of the actual statement
> itself, which on any particular occasion is being made about
> the world.[228]

What is taken diagnostically to be evidence of a technical failure or
breakdown communicates to the technically fluent about unseen past
operations. Any encounter with a glitch, while it may be a thing in the
world, is not an encounter with the reality of its creation, but actually
an interpretive "bet" which communicates the idea of "error" to the
fluent observer—Danto's "semantic function" thus links perception to
reality. But the encoded nature of digital media means that any *actual*
error can only be expressed via the 'iconography of error.' Making an
indexical claim for glitches thus reveals the Formalism at the heart of
'aesthetic ontology' for digital media.

Assuming the glitch is an instance of 'the real,' the *thing–in–itself*,
understands it as a product of direct/autonomous actions of the
machine creating it, thus rejecting the role of enculturation that shapes
this identification. However, all these assertions always already
activate the audience's encultured knowledge. This symptomatic
analysis of glitches as *mal*functions asserts the expertise provided by
technical fluency as a qualifier for perception, but at the same time,
efface how the 'iconography of error' used in that identification also
represents glitches, a superficial paradox that is resolved because it is
an illusion. This artifact of 'aesthetic ontology' disappears with the
acknowledgment that the distinction of diagnostic versus symbolic
variants of interpretation both depend on semic conventionality. There
is no paradox in the diagnostic recognition of a glitch. For glitches
to become symptoms they require at the moment of recognition a
learned fluency derived from expectations for a particular formal
appearance which evaporates into invisibility to mask its basis in
symbolic interpretations because the diagnostic identification of
"broken" is not an expressive feature.[229]

4.2 "Real" Sources

What ontology describes, in a Hegelian turn, is a reality of the mind,
not perception. Accepting the diagnostic recognition as an indexical
proof of failure thus creates an ontological fallacy by hiding its own

signification: **the ontological relationship between any /glitch/ and its generative source is irrelevant for interpretation.** The interdependent contingencies of 'the real' might not appear to perception at all, which is always limited to the empirically present features (perceived semantic cues) that provide the inchoate substance becoming apperception. Disentangling 'aesthetic ontology' from the recognitions of glitches and diagnostic or symbolic interpretations demonstrates these empirical and cultural values are connected, but must remain separate.[230] While the 'ontological nature' of a thing is of philosophical interest, it is at the same time inaccessible to perception, an immaterial concept of reflective reasoning, not present to *any* material or empirical encounter. Any ontology of errors must refer to these visible mistakes and acknowledge that what appears as "glitch" is a correlation between hidden and absent actions and the artifacts generated— revealing the fallacy of Modernist aesthetic "purity."

Nevertheless, maintaining this duality of address allows Glitch Art to apprehend the /glitch/ aesthetically, while acknowledging the role of 'technical failures' in articulating and designating these works *as-error*. Semiosis splits denoted and depicted contents as the diagnostic appraisal and/or the infinite recursion of symbolic analysis, apparent in the immanent capacity to change from breakdown to a *symbolic* rupture in typical function. The diagnostic mode's indexical claim to refer to the *thing–in–itself* must remain separate from any ontological claims to 'the real,' even while /glitch/ entangles all these different interpretations ever more tightly as contingent modes. This ontological exhaustion weakens the indexicality of technical media allowing the /glitch/ to become a liminal encounter demarcating the transition and point of contact between incompatible states.

4.3 The Diagnostic Fallacy

The 'diagnostic fallacy' is a pernicious error for technical media, shaping the paradoxical duplicities of assuming communication that conflates denotation and enculturation with 'the real,' masking their existence as cultural constructs. Unlike the symptomatic view of "if smoke, then fire" that posits a *reactive* association, the reification of glitches and what produces them in the computer's operations displaces the role of learned fluency and the cultural expectations that identify all errors as unintentional disruptions. The conception *as-error* informs the mathematical theory of communication by presupposing the intentional structuring of semiosis.[231] "Information theory" does not describe an individual message (as with the concept of meaning), but rather identifies the situation of 'meaning communicated' as a whole.[232] It proceeds by addressing ways to maximize the capacity to convey meaning (information); the diagnostic defines the material cues displayed by glitches in the strictest literal sense: it treats what emerges as directly linked (indexical) to a physical cause (*mal*function) that requires action (correction or repair). This minimizing process restricts glitches to being distortions and/or corruptions of "signal." This *a priori* decision converges on the indexicality of 'aesthetic ontology' as not a metaphor, but as an instrumentality for engaging glitches via *failure-as-failure,* allowing analysis to "fix" the problem. By affirming what appear to be "common sense" (conventional and correlational) assertions, the diagnostic fallacy transforms the complexity of perceiving technical media into an ontological claim about encountering 'the real.' There is nothing novel about this error; only its persistence is notable.

Repair handbooks such as the *RCA Television Pict-O-Guide* ratify this use [Figure 4.1] via photographs of various analogue technical problems accompanied by instructions for their correction; however, their identity *as-noise* in one context does not preclude their expressive use in another—these "failures" resemble the distortions and other visuals appearing in the techniques of "signal processing" used in/by video art.[233] Every attempt to repair a problem employs symptomatic analysis to recognize the nature of the failing. These protocols for revealing glitches *as-error* to eliminate or minimize are deeply embedded in the conception of technical media. Historical aspirations to document 'the real' illuminate how linking depictions to specific computational processes renders all glitches as an artifact that can be used to reference the operations that may have produced them in the same ways and for the same reasons that a footprint is indexical—a representation of experience, contingent and artificial, entangled with the encounter.[234] But the *digital* glitch is not a footprint. The semiotic basis of the digital machine's operations contrasts with the translations effected by earlier analogous media: the human readable display is a generative product, different from earlier analogue media where the display is linked to a specific material source through a causative action such as the electrical voltage that excites a phosphor on a cathode ray tube. The examples shown in Figure 4.1 are typical.

The initial identification of "error" maintains indexicality, even when it is radically reconceived without an ontological basis, because the audience's desire for a direct grasp of the contents of technical media addresses depiction as *spectacle.*[235] The technological basis of glitches understood as artifacts of automated processes (typical machine operations)[236] inherent in their diagnostic function reveals how Greenberg's arguments for "purity" are contained in the 'aesthetic ontology' critiqued by Glitch Artist Rosa Menkman, whose challenges to the separation of 'real' from 'fake' glitches show how persistent this heritage,

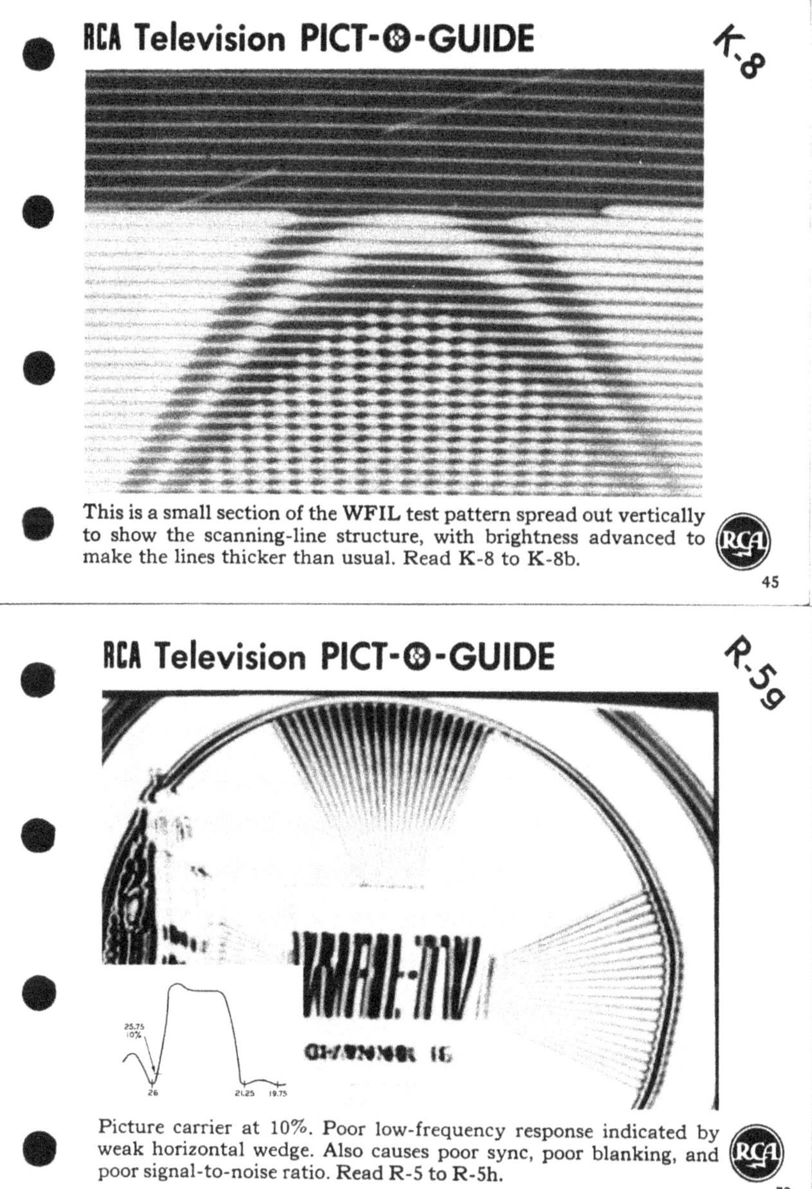

4.1   Examples of technical breakdowns that converge on the visual
distortions utilized in early analogue video art; from John R. Meagher's
1949 television receiver repair handbook *RCA Television Pict-O-Guide:
An Aid to TV Troubleshooting, Volume 1* (Harrison, NJ: Radio Corporation
of America, Tube Department, 1949) pp. 45 [TOP], 73 [BOTTOM].

value system, and influence remain.[237] Her projects, such as the *Vernacular of File Formats* (2009-2010), and her essays, for example, the *Lexicon of Glitch Affect* (2019),[238] demonstrate how persistent the embrace of Modernist beliefs about "real errors" divorced from significance and offered as a pure engagement with 'technical failure' is: Formalist approaches depend on *being* rather than *signifying*—'the real' rather than mere representation—all the interpretations that the ambivalence of /glitch/ undermines. Her projects articulate the limits of these protocols, deconstructing the certainties that Formalist methodologies assume by demonstrating the broader limitations of "purity." Her taxonomies reveal that any attempts to provide a fixed universe of signs and cultural importance is untenable.[239] By documenting the ambivalences attached to the material appearance of glitches she counters assumptions about the diagnostic mode and its suggestions of an essential definition of 'real' or 'fake' errors: there is no simple way to distinguish between one and the other since all the glitches shown are recordings that exploit the convergence between an unpremeditated technical failure, unstable and transitory, and those audio or visual artifacts that coincide with these incidental errors, but are stable and repeatable. No categorical distinction can be determined from the glitches in themselves. The semantic cues for recognizing them lie not with being ontological proofs of breakdown, but with iconography; thus the challenge to the ontological status of glitches must be total.

4.4 Contextuality

Resolutions of /glitch/ are always unstable, a fact that is obvious from Glitch Artist John Bumstead's works [Figure 4.2] presented as "broken laptops." When encountering them, their immanent and interactive transformations invite being understood *as-errors*, yet this recognition remains unstable because they also invite an 'intentional function.' The assessment of the symbolic modulations of Glitch Art transform what would otherwise be *mal*function into *mis*function, producing an ontological exhaustion that renders the origins of any particular glitch irrelevant. Any *meaning* (even the separation of "real" from "fake") is co-dependent on the encounter and on enculturation.[240] Their *presentation* matters: **context**—*where* and *how* a glitch is encountered informs the potential interpretations accepted by the audience, while shaping signification *a priori* to semiosis; the encounter

4.2   John Bumstead, *untitled*, presented at the Experiential Sensory Collective (ESR) V3.0 show, REM5 VR gallery, St. Louis Park, Minnesota on March 26, 2022; used with permission.
This array of laptop computers displaying visual glitches produced by their built-in cameras which transform the audience as they encounter the device.

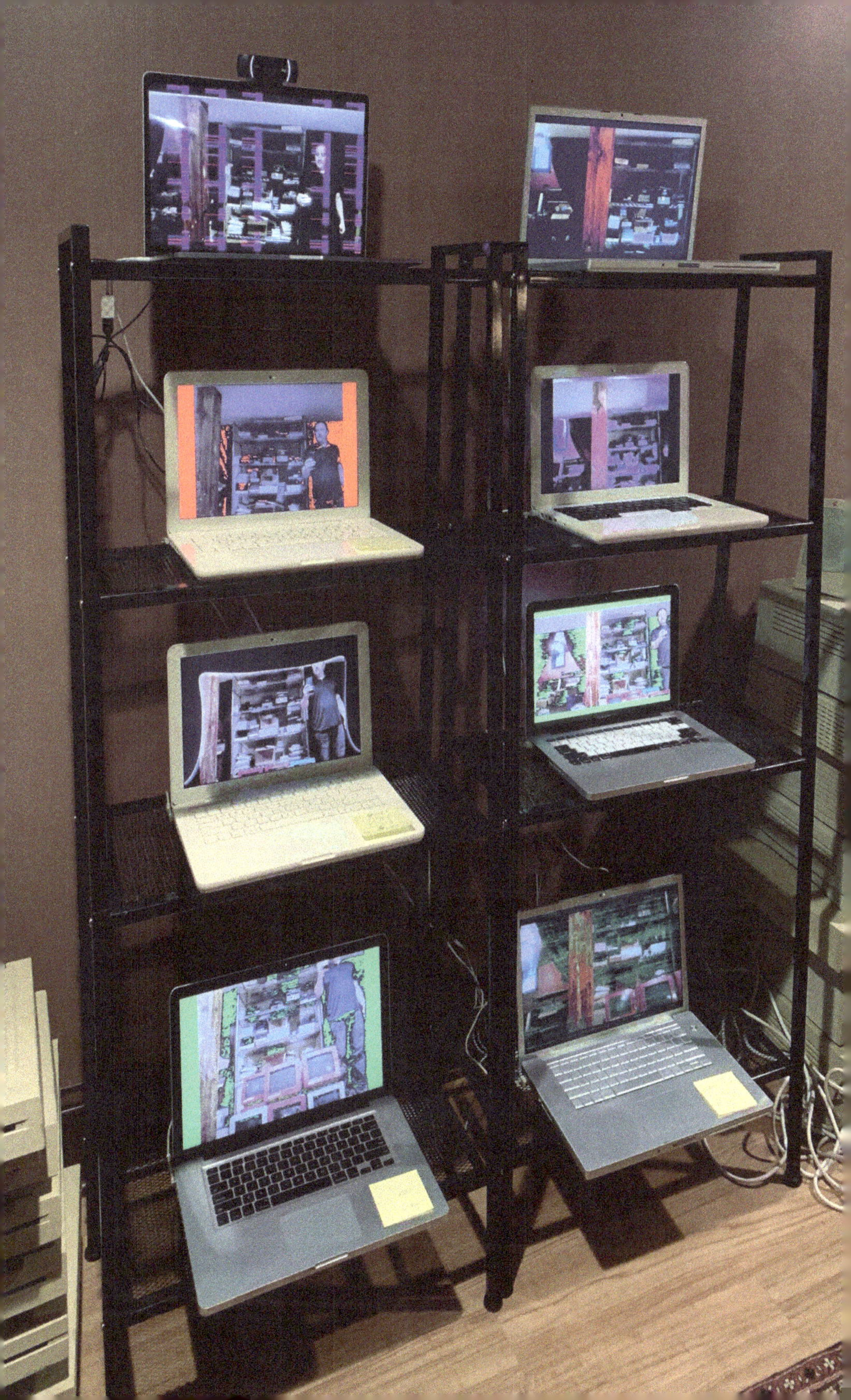

is an extraneous dimension of the object, but nevertheless directs its meaning. These factors are separate from the formative role of the 'intentional function,' creating a parallel and intersecting framework shaping all hermeneutic responses. This recognition is implicit in the Modernist invention of the "white cube" gallery space that purged externalities of everyday reality. This invention of a decontextualized *mise-en-scène* enforced ideological effects that focus, restrict, and direct attention to the art object,[241] but these attempts to eliminate external context from the interpretations of art via a durable presentation merely facilitated, rather than limited, the scope of transformations that change semantic functions into semantic vehicles.[242]

Bumstead's work thus reveals the external role of context in mediating between perception and semiosis. The exhibition context parallels how a glitched image seen online and presented in a forum focused on such errors will be understood in very different ways than the same glitched image encountered on an otherwise *unglitched* webpage with no indication that these errors are *not* some type of technical failure.[243] Separating this documentary role from context is precise: this distinction is the difference between a diagnostic apprehending the *thing–in–itself* and a representation of that thing. These are the problematics of ontology returning in a new guise, but with the same 'diagnostic fallacy.' Documentation is evaluated as *spectacle*, based what information it presents, not how aesthetically it presents that information, while *context* identifies the ways that the presentation can cue the interpretation of the work: they are a repetition of the opposition between diagnostic and symbolic interpretations, but addressing *context*.

While there is nothing to prevent a glitched image from being addressed as an aesthetic object in either, both, or neither setting, it is much more likely to be considered *as-if* encoded in the first context than in the second. The enframing produced by the "art exhibition" context sets an expectation for the shifting and ambivalent semiosis of *poesis*, converging on the same problematics of encoding raised by Humpty Dumpty's statement about "a nice knock-down argument" that reveals the ways audiences categorize their encounters determines sensibility.[244] The *mise-en-scène* of the "art exhibition" contains the mediating role of past experience through contextuality, a factor apart from and yet integral to *poeisis* that Danto recognizes as an essential shift in attention:

> In life as in art it is easy enough to overlook things that do
> not fit the spontaneous hypotheses that guide perception. In
> life, where perception is geared to survival and guided by
> experience, we structure the visual field in such a way as to

regulate to inessential background whatever does not fit our schemata, and such habits of looking are carried over into the gallery, much in the way that the habit of scanning, which is essential to reading, is brought with us into the study, where we may find ourselves reading texts, until we deliberately intervene, somewhat as we would read a newspaper article.[245]

These horizons of expectation delimit the 'intentional function.' Context imposes a real constraint on this assertion of /intent/ in a recognition of invisible yet omnipresent parallels provided by the 'habits' that Danto describes. Encultured assumptions are essential for understanding *mise-en-scène,* which complements the 'intentional function' by clarifying and supporting the audience's "bet" about *when* it is appropriate to analyze technical media *as-if* they were vehicles for symbolic meaning (i.e. intentionally encoded[246]) and thus subject to the same expressive modulations as language.[247] This non-semic dimension defies the limits of 'aesthetic ontology' and concerns with 'purity' by separating the issues of syntagmatics from questions and processes of sign formation that have been problematic for technical media since the invention of photography and its conception as "the medium of absolute realism."[248] The nineteenth century debate over intentionality in photography[249] and the role of contextuality for Glitch Art is the same concern with the appropriateness of when to engage *as-if* encoded.[250] The context that encourages and facilitates this change in perception is not a feature of the work—neither contained by perception, nor present in their apperception of the semantic cues—but resides in how enculturation shapes context to create a *mise-en-scène* that instructs semiosis, a factor that must be learned from past experience.

4.5 Semic Ruptures: the *Verfremdungseffekt*

Modernism, for all its faults and fallacies, was an attempt to formulate protocols for an autonomous, critical art that conceived interruptions and disruptions as aesthetic interventions in form whose axiomatic assumptions continue to shape the interpretive "space" that all technical media occupies. This lineage creates fallacies for the interpretation of the specific ambiguity of /glitch/ and its indeterminate operations for apperception; Glitch Art makes these Formalist precedents its frequent hobgoblin, beyond questions of ontology. Philosopher Vilém Flusser's scientistic argument for an "uncanny" art asserts this Modernist paradigm for technical media via instabilities that subsume what are ideological and subjective biases about class and social position into an "objective" aesthetic encounter:

> "Art" is any human activity that aims at producing
> improbable situations, and it is the more artful (artistic) the
> less probable the situation is that it produces. Such a "new"
> situation is terrifying if seen from the context it emerges
> from, because it is unexpected and therefore experienced as
> something hateful, ugly. Thus "art" is that human activity
> which aims at producing hateful, ugly situations, situations
> that cause terror.[251]

Flusser's attempt to create a "science of beauty" is a denial of
contemporary aesthetics[252] to return to an earlier Modernism that
synthesizes the influence of Surrealist aesthetics (their emphasis on the
"marvelous"[253] converges on his "terror" and the *Unheimlich*) to propose
a conception of "art" that articulates an avant-guardiste rejection of
anything that is not explicitly novel,[254] thereby enshrining the Modernist
demand for "originality" in the aesthetic valuation of work.[255] Elitist
values are implicit in his proposal: the concept of "kitsch" is associated
with the people whose labor, through industrialization, made a small
number of bourgeois (the factory owners) rich. His refusal—anything
insufficiently novel is disregarded as "kitsch"[256]—marginalizes whole
categories of art, and by association, those people who enjoy that
work in a proposal that converges on other Modernist critics such as
Clement Greenberg.[257] Unlike critic Susan Sontag's idea of "camp" (i.e.
"kitsch") which is founded on being "fun,"[258] his rejection of kitsch
derives from its aspirational nature and its imitative function: these
works are embraced by are the classes which comprise the "petit"
bourgeoisie who strive to become fully bourgeois.[259] They adopt the
formal appearances of their aspirations without understanding or
acknowledging the meaning of those symbols.

Flusser's proposal of "terror" as the essential feature of 'novel'
aesthetic work[260]—the more the interpreter experiences something
new and unexpected, the more their encounter is terrible, hateful,
or "ugly"[261]—is the same affect that defines *rejective encounters*
with glitch: but not everything new produces terror, and those
things which are initially terrifying[262] often lose this dimension as
they become familiar.[263] As it becomes habitual, the "terror" of the
uncanny fades and it returns to the realm of the *Heimlich*.[264] This
process is internalized with digital media via the aura of the digital
that is always a return to the *Heimlich*, a term that is appropriate:
the safety and familiarity of an unquestioned and expected order.[265]
These transformations are predictable as each avant-garde dies
when a new fashion or movement replaces it,[266] rendering earlier
innovations familiar and commonplace.[267] This counter-revelatory
engagement undermines any potential rupture because "at
homeness" forecloses on potential opposition by protecting and

maintaining the transparent fantasy of digital perfection, separate from the mere materiality of its presentation. To return to any familiar and stable semiosis requires a disavowal recoding the glitch either as irrelevant (noise) or as a material sign for the technology that is a novel but syntactical part of enunciation as with fades, dissolves and other graphic, visual effects that serve as transitions or markers within the enunciation of cinema. However, Flusser's interpretation of "terror" converges on Bertolt Brecht's performative theory of *Verfremdungseffekt* (distancing or alienating effects, an uncanny sense of violated rules and conventional expectations) that relies on narrative conventions to establish a transformative paralogy that disrupts the codes of its own construction. "Terror" describes the superposed, modal uncertainty which defines glitches as more than the technical operations of computer systems:

> The audience can no longer have the illusion of being the unseen spectator at an event which is really taking place. [...] The artist's object is to appear strange and even surprising to the audience. He achieves this by looking strangely at himself and his work. As a result everything put forward by him has a touch of the amazing. Everyday things are thereby raised above the level of the obvious and automatic.[268]

The *Verfremdungseffekt* (defamiliarization) arises in encounters where established codes and interpretive schemas that suggest contradictory (if not mutually exclusive) understandings (i.e. they are instances of paralogy) are parasitical on established, normative interpretations without expanding on them. The critical affect of Brecht's transformation / violation of expectations depends on *aesthetic* ruptures with 'transparent' enunciation and articulation that renders them 'opaque': this "terror" is a conceptual product of a semiotic mismatch between anticipation and immanence that arises spontaneously and unexpectedly to produce an *Unheimlich* experience.[269] This semiotic protocol redefines Brecht's argument. These subjective responses redefine and transform via the / glitch / whose interstitial breach violates established, familiar distinctions. By separating these potentials from Brecht's Marxist dialectics that conceived viewers as *passive*,[270] it recognizes they do not need to be 'shocked' out of their complicity. Reconsidering these dynamics via semiotics shows that the defamiliarized opens away from the easy duality of class and political economy. These effects correspond to the relational evaluation immanent in Glitch Art: to recognize any "glitch" depends on the vernacular association with its being the *effect* of a hidden *cause* that originates within the technical functioning of the machine. This basis must either symptomatically return to the 'iconography of error' or abandon it for the deeper complexity of an *Unheimlich* which addresses the interpretive relationship between immanent encounter and past experience, symbolically repeating the same violation of expectation and anticipated form that produces the diagnostic recognition of "glitched" from the 'iconography of error.'

4.6 Varieties of Rupture

Digital media are governed by the nested, matryoshka-ambivalences of perception, past experience, lexical fluency, and the conventions of art. Conceiving /glitch/ as an automatic vehicle for the *Verfremdungseffekt* is a fallacy: this critical rupture depends on its relationship to the commonplace 'transparency' of interpretive engagement that is interested in the meaningful, symbolic content, but not necessarily in the vehicles of its presentation. By violating the 'transparent' reading linked to the immanent encounter (an *intra*textual engagement that remains fixed upon the enunciations and order arising from accepting its articulation) Brecht's techniques for prompting a critical reading challenge any immanent elaborations through *inter*textual information *absent* from the encounter, throwing its interpretation open to alternatives and competing systems of meaning—*paralogy*. His protocols for creating a reflexive ambivalence are a product of the period in Europe between World Wars 1 and 2, and have now become familiar aspects of media semiosis:

[1] direct address to the spectators

[2] the quotation or disruptive non-sequitur

[3] breaching the "fourth wall"

[4] presenting directly critical content

[5] drawing attention to the artifice

[6] the intrusion of "noise" that disrupts the work
     (typically ignorable as external to the media,
     as glitches often are rejected/ignored)

The capacity to create disruptions, to invoke paralogies, is attenuated or even eliminated over time. Each of these aesthetic protocols stands apart from established, normative engagement, yet they all can be assimilated back into it—a transformation from *Unheimlich* to *Heimlich*, alienation to everydayness—giving their roles an ambivalent character. All six aesthetic types are well-known and familiar, yet only the responses to [5] and [6] do not necessarily entail a return to a 'transparent' semiosis—they must be expelled as insignificant to reassert transparent semiosis (normalcy). The identifications described by [1/2/3/4] all depend on the symbolic elaboration of the work; they require analysis, and rely on past experience, interpretive fluency, and lexical expertise being informed by context. The change from *intra*textual organization to *inter*textuality [1/2/3] defines the central place of 'transparency' and expectation in setting the parameters that define articulation. Glitch Art does not change/ challenge this semic role of the *Verfremdungseffekt* or the *Unheimlich*. Instead, /Glitch/ exploits how mutually exclusive positions are central to these "terrors" that establish impossible alternatives. Their superposed potentials, identified by points of maximum difference, simultaneously lie within the same range. They *all* remain true, revealing how enculturation asserts the utterance and articulation. Playful possibilities are always paradoxical; however, these "terrors" posed by the shifting identification-acknowledgement of /glitch/ depends on the interpreter's initial and proximate decisions to resolve the entanglement of diagnostic and symbolic interpretation.

The challenge offered by defamiliarization transforms technical media into an alien and ambivalent autonomous under coded product that is simultaneously encoded. The *Verfremdungseffekt* anticipates how the mere presence of a glitch will *not* produce defamiliarization because this encounter is not experiential but interpretive, complicating its unmasking of artifice.[271] Brecht argues the violation of expectations is not simply a formal device, but something that arises as a challenge to established and familiar articulations that liberate (activate) and capture (pacify) audiences.[272] This paradox is resolved when these potentials are not considered as antitheticals, but as a process that ungrounds all established expertise—*both the expectations established in the work (normative) and those invoked through its context (critical).* Although it is an aesthetic, thus *formal*, dimension of articulation, it is neither a material, nor an ontological, nor an indexical feature that can be manipulated directly. By acknowledging the contingency and the artificiality of interpretations this "terror" clarifies the discernment of Glitch Art as a shifting recognition based on an unstable and impossible indexical claim to be 'the real.'

The convergence between /glitch/ and the destabilization of the *Verfremdungseffekt* does not concern the thing perceived, but the perceiving-process. Each revelation of contingency and artifice potentially becomes an *Unheimlich* disabusal of anticipated progression, morphology, and structure. Brecht's aesthetics of defamiliarized articulation emerge from /glitch/ as neither representative of general rules, nor the unique properties of singular works. They reflect the role of past experience in framing analysis, a precise demonstration of ambivalence. This *poeisis* subverts any and all established systems: the disruptive effect that "shocks" depends on a 'transparent' concern for the meaning communicated. The defamiliar consciousness may be produced from any *un*anticipated deviation from an expected ordering.[273] Glitch Art renders existing orders as sets of potentials within a range of possibilities, destabilizing their authority. The awareness it can prompt of *both* normative and critical modes as contingencies (created by social, economic and political factors that defamiliarize familiar, comfortable relations) is the threatening and capricious modality of the *Unheimlich*—neither dependent on Modernist, nor Formalist devices—arising from its upset of fixed semic ordering. /Glitch/ identifies this superposed state without prescribing its functions or features.

4.7 Recoding Errors

Both digital objects and their human readable presentations rupture the indexicality that has been assumed for technical media since its inception in the nineteenth century photograph, dispelling the 'aesthetic ontology' that conceives of glitches via 'the real' as symptoms of *failure–as–failure*. The accumulated cultural fluency, extratextual experience, and intertextual knowledge that defines the interpreter's past experiences as the "plastic intelligence"[274] of perception separates the diagnostic recognition from its symbolic interpretation. The semiotics of perception requires a "mobile articulation"[275] that reconsiders both glitches and Glitch Art at different levels of interpretive engagement. These semantics prevent fallacies arising from category mistakes[276] that identify the glitch ontologically as "real" or "fake" and suggest that glitches are an autonomous signifier *for* criticality. Fallacies of this type mistake the conclusion for its syllogism, and lead to the false belief in aesthetics whose signs offer stable, specific, inherent meanings—thus perversely recreating the same *normative* engagement traditionally challenged by critical analysis. The challenge posed by glitches is always subject to alternative re/organizations and disruptive counter-readings (paralogies) even though shifts to alterity are often captured in advance by the conventionality of signification. The assimilation of the 'iconography of error' in/as a conventional demonstration of materiality belongs to this process of re/coding, a normative reflection of the autonomous facility to adapt, recoding critical ruptures as structural and expected features of the art object—their *aesthetic* nature returns any novel morphology to the realm of the *Heimlich,* and so denies any disruption it might produce. This conventional function shifts from defamiliarized to familiar, a transition that makes the ambivalent role of mobile articulation and the analytic reversibility of glitches apparent. Ambivalence is essential to these shifts; all aesthetics emerge from already-known and internalized codes offer the same potential for disruptive and transformative 'shock'—defamiliarization of their enunciation—by creating a mismatch between their articulation and interpretation. This disruptive alterity is often captured in advance, rending its challenges moot.

The viewer's autonomous choice/decision to transit between diagnostic and symbolic modes enables the mystification of this process as an "ontological concern" for the nature of the object considered. This error is a refusal of how experiential, non-lexical signs, as in visual art, are articulated by their re/use and contextuality, not by double encoding as with language. Critical signification happens when audiences choose to direct their attention towards another level of complexity *not* immenent in the 'event,' but arising from fluency—past experience and established expertise.[277] This change from perception to apperception is an autonomous decision made unconsciously and unrelated to the iconography, ontology, or signs within the work encountered because it is the sign formation process. Coherence *is* the desired result of recognizing familiar orders. The audience's apperceptions *are* the expectations challenged or undermined by the glitches that appear in the actual progression of the encounter.

Brecht's concerns for defamiliarization and reflexivity converge on Umberto Eco's analysis of serial narratives where potential responses to any mismatch between applied schema and novel (immanent) ordering threatens to become the rejection of these irruptions *as-noise*. Brecht's *Verfremdungseffekt*, and its *Unheimlich* impact, arises from its aesthetic ordering and the audience's anticipations of progression, a direct reflection of *who* the interpreter is.[278] Yet what is of critical interest are those situations where this changed approach appears to provoke its consideration as a specific feature, an aesthetic *attribute*, rather than being a capricious decision made by independently the audience as they encounter the work:

> It is evident that even the most banal narrative product allows
> the reader to become by an autonomous decision a critical
> reader, able to recognize the innovative strategies (if any).
> But there are serial works that establish an explicit agreement
> with the critical reader and thus, so to speak, challenge him to
> acknowledge the innovative aspects of the text.[279]

Eco recognizes the problem of criticality: there are no precise or specific formal elements that provoke this changed approach—they are dimensions of signification, not articulation, and thus depend on the audience's *desire*. Although the recognition of Glitch Art is a distinction made by the interpreter, it requires a specific identification of signification at more than just the immanent level of encounter 'signaled' by formal elements (semantic cues)—in Glitch Art the glitches are not occasional interruptions, but become the aesthetic

substance. Their disruptions and transformations are expected,
total, and at the same time subsumed, invisible, 'transparent.'
Their recognition *as-art* demonstrates how audiences recode their
expectations and semic engagement following the model descriebd in
critic Brian Larkin's analysis of the circulation of pirated and broken
media through the informal distribution systems of Nigeria:

> If infrastructures represent attempts to order, regulate, and
> rationalize society, then breakdowns in their operation, or
> the rise of provisional and informal infrastructures, highlight
> the failure of that ordering and the recoding that takes
> its place.[280]

The failure of one signifying system does not result in a wasteland,
abyssal, but rather an emergent replacement—a reorganization of the
(dys)functional elements around the precise (dys)function—what was
a point of failure becomes the central feature of a *return–to–normal*:
hence a *recoding* of the existing order to integrate the 'failure.' The
transformations produced by Glitch Art depend on the audience
recognizing the work's semic organization. It relies on a bias
inherent in the audience's *desire* to comprehend what they encounter
that produces both the 'intentional function' and communication.
The glitch ceases to be rupture and becomes instead meta-stable;
disruption is always relative. What *may* provoke *Verfremdungseffekt*
changes based on the context within one work may be a re-assertion of
continuity in another. This *Heimlich* return to normal 'transparency' is
a feature of how the aura of the digital imbues digital media with their
specific valence *as-immaterial*, quite apart from whatever semantic cue
may be encountered at any given moment. Semiosis always enables
the potential rejection or discounting of the glitch *as-noise*, in a specific
elision where the glitch is conceived as momentary, a feature of *this*
presentation, thus irrelevant to consideration.

Materiailty is a sign that points to itself, but the idea of materiality,
the physicality of media, and questions of an innate ontological basis
are neither convergent, nor equivalent. The viewer is *not* liberated by
the materiality of digital facture; Modernist concerns with ontology
cannot resolve the problematics of the *Heimlich* and the *Unheimlich* for
Glitch Art. Any appeal to an essential nature of glitches undermines
their ambivalent potential for paralogical transformation by foreclosing
on the "openness" of these texts.

The capacity of glitches to violate expectations is responsible for
the "critical" illusions that envelop the interpretive superposition
produced by /glitch/ or glitches, and their roles in Glitch Art.
The Formalist approach reduces these questions to an immanent
consideration whose identification of the 'substance' rendered for

humans by the digital apparatus operating invisibly, continuously, autonomously inevitably returns to familiar and stable orders whose critical potential is neutralized. Attempts to restrict glitches to an ontology of technical failings, as Menkman's the *Vernacular of File Formats* demonstrates, merely amplifies these fallacies. Any attempts to produce challenges via a diagnostic treatment of glitches as instances of *mal*function invokes the aura of the digital, which mystifies how the audience returns to a familiar symbolic order.

The potential for paralogy that defines Glitch Art lies in the shifting relationship between expectation and encounter, recognition and irregularity, whose status *as-error* and *as-not/error* moves into a conceptual realm apart from materiality and physical engagements with media: the assumption of a medium's innate properties creates an *a priori* conception of "purity" that is separate from philosophical ontology. The denial of 'aesthetic ontology' required by embracing a semiotic approach to glitches and Glitch Art is a refusal of Modernist Formalism that escapes from its strictures and fallacies that confuse the 'intentional function' for the intentions of the artist, and that simultaneously mistake the diagnostic function of indexicality with an encounter with 'the real.'

Glitch Art thus continues the Romantic tradition of transcendent art despite the Formalist doctrines of medium specificity. Disentangling the diagnostic and symbolic modes shows how the heritage of a Formalist aesthetic conflates the semantic function of the 'material markers' that cue glitch identification with their role as a semantic vehicle for expression: Greenberg's 'aesthetic ontology' requires a negation of symbolic articulation and derives from idealism, unlike a realist philosophical ontology such as OOO which acknowledges reality's withdrawal from direct perception. Glitch Art's generative basis demonstrates the need to break from this Modernist "purity" by acknowledging the role of enculturation in identifying glitches and revealing their contingency as /glitch/ denaturalizes expected orders and conventions. This power of glitches to demonstrate the artifice of sign formation thus does not depend on *any* innate properties, making their active participation in the unresolvable ambivalence of /glitch/ (which is their assumed definitional condition) a direct illustration of the role audience *desire* has in shaping the recognition of encoding itself as a reflection of subjective proclivities.

5

THE 'ICONOGRAPHY OF ERROR'

Automatic processes define all technical media, but interpreter recognitions of the 'iconography of error' provides the necessary semantic cues for the 'intentional function' which identifies *when* to interpret any perception *as-if* it is encoded, and thus invokes the 'material function.' This autonomous shift to semiosis by the interpreter / reader / viewer / spectator / listener / audience is structured by the encultured modulations of past experience and beliefs in intentional encoding: symbolic functions replace the diagnostic recognition, shifting apperception, while being directed and informed by the role of context—the *where* and *how* of presentation matters to the emergence and identification of signs guided by the harbinger of symbolic encoding whose identificatory iconography is always already an action that impugns the 'intentional function' to the structure and organization of perception: the transformation of glitches from a material artifact (diagnostic) to an encoded form (symbolic) is a product of past experience with the lineage of semantic vehicles ('iconography') that is the secret of these / objects / becoming signs. However, this heritage must remain contingent for glitches since, unlike the marks and glyphs of letterforms and written language, they are ambivalently superposed between being the 'material markers' for *mal*function and being *mis*functions demanding semiosis.

Because all communications—performative (speech, music), analogue (images, writing), and digital (generative)—are inherently implicated in human agency and activities, their 'intentional function' is inherent and unavoidable; technical media exacerbate this foundation, even if they were in fact produced unintentionally (as when a photograph is made unconsciously or accidentally) because of their ontological basis in human action. These residues of artifice arise from the nature of the technical medium; in themselves they are insufficient to assert an 'intentional function,' as is apparent even or especially in ambiguous circumstances where perceptions of encoding requires a conscious evaluation to decide its presence or absence. What the digital code renders is never only arbitrary, no matter how unanticipated the form presented by any glitch is. Although they may appear random to their human interpreters, glitches remain determinate operations performed by machines that will produce the same result so long as the system remains constant: this immobility makes the diagnostic approach to *failure-as-failure* possible and enables its 'material function' as an encoded, symbolic form. These metastable modes of analysis are the necessary precondition for the articulation of any expressive medium: those unintentional pre-coded elements that identify *when* to engage something in perception *as-if* "intended" are always empirically present to perception, but are not formally isolated—the 'intentional function' is not only an issue of morphology and structure, but is constrained by context, and additionally complicated by the autonomous organization created by the technical system. Cues that can indicate encoding are multivalent, present in every dimension of the apperception and contributing to the imposition of articulation (sign formation).

5.1 Expressive Signifiers

Constant, recurring elements derived from the empirical features of glitches define the 'iconography of error' in Glitch Art. Their capacity to prompt diagnostic recognition of glitches *as-error* is foundational for their use, but they also continue the lineage of abstraction known as "visual music" apparent in the early Modern embrace of synaesthetic forms as a metaphor (and model) for visualizing spiritual beliefs through the relationship of sound to color;[281] these early avant-garde artworks, "synaesthetic abstraction," are sometimes identified as "kinetic abstraction"[282] and they inform the iconography of abstract films and the historical avant-garde cinema. The abstraction presented by Glitch Art reassesses the form and meaning of early abstraction produced at the start of the twentieth century. Art historian Jeffrey T. Schnapp has argued this type of abstraction is not a withdrawal into a self-referential and Formalist contemplation of materiality, but is instead something hybrid and ambivalent:

> As initially employed in twentieth-century cultural debates, "abstraction" signifies less a distinctive pictorial practice that disrupts naturalism in the name of autonomy of art than a mode of unfettered exploration of the world—hence the referential trace embedded in the word "landscape"—closely allied with visionary states: meditation, dreaming, delirium, hallucination. [...] So understood, "abstraction" opens up the prospect of an art that, following in the footsteps of pure philosophical inquiry, symphonic music and certain expressions of spirituality, finds in geometry not only the new vernacular of the era of industry but also the secret language of the psyche or of the world.[283]

This initial conception of "abstraction" merges "subjective" and "objective" realisms to create an expression that is ambivalent in its concerns for 'the real': by depicting a reality "of the mind" it eschews the familiar appearances of everyday life. This art critical use of the term "synaesthetic" differs from its use in psychology where it has a limited and precise, technical meaning: "cross-modal sensory experience" that describes a real, physiological condition where two distinct senses (such as seeing and hearing[284]) are linked, producing simultaneous sensations from a singular experience (such as seeing colored forms while hearing music).[285] This history involves those artists working in film, painting, and live performance during the twentieth century whose creations are unified by the attempt to render a metaphysical reality immanent by creating analogues to the rhythmic and compositional structures familiar from music visually, in painting[286] or film.[287] What Glitch Art's return to an alternative 'abstraction' brings into question is the nature of the image, revealing these mutually exclusive positions depend on the same presupposition: the image encountered is fully formed, complete, a *function* of decoding/display: procedurally generated errors suggest a reconciliation of this Romantically-inflected conception of abstraction with the ambivalence of semiotic theory and the demands of medium-specificity.

Disrupting naturalism in the name of autonomy for art[288] has historically defined this type of abstraction, influenced by nineteenth century Romanticism, that cultivates hybrids and transfers between media.[289] This model of abstract art differs from Formalism's concerns with ontology, even though its early development parallels the Formalist concern with a demonstration of 'the real' through art. in place of a self-contained and hermetic art, the synaesthetic abstraction of the visual music tradition identifies a withdrawal from the realm of everyday appearances into an attempt to present the noumenal: a specific concern with developing analogues between sound and image that defies the demands of purification and an *a priori* ontology for aesthetic form.[290] The avant-garde took these subjective experiences as an inspiration for their work, no less an explicit statement in Vassily Kandinsky's theorization *Concerning the Spiritual in Art*,[291] than an implicit dimension of filmmaker Stan Brakhage's argument about "closed-eye vision" in *Metaphors on Vision*,[292] while the pioneering automatic drawings by Georgiana Houghton made in the 1860s,[293] and later esoteric paintings of Hilma af Klint[294] explicitly linked abstraction, spiritualism, and synaesthetic experiences. The graphic forms shown by these works spontaneously reappear in some types of generative glitch, such as those produced by databending JPEGs or MPEGs: recognitions of the continuities between early abstract art (such as painting or the visual music film), the productions of the mid-twentieth century film avant-garde, and the contemporary abstractions generated by digital processes are not new.[295] The contemporary phenomenon of Glitch Art extends this history of synaesthetic abstraction into the present, developing its iconography as a discursive aesthetic directing attention to an idealized and absent perfection.

5.2 Synaesthetic Media

Expressive visual iconography based on the hallucinatory "synaesthetic form constants" that would be later identified by German psychologist Heinrich Klüver[296] are foundational for the invention of Modernist abstraction between 1900 and 1920,[297] apparent in both abstract painting and avant-garde film,[298] and continue to appear in later video art,[299] computer art[300]—and contemporary Glitch Art. This nexus of ideas about sound, color, form, and realism that offered a demonstration of a transcendental order converged in the years immediately prior to World War I with the widespread embrace of abstract art.[301] These historical interrelationships are complex, and suggest a specific aesthetic predicated on an analogy between visual form and sound/music. The emergence of "visual music" continues the lineage of nineteenth-century Romanticism in the analogy between imagery and music that understands the *experience* of synaesthesia as a merging of "subjective" and "objective" encounters with reality.[302] Formalist art critic Roger Fry predicted the transition from recognizable forms to abstract shapes and colors arranged on the canvas by using the established abstraction of music to explain the on-coming shift away from representation in visual art in 1912:

> [These painters] do not seek to imitate form, but to create
> form; not to imitate life, but to find and equivalent to life.
> By that I mean that they wish to make images which by
> the clearness of their logical structure, and by their closely-
> knit unity of texture, shall appeal to our disinterested and
> contemplative imagination with something of the same
> vividness as the things of actual life appeal to our practical
> activities. In fact, they aim not at illusion but at reality. The
> logical extreme of such a method would undoubtedly be the
> attempt to give up all resemblance to natural form, and to
> create a purely abstract language of form—a visual music.[303]

Fry's review of paintings by Henri Matisse, Pablo Picasso, André Derain, Auguste Herbin, Jean Marchand, and André L'Hote makes the connections between the new abstract art and the earlier "color music" immediately apparent in how explains their movement towards a fully abstract iconography. "Music" is the first model for abstraction because it is free from representational links that subjugate art to the world of sensory experience and its organization in the form of everyday objects,[304] thus "visual music" identifies a transcendent aesthetic based on using musical form as a metaphor. This model is commonly used by the artists, writers, and critics developing abstract art to deny representation's immediate, recognizable forms of everyday life to argue for the presentation of an unseen, transcendent reality that is otherwise invisible to perception: without this informative role of past experience and prior knowledge shaping apperception, abstraction can easily collapse into a non-signifying, "decorative" pattern. This established cultural fluency is required for all aesthetics, yet with abstract art it becomes central. Abstract art does not produce a diagnostic recognition with its imagery; the audience that encounters abstraction and asks *"but what is it?"* is not addressed by the work.[305]

Fry theorizes a formalist tendency towards a "logical extreme"— abstraction comparable to music, a "visual music." This change in the subject matter of art was being achieved as he wrote his review, first appearing in the abstractions produced by painters František Kupka and Vassily Kandinsky. The harmonious arrangement of colored forms that Fry discerns in the *near*-abstraction of Matisse's or Derain's paintings will rapidly become devoid of familiar appearances with the invention of both geometric and painterly abstraction over the course of the decade following his review. His discussion anticipates these "novel" aesthetic developments: in the 1910s, both the expressionist and constructivist strands of abstract painting, such as Kazimir Malevich's *Suprematism*,[306] attempt to create what Fry proposes—a "purely abstract language of form." Paintings by Kupka, Malevich, and Kandinsky present a "deeper realism" born of the mind, visualized as a realm of pure geometry and color, but arranged as an analogue to music.[307] Glitch Art recapitulates their iconography.[308] The same bars, grids, lattices, and tessellations appearing in glitches match those of synaesthetic hallucinations,[309] and are described in both writing and art by Kandinsky,[310] Malevich,[311] and Viking Eggeling[312] among others.[313] This heritage situates the generative products of Glitch Art within the larger tradition of early abstraction[314] whose specific iconography reproduces the same four classes of "synaesthetic form constants"[315] [Figure 5.1] seen by color-sound synaesthetes, and documented in Heinrich Klüver's psychological study *Mescal and Mechanisms of Hallucination*, published in 1932:

[a] grating, lattice, fretwork, filigree, honeycomb, or chessboard

[b] cobweb

[c] tunnel, funnel, alley, cone or vessel

[d] spiral[316]

These graphic patterns/forms common to synaesthetic hallucinations also provide a framework that describes the visual character of

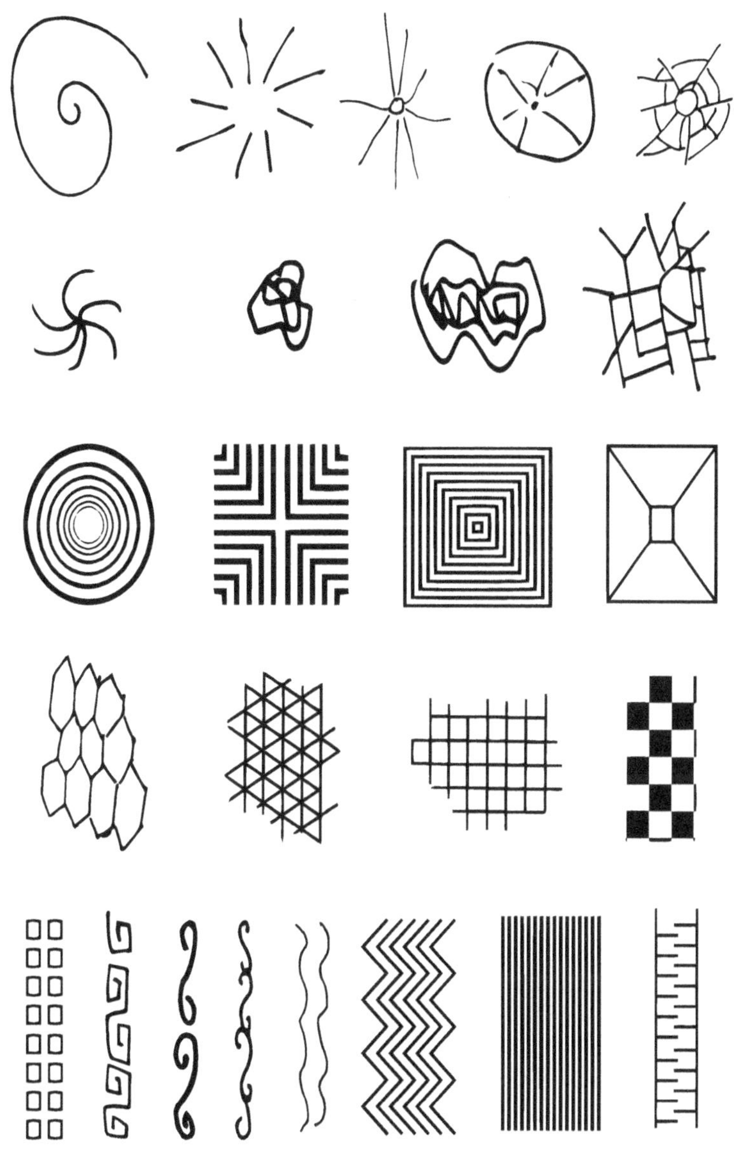

5.1   Graphic examples of Heinrich Klüver's "synaesthetic form constants" seen by subjects experiencing sound-image cross modal hallucinations, as described in *Mescal and Mechanisms of Hallucination*.

abstract art generally.[317] These shapes are common formal descriptions reappearing throughout the abstract art made in the nineteenth, twentieth, and twenty-first centuries. These visual constants are also obvious in abstract film, video art and digital art, masking the alienation and disruption that all new media potentially offer by converting novelty into familiarity and rendering the unfamiliar mundane.[318] Recapitulation of the established and familiar iconography of historical abstraction is a factor in the development and acknowledgement of new media such as Glitch Art that rely on the generative processes of computers: the artifacts generated by computer *mis*function (and occasional *mal*function) produce a wide range of graphics that resemble Klüver's "synaesthetic form constants"—especially the highly geometric gratings, lattices, and chessboards—enabling the aesthetic continuation, elaboration, and further development of familiar iconography (synaesthetic abstraction) in a new medium. The continuity this lineage creates transforms the disruptive and alienating aspects of Glitch Art into part of a familiar aesthetic heritage whose significance is readily understood. These recognitions are simultaneously startling and predictable: familiar and already-established aesthetics from historical media and art are prioritized in art made with new technology, maintaining the stability of traditional aesthetics.[319]

5.3 The Lineage of Visual Music

Glitch Art belongs to the lineage of those abstract works made in the convergences between live performance, motion pictures, and abstract painting.[320] It continues the hybrid and intersectional practices of early visual music practitioners who typically worked both as painters and as animators because they wanted to abandon static compositions for the direct presentation of real movement and the synaesthetic potentials afforded by the new technical art, cinema. The apparatus that made this transfer possible, a cardinal invention of this age—the motion picture camera and its projector—was a fusion of nineteenth century technologies (photography, electricity, the incandescent lamp) that allowed a Modern realization of a much older aspiration[321] to demonstrate a transcendental link[322] between light and sound.[323] These transfers are common among the historical avant-garde at the start of the twentieth century. Futurists Bruno Corra and Arnaldo Ginna explicitly connected synaesthesia to abstraction; their development is typical of later artists who often shift/divide their efforts between painting or film and the construction of a live performance instrument or "color organ."[324] Corra and Ginna created the first avant-garde films as direct animations drawn on clear film stock between 1909 and 1912, explaining their now-lost films in the manifesto, "Abstract Cinema—Chromatic Music."[325] Their discussion and experiments with live performance and direct animation link the nineteenth-century conception of the immobile framework of a "color organ" that demonstrates "color music," (via an assignment of colors to notes in an attempt to demonstrate the pseudo-scientific belief that "light and sound are similar"[326]) to the first invention of direct animation. Their fluid movement between these two activities is not unusual; the change of medium was neither a failure of aesthetics nor a conceptual deficiency, but a technological one because their "color organ" apparatus, an electrified piano, was incapable of producing the desired effects.[327] These visual music animations fulfilled an ambition to illustrate the "true nature" of the world that has directed avant-garde media art from the beginning.

Because of the difficulties presented by animation in early cinema the histories of abstraction on film and in avant-garde painting are not simply parallel evolutions. Issues of formal arrangement, timing, and design, but also the problems of audio-visual synchronization marks all the first abstract animations as innovations, inventions, and experiments attempting to produce a kinetic analogue to then-recent developments in avant-garde painting.[328] Visual music and abstract painting intersect and share the influence of Theosophy,[329] an esoteric cult that incorporated Buddhism and Brahmanism, fusing them with spiritualist beliefs common in the nineteenth century.[330] The iconography apparent in these early films resembles the imagery in Anne Besant and Charles Leadbetter's Theosophical treatise *Thought Forms* (first published in 1901) [Figure 5.2, Top] that gives the "synaesthetic form constants" that Klüver will describe in the 1930s a specifically transcendent meaning as visual projections of mental/emotional activity.[331] Transfers between Theosophy and these abstractions are especially obvious in the "absolute films"[332] made in Germany in the 1920s by Walther Ruttmann [Figure 5.2, Bottom]. His animations used increasingly geometric imagery in each of the *Lichtspiel: Opus I – IV* (1920-1925) series, developing an increasingly non-narrative and non-representational style: the brushy, Expressionist forms appearing in *Opus I* become Constructivist bands and curves in *Opus IV*, demonstrating the direct connection between avant-garde abstraction in painting and these earliest surviving "visual music" animations which render those forms kinetic.[333] This translation of the synaesthetic forms employed in abstract painting and film was of both practical and theoretical concern to these artists. It figures prominently in Ruttmann's statement on his own work, *Malerei mit Zeit* (*Painting with Time*), that attests to his ambitions to link musical form and kinetic, visual articulation:

> An art meant for our eyes, one differing from painting in that
> it has a temporal dimension (like music), and in that its artistic

> foci are not to be found (as in the picture) in the rendition
> of a (real or stylized) moment in an event or fact, but rather
> precisely in the temporal unfolding of its form. [...] This new
> art form will give rise to a totally new kind of artist, one whose
> existence has been only latent up to now, one who will more or
> less occupy a middle ground between painting and music.[334]

This statement was written during the production of Ruttman's
first abstract film, *Lichtspiel — Opus I* [*Lightplay: Opus I*], that
was completed in 1920. "Music" occupies a crucial role in this
theorization as a metaphor for what his work attempts, conceived as
belonging to the "middle ground between painting and music." The
iconography that demonstrates this new art is typical of his fellow
"absolute" film makers Viking Eggeling,[335] Hans Richter,[336] and Oskar
Fischinger[337] whose abstract films also display the same "synaesthetic
form constants."[338] The use of iconography that can be linked to
synaesthesia is common to early avant-garde attempts to translates
a "spiritual realm" into visual form—expressed directly in their link
of sound to image, and initially accomplished by composing musical
scores designed for a synchronized live performance that would
create a counterpoint of sound::image. The development of the "sync
sound" recorded soundtrack only accentuated this linkage.[339] Absolute
film thus demonstrates the same spiritual concerns expressed in
Thought Forms by animating an iconography derived from the
synaesthetic form constants to reject the familiar realism of cinema
via a "rendition of a (real or stylized) moment," to visualize instead
an unseen realm aspiring to show the "true nature of reality." What
matters for later abstract and visual music works is the precedent of
these initial linkages of kinetic abstraction to the static abstraction
of painting: theyt express an unseen, spiritual, or transcendent
order that becomes immanent via an iconography evoking the
"synaesthetic form constants."

These twin developments are essential to understanding abstract art
as having a metaphysical significance. Ironically, this iconography for
visualizing the noumenal by attempting to render a metaphysical order
that lies *outside* perception is also concerned with immanent forms
that can be perceived. This iconography whose "attempt to give up all
resemblance to natural form, and to create a purely abstract language
of form" by reducing and eliminating familiar details is understood
as a refinement of perception that presents what the German Idealist
philosopher Georg Wilhelm Friedrich Hegel described in the
Phenomenology of Mind:

> The simple ultimate spiritual reality (*Wesen*), which, by
> coming at the same time to consciousness, is the real

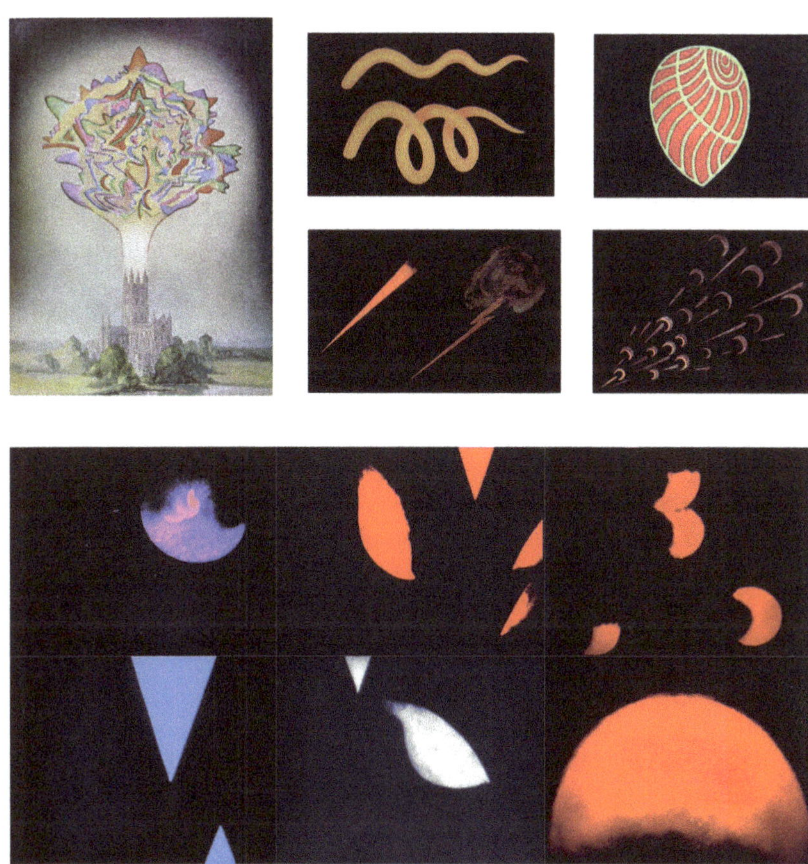

5.2   The esoteric tradition of spiritualism and Theosophy understands
      Klüver's "synaesthetic form constants" as demonstrations of an
      unseen, metaphysical realm:

      [TOP] Annie Besant and C.W. Leadbeater, "Illustrative Thought-Forms"
      from Plates G, 19, 23, 27, and 37 in their Theosophical treatise
      Thought Forms, published in 1901;

      [BOTTOM] Walther Ruttmann, Eva Riehl restoration, selected
      stills from *Lichtspiel — Opus I* [*Lightplay — Opus I*] (1920).

> substance, into which preceding forms return and in which
> they find their ground, so that they are, with reference to the
> latter, merely particular moments of its process of coming
> into being, moments which indeed break loose and appear as
> forms on their own account, but have in fact only existence
> and actuality when borne and supported by it, and only retain
> their truth in so far as they are and remain in it.[340]

The "spiritual" meaning associated with visual music and abstract
art generally derives from an aspiration to make a transcendent,
metaphysical reality perceptually immanent: the "absolute knowledge
of the world" that becomes evident in these works provides an insight
into the "first principle of the world"[341] that then becomes an elevation
of humanity towards a similar level of spiritual consciousness. The
metaphor of "insight" is not coincidence. Hegel understands this shift
as the transformation of the external reality into an internal, mental
order that changes mere appearances (perception) of the everyday
world: it requires a qualitative change to become *universal* reason apart
from the normal resemblances of familiar reality. His approach to the
"realism of the mind" through a process of advancement towards an
essential "purity" apparent in the Formalist demands that became
increasingly important to abstraction in the twentieth century.[342]

5.4 Realizing an Iconography of Transcendence

Just as Hegel's assertion of knowledge through vision is an ordering
of the world that implicitly demands specifically *visual* proof,[343] the
development of abstraction provides that proof in a demonstration
effected through the identification of the cross-modal experience of
sound-color synaesthesia. The belief this experience was presenting
a metaphysical experience led to its use as a means for escaping
the predetermined, mechanical world of empirical science and
behaviorist psychology.[344]This directive gives the transfer of the
characteristic, hallucinatory visual forms of synaesthetic perception
into abstract visual art the characteristic "spiritual" meaning as a
material description of the hidden nature of 'the real,' which Abstract
Expressionist painter Hans Hoffman termed "surreal" in his article
"The Search for 'the Real' in the Visual Arts":

> Although these forces are surreal (that is, their nature is
> something beyond physical reality), they, nevertheless,
> depend on a physical carrier. The physical carrier (commonly
> painting or sculpture) is the medium of expression of the
> surreal. Thus, an idea is communicable only when the surreal
> is converted into material terms. The artist's problem is how

> to transform the material with which he works back into the
> sphere of the spirit.[345]

Hoffman identifies "spiritual significance" as an intangible factor of
Art that only impacts its interpretation when it becomes immanent
in the work, i.e. when it is demonstrated in material terms as a *fact*:
this "surreal" dimension is not precisely that of the French avant-
garde movement.[346] Hoffman's term is consistently supernatural, a
transfer from metaphysical interpretation into immanence that places
the appearances of the work within the realm of realism, not only as
physical objects, but as works whose understanding is connected to
reality rather than merely to depiction. The diagnostic search for 'the
real' blocks the ambivalences of cultural entanglement, illustrating
the links between the transcendence of synaesthesia and the
universal, utopian aspirations that inform Hoffman's argument about
transcendent realism. This utopia/decay dialectic frames the meaning
of abstraction in an opposition between a transcendent state visualized
by Klüver's "synaesthetic form constants," and the rationality of
materialist science that transforms them into everyday appearances.[347]
This opposition between physicality and transcendence enables the
subjective understanding of the world offered by abstraction as an
objective 'fact': visual music thus becomes a revelation of higher levels
of reality than those normally available in the mere appearances of
the world. These conceptions of a metaphysical and spiritual realm
visualized through abstraction provides not only a foundational
framework of imagery, but a collection of meanings for those images,
distinguishing these synaesthetic compositions from simple decorative
patterning via their signification.

These "synaesthetic form constants" have a distinct graphic nature
that makes their translation into the flat geometries of abstraction
an easily understood application of these forms, one which gives
the resulting iconography an immediately recognizable meaning for
interpreters familiar with the synaesthetic tradition of visual music. The
nexus of convergence between the physiological process of synaesthetic
sound-color perception and the articulation of spirituality in painting
and visual art are a formal heritage that is immediately obvious in the
graphics and imagery generated by digital computers. This relationship
between the forms of historical abstraction and computationally
generated imagery was initially noted at Bell Labs in Murray Hill, New
Jersey by computer scientist A. Michael Noll.[348] The generative nature
of early computer graphics reflected the limitations of computational
power—both in terms of resolution and in the initial constraint on
imagery as patterns of geometric forms.[349] The limitations on digital
imagery that Noll described are readily apparent in the graphics
produced by Kenneth Knowlton in his film *A Computer Technique for the*

Production of Animated Movies (1964) made at Bell Labs using BEFLIX, an animation programming language that expanded on commands and structures in FORTRAN [Figure 5.3,Top]. The low resolution of the imagery (252 by 184 pixels with 6 levels of gray anchored by pure black and white for a total of 8 values) meant that both the pixels and their arrangement on-screen necessarily became features of their aesthetic form.[350] The patterns that are easily generated by computers have the same repeating, graphic patterns of Klüver's form constants, but at the same time suggest circuit boards, anticipating the Post-Modern paintings by Neo-Geo artists such as Peter Halley in the 1980s.[351]

Lillian Schwartz, during her time as artist-in-residence at Bell Labs, identified the formal connections between early abstraction and flat, geometric graphics of computer imagery as the direct inheritor of this tradition that becomes immediately apparent in her work as kinetic, flowing patterns that change shape and spread across the screen in her abstract, computer-generated films such as *Pixillation* (1970), *U.F.O.s* (1971), *Olympiad* (1973) or *Metamorphosis* (1974). The tension between recognizable "runner" in *Olympiad* and its decomposition into abstract geometry creates fields of repeating graphics across the screen, leaving traces of its motion-path readily visible.

How limited the early computer graphics of the 1970s were is evident in the ways technical restrictions became part of the "grammar" of her first computer film: *Pixillation* employs extended montages that contrast live action painting showing geometric patterns with the same types of forms generated by computer, making the differences between these types of imagery fully apparent. The opposition this intercutting sets up between analogue and digital is also a transformation of the same imagery: a concentric, rectangular pattern familiar from Klüver's research. These "synaesthetic form constants" are an immanent feature of this film, one which reappears in her later films as well—they are especially obvious in her computer animated films *U.F.O.s* and *Metamorphosis*.

Multiple, repeating linear and concentric shapes—what are initially squares in *Pixillation*—become increasingly "organic" blobs as that film progresses, but their visual repetition and tendency to form tessellation patterns remain constant. These forms have the same, distinctly serial nature as the repeating geometric patterns of the first glitch video, *Digital TV Dinner* (1978/79) by Jamie Fenton [Figure 5.3, Bottom] that displays imagery produced by a physical assault on the *Bally Astrocade: The Professional Arcade Expandable Computer System*.[352] These glitches were generated by striking the machine hard enough to cause the game cartridge to pop out. What appears on-screen are the visual results of a partial system crash that happened while the machine was drawing the on-screen menu.[353]

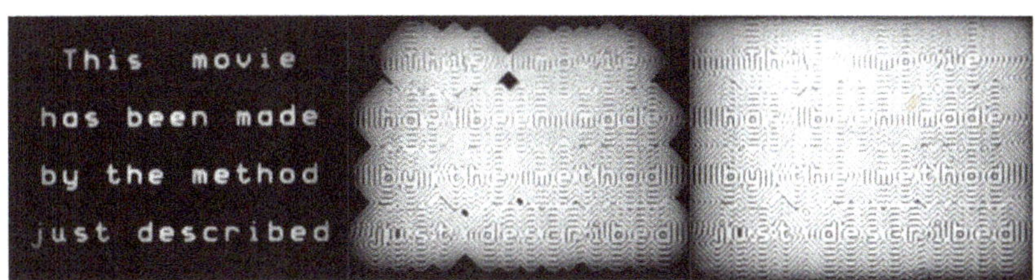

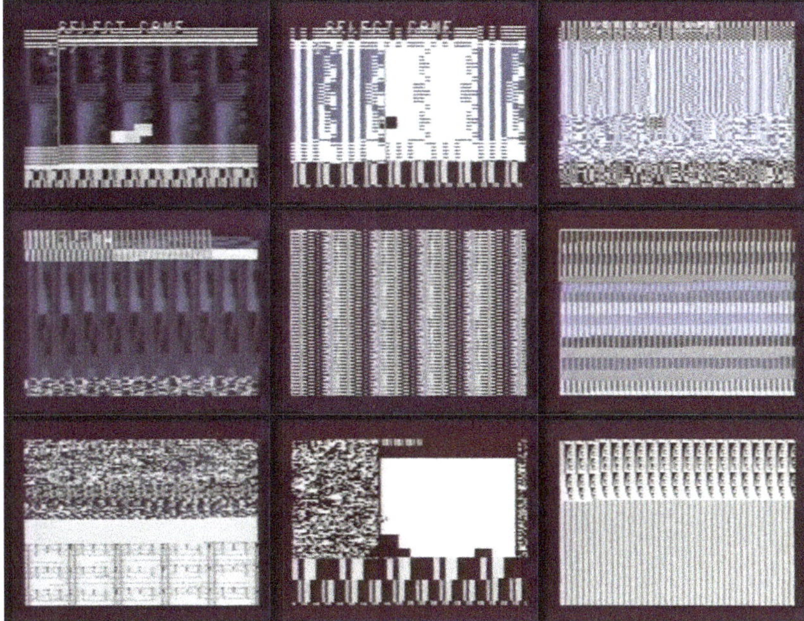

5.3   [TOP] Kenneth Knowlton, selected stills from
       A Computer Technique for the Production of Animated Movies (1964),
       produced at Bell Labs, Murray Hill, NJ;
       [BOTTOM] Jamie Fenton, selected stills from *Digital TV Dinner* (1978).

These images are the instrumental product of a partially (in)complete mechanical operation; they are potentially present at all times for these devices, but are rarely acknowledged or identified as anything other than a momentary breakdown that can be readily fixed. "Noise" *is* and *is not* the particular affect of the patterns generated by the breakdowns that Fenton instigated: these eruptive patterns replace the familiar, comprehensible image/text with abstraction, a presentation that reveals the 'material function' is the starting point for a semantics whose linage attempts to express Hegel's "ultimate spiritual reality" in the iconography of abstract art.

Nevertheless, any potential for a transcendent signified can only be cued by the 'iconography of error', but must nevertheless remain only one potential among many: this interpretation of glitches is contingent upon the audience's interpretive expertise and past experience moving beyond mundane semiosis into the high level re-articulation that defines *poeisis* in what Jakobson's *'poetic function'* identifies as a "focus on the message for its own sake."[354] These semiotics require "the poet and his audience remain constantly aware of the metaphorical character."[355] The 'poetic function' is an interpretive bet justified by its utility in parsing ambivalence[356] to integrate the signs identified in perception with a new set of signifieds.[357] *Poeisis* changes already produced meaning via a spiraling re-encoding whose mobility transforms signs, signifiers, and signifieds. These re-articulations accentuate and produce ambiguity, rather than resolve and diminish it in a redoubling of the instabilities that already surround /glitch/ to reveal that 'transparency' is a precarious construct.[358]

5.4 Technesthesia

Orchestrating the ideological concerns of synaesthetic form and the visual music tradition to emerge within the technical fluency that identifies the 'material markers' of digital media is a logical consequence of the recurrent *desire* to render transcendence immanent in art: to make the immaterial material gives this empirical attention to the material dimensions of media its particular currency in art, unveiling the paradox at the heart of the 'material function.' Attempts to render the unseen "universals" of human experience visible[359] develops through this network of relationships between abstraction, synaesthesia, and technology that are more than just a set of coincidental congruencies.[360] A concern with them as a literal *material* that crystalizes the invisible has been a part of their aesthetics since the 1920s,[361] a recurring aspect of how artists have addressed the generative technologies of motion pictures, video art, and computer graphics.

Perceptions of Glitch Art via the 'iconography of error' begin with the same visual structures shared by historical abstraction: the iconography of linear and graphic elements which form repeating patterns continue the lineage of early abstraction—specifically the grating, lattice, or checkerboard—but arrayed in novel ways beyond merely the grids of squares that are a reflection of the technical organization imposed by digital compression [Figure 5.4]. This instability is precisely the purpose of those aesthetics understood as *transcendent*—the convergence of representation with the represented that is an essential goal of *all* realist arts.[362] The empirical convergence of the imagery created by digital breakdowns with the set of synaesthetic forms described by Heinrich Klüver produces a convergence of the abstract imagery of visual music with the 'material markers' common to Glitch Art.

However, gltches have a different, generative basis that separates them from the synaesthetic patterns and forms appearing in traditional visual music animations which must be planned and then consciously executed to appear at all. The diagnostic understanding of glitches depends on the apperance of a generative autonomy for the technical system which enables the 'material function' to pose glitches as revelaing an underlying reality as these machinic operations become a presentation of that which is *not* apparent to everyday perceptions. The assumption dominating discussions of aesthetic synaesthesia in relation to any technical apparatus is that an analogous transfer of iconography and procedures following a human-determined and controlled paradigm based in perception results in a technical expression of perception—in the case of synaesthetic abstraction, its "synaesthesia" is actually a stylized realism.

Glitch Art continues and extends the lineage of historical synaesthetic aesthetics common to both painting and abstract animation within a new digital matrix, a technesthesia,[363] whose metaphoric addressing of *mis*functions unveils the 'iconography of error' as the inheritor and continuation of the avant-garde tradition of visual abstraction in painting and media begun in the early twentieth century. Quite apart from the *mal*functions that it began with, this 'iconography of error' belongs to the lineage of synaesthetic abstraction whose heritage as simultaneously *expressing* and *being* a transcendent revelation of an underlying or hidden reality becomes immanent in the duality of diagnostic and symbolic interpretations. The *mis*function that defines discursive reasoning creates these revelations of an unseen reality as "immanent" in the ambivalence of the /glitch/. This denial of dialectical modes of thought makes synthesis impossible since the mutually exclusive potentials (thesis, antithesis) are themselves contingent and imaginary, their distinction subject to the same ambivalence that /glitch/ describes. These interpretive relationships are circular, continuously returning to the same intertextual meaning—a *technesthesia*—originating with historical synaesthetic/abstract art. The visual forms autonomously generated by the technical failures of digital systems coincidentally converge with the formal, visual features of historical abstraction, allowing the embrace of misfunctions as a continuation of this intentional iconography, thus authorizing Glitch Art as the continuation of an aesthetic tradition that sought to demonstrate transcendence via the immanence of art. The autonomy of digital systems' generation of this familiar iconography, whose foundations lie in the synaesthetic hallucination, authorizes the glitch's claim to perpetuate this approach to abstraction and its significance; it also masks the role of enculturation in this interpretation established by earlier abstract art. The contemporary embrace of digital errors adapts the *un*intentional recapitulation of encultured significances in the happenstance of glitches, thus asserting the cultural continuity between Modern, Post-Modern, and Contemporary works which are otherwise dissimilar in production, exhibition, and dissemination.[364] By reconfiguring the iconography developed in painting and animation, Glitch Art facilitates an imaginary transfer between electronic imaging and human perception that sustains the continuity of historical meaning for these visuals. By maintaining this traditional iconography, the radically new abstraction produced by digital technology becomes familiar instead of alienating, a change in perception that elides the novelty of new technology by asserting its familiarity.[365]

Recognizing the viewer's ability to conceptualize and interpret these procedural abstractions via this iconography depends upon their familiarity with the varied aesthetic traditions and contexts of abstraction, as much as their technical fluency and culture expertise require past experience to effectively navigate subtleties of materiality, expression, and usage—a role for encultured knowledge that remains constant throughout the history of the avant-garde art addressing new technology.[366] These recognitions of "visual music" abstractions, whether in traditional art or contemporary digital media, depends on the interpreter's attentiveness to the iconography of synaesthesia as much as to the relationships of audio-visual synchronization. These images and movies are understood as a visual, graphic parallel to the formal designs that create musical order. The synaesthetic experience and its hallucinatory imagery lies at the foundations of this visual music tradition—a connection between subjective experience and aesthetic form documented by the graphic patterns and structures recognized by Klüver's "synaesthetic form constants." Their presence and recurrence throughout this history is neither surprising nor unusual. It is the evidence for the continuity of this tradition independently of its means of production.

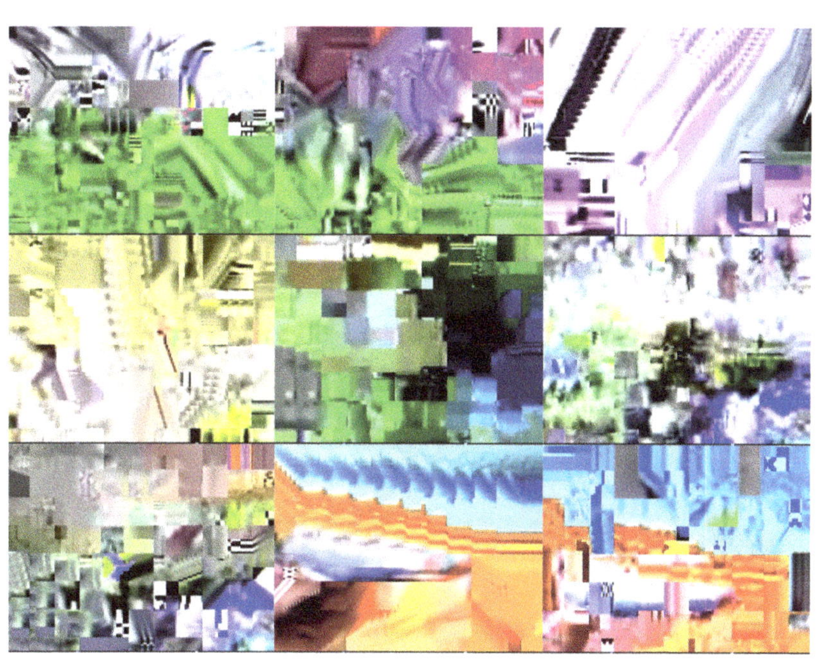

5.4   Michael Betancourt, selected stills from *malfunction* (2000) showing
       digital glitches produced by video codec failure.
       Copyright © 2000 by Michael Betancourt / courtesy Artists' Rights Society (ARS).

6

POESIS, QUOTATION, AND THE TRANSCENDENT DIGITAL

All technical media remain the "same" each time they are played. This fact creates a series of possibilities for quotational and intertextual engagements around both the reuse of media and its reviewing. The cultural fluency that identifies something as an echo of 'something else already encountered' produces a range of relationships in which the necessity of this connection to established knowledge decreases, bounded by the original work where intertextual knowledge is minimized and the appropriative work where intertextuality is paramount [Figure 6.1]. The variant of an "open text" created by these recognitions continually defers meaning as a contingent product of context and past experience—thus offering a spectrum with three distinct modes: two directly intertextual modes, *appropriation/collage, transformation/remix,* and the implicitly quotational mode of *intervention/glitch* whose displacement of the immanent encounter by cultural knowledge can bring an instrumental transcendence into consciousness as the 'discursive aesthetic.' Direct, quotational intertextuality may be entirely absent from *intervention/glitch*.[367] Unlike the metaphoric transformations created by the historical approaches of *transformation/remix* and *appropriation/collage* whose intertextual relations are defined by recognizing *something* as being-extracted from an already known and familiar form, the 'canonical' source. In *intervention/glitch* this quotational linkage is ambivalent, always discursive, apparent in how glitched media create a (hypothetical) quotation of its *un*glitched self; the embrace of *intervention/glitch* and Glitch Art thus becomes inevitable due to the vicissitudes of digital media production, transmission, and presentation. The apprehension of glitches as deviations from an idealized, pre-existing work creates a discursive aesthetic by discarding the immanent encounter for its absent alternative because transcending that encounter is always a potential for the transformative impacts of technical fluency's engagement with glitching.[368] This instrumentalist understanding of digital artifacts renders their iconography as an expressive vehicle for historical consciousness, a *telos,* that makes the transcendent immanent in the operations of digital technology.[369]

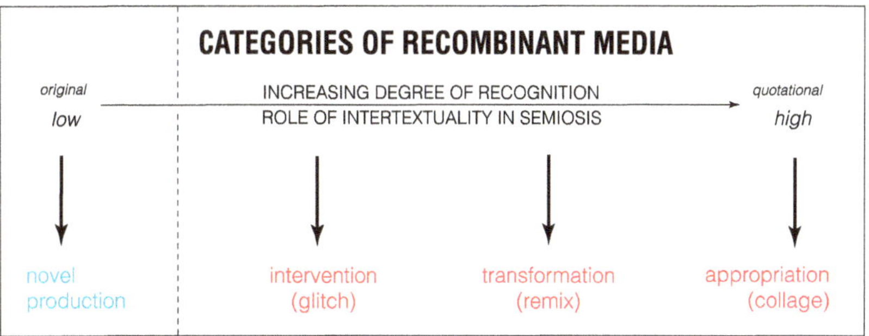

6.1   The range between original productions and those relying on a quotational recognition produces intermediate positions where the degree and importance of intertextuality is diminished, but not eliminated from any semiosis.

6.1 The Pseudo-Diagnostic

All communication depends upon past experience—*fluency*—whose intertextuality is already present for any lexical statement.[370] Semiotic processes depend on the interpreter's expertise with the encoded nature of utterances that are transformed by circulation through a variety of displays and presentations: the author's "only power is to mix writings, to counter the ones with the others, in such a way as never to rest on any one of them."[371] While these relations are endemic to all types of reproduction, and instrumentalized by digital media, how quotations mobilize past experience is qualitatively distinct from fluency: a quotation is not merely the *déjà* of "I've seen that before."[372] The pseudo-diagnostic defined by past expereince replaces perception with cultural knowledge because there is no quotation unless audiences allow their cultural knowledge to shape semiosis; that intertextual connection is the necessary and sufficient condition for *all* recombinant media, self-evident in the assumption the audience will identify the original sources being combined and altered.[373]

Quotations guide interpretation by replacing perception with features recalled from memory: the *déjà* that must be identified by the interpreter for the semiotic chain to begin. This pseudo-diagnostic recognition—*a quotation!*—turns the novelty of immanent encounter into a variation on an already known and evaluated experience.[374] It shifts from identifying *things–in–themselves* present to perception, to a re-evaluation of perception in relation to encultured knowledge. While past experience always mediates how any immanent work is understood, their identification as a quotation redoubles and redirects attention from the immanent to the remembered, reassessing the novel production via recognized connections to historical material. When confronting the specifically intertextual phrase *"four score and seven years ago,"* semiosis is not limited to knowing component terms but includes the *déjà* of their earlier configuration as the opening of United States president Abraham Lincoln's *Gettysburg Address*, famously delivered at the dedication of the Soldiers' National Cemetery in Gettysburg, Pennsylvania on November 19, 1863. The meaning of this phrase *as-quotational* gives the statement a second meaning apart from mundane concerns with lexical content, a doppelgänger that augments the terms' direct significance, altering semiosis.

Déjà apprehensions are specifically nostalgic, a reconsideration of past experiences. This product of the immanent encounter and its relationship to an imagined/remembered past encounter emphasizes the repetitions, repeats, and replays of technical media to instrumentalize a return to the same thing, allowing audiences to have a different experience with something they already know because it is fixed, stabile, unchanging. Although any copy of a digital file will be functionally identical no matter when or where it appears, apart from the vagaries of presentation, the discursive aesthetic originates in this normally ignored variability: entangled with the pseudo-diagnostic recognition, it reflects how any particular encounter differs from an ideal form that never appears and may not actually exist. These returns deflect immanent encounters via anticipation, enabling the longing for a repeat of the original experience that is saudade. Intertextuality creates this nostalgic reverie paradoxically without any direct or explicit longing for the past. Philosopher Bernard Stiegler described this appeal as a shift in consciousness whose changed engagement allows expectation to dominate perception in a transfer from a diagnostic recognition of what is encountered to an evaluation via memory and enculturation, the pseudo-diagnostic:

> From one hearing to another it is a matter of different ears, precisely because the ear involved in the second hearing has been affected by the first. The same melody, but not the same ears nor, thus the same consciousness: consciousness has changed ears, having experienced the *event* of the melody's first hearing. [...] Inscribed in my memory, the anteriority of the melody's first hearing arises from secondary memory, i.e. from the imagination and from fiction. What is strange is obviously that this already gives rise to the *not-yet*; that the already-heard gives way to the not-yet-heard, echoing a protentional expectation that has entered a play of archi-protentions.[375]

The work is constant, what has changed is the audience: quotations produce the *déjà* connection by asserting a link to a past source—whatever the nature of that source may be—to re-establish novelty within the *familiar* encounter as those aspects of the old that were forgotten, misremembered, or just initially ignored. Although *déjà* parallels the lexical fluency that makes communication possible, the "anticipation" central to this connection depends on foreknowledge, but replaces the immediate experience by considering it as variant of an internalized 'ideal,' the already-seen. This emergence of the *self-as-quotation* defines the *déjà* as a diagnostic rearticulation. It is a dynamic capacity which continuously re-engages perception in a hall of mirrors that confuses semblance and resemblance via spiraling associations and reiterations that do not create signs but deflect them, modify them, change their significance without altering them as the givens of communication—an expressive *diagnostic* articulation.

Digital quotations are different from those of analogue media because digital media are divergent variants of a consistent and unseen 'canonical source' that creates surplus relationships not only with the digital media-object's technological foundations as data, but also with its rendering for a human audience. Multiple returns to the same media-object enable changes in consciousness about that work *as it happens*; however, this change in consciousness (the use of *quotational* knowledge to shape expectations) displaces the encounter with a subjective apperception of intertextuality. When anything repeats—either as a quotation, or via replaying, or in a loop—*déjà* apprehension brings the audience's memory into consciousness, each new iteration becoming a variation, allowing each 'new' experience of the same recording to be modified by previous encounters with it. The implicit transcendence of this deferral complicates the quotational identification: *déjà* precisely mirrors the symbolic because quotations diagnose a connection to past experience, a fact that further ties the discursive aesthetic to all digital media because they are rendered anew for every presentation. Thus *déjà* apprehension defies novel articulation by relying on the audience's encyclopedic knowledge, but its quotational intertextuality also estranges what the audience identifies, no matter how familiar, until it becomes misrecognition.[376]

What were "essential facts" about analogue technical media are simply contingencies resulting from a particular apparatus and presentation; the variability of digital files as they circulate through a variety of displays and presentations accents the essential difference between analogue media and its digital doppelgänger.[377] For Glitch Art, the recognition of glitches implies the existence of an *unglitched* original, thus revealing how fluency, memory, and knowledge dominate quotational recognitions because each repetition must also always resemble itself; technical media are always potentially understood as self-quotations. Only interactive media such as video games make this *déjà* quality part of their semic articulation since a game changes each time it is encountered, and yet these changes remain within the tightly bounded *a priori* essential to its recognition.

Glitch Art problematizes the constancy assumed by normative readings[378] by presenting quotations that are sufficiently changed that they appear novel,[379] raising the question of whether the 'canonical' source material even remains evident [Figure 6.5].[380] The techniques of "databending" and "datamoshing" introduce instrumental changes to the data file. The variations, ruptures, and "noise" that fragment Hollywood actress Mae Murray in Figure 6.2 create new features not present in the source.[381] The transparent engagement with her glitched image is actually a contingent product of complex processes happening invisibly. Recognizing these glitches shifts semic awareness from the immanent encounter to the technical fluency which understands digital media as data processing; however, the familiarity of recognizing these glitches superposes that diagnostic of failure with their expressive use, allowing a pseudo-diagnostic recognition of "being digital" to emerge directly from technical fluency. The *poesis* of Glitch Art ironically superposes the rejection of digital materiality by embracing its 'iconography of error'. The hypothetically *un*glitched source necessitated by every glitch is a metaphysical fantasy that denies critical engagement because the diagnostic is a semantic function addressing 'the real.' It mediates between the imagined *un*glitched source and the technical fluency that understands the glitched presentation as quotational *of itself*. These disruptive affects are products of the pseudo-diagnostic recognition immanent in understanding glitches as deviations from a 'canonical' source whose imaginary identification masks an ironic desire for an impossible perfection[382] and authenticity of expression[383] that escapes the repetitions and variations inherent to all *déjà* apprehensions of digital media. This transcendence defines the discursive aesthetic.

6.2 Quotational Rhizomes

Although the aesthetic protocols for reusing existing media were commonplace in avant-garde literature, media, and art by the 1920s,[384] they do not achieve a wide spread, vernacular embrace (as "memes") until the digital transition of the 1990s and the commonplace emergence of the Internet.[385] However, Contemporary recombinant media is not limited to repurposing the 'givens' of past production. Digital assets are 'found objects'[386] that produce novel examples of existing media by fusing the fixity of the shots used in traditional 'found films' with the control over those shots provided by using digital assets such as 3D scans, architectural models, programming code, and high resolution digital artworks to render novel productions that can be 'directed' in the same ways as live-action filmmaking.[387] Quotational rhizomes reflect the robust and varied contents of online archives that have expanded the degrees of freedom afforded to recombinant productions by offering new potentials for intervention

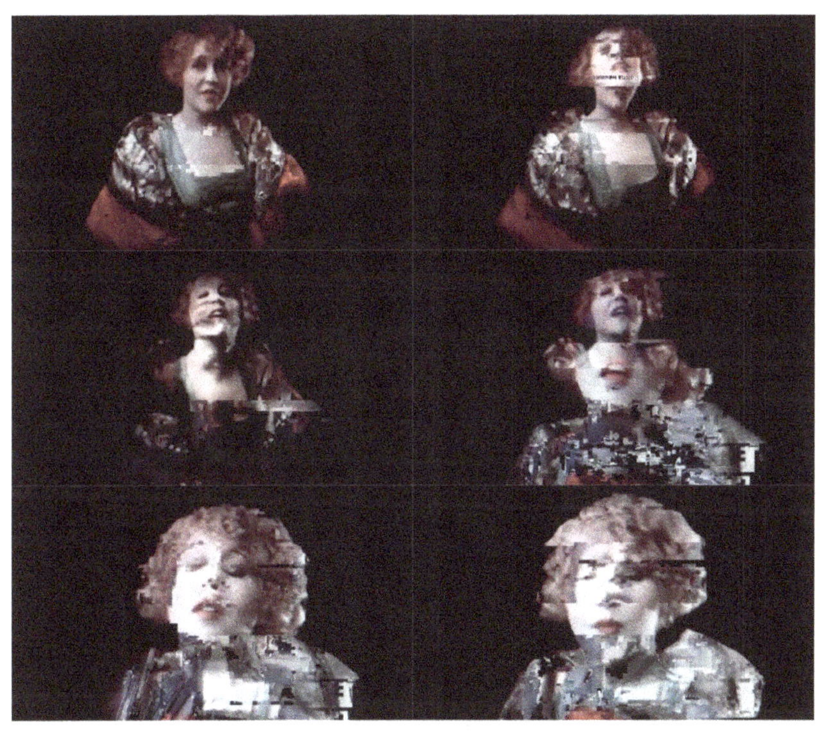

6.2　Michael Betancourt, a series of successive frames from the movie *The Kodak Moment* (2013) where the glitches mask the edit between two shots by integrating elements of multiple 'shots' on-screen simultaneously.
Copyright © 2013 by Michael Betancourt / courtesy Artists' Rights Society (ARS).

that are impossible for analogue media. The synthetic media created by machine learning (AI) further expands these potentials. The training data that generates AI outputs according to the models organized in/by a database are also 'found objects' subject to divergent and appropriative uses. These systems increase the degrees of freedom offered by more traditional generative media without altering the ontology of these media-objects as novel outputs from fixed and pre-determinate sources.

Quotational signification demands an explicitly established knowledge of sources. The audience's ability to recognize variation and repetition bridges the difference between concerns with the *semblance* and the *resemblance* that always descends from their knowledge of an original model. Each new variation acknowledges an endless procession of likenesses and reduplications distinguished by the fidelity of each copy to their source.[388] Generative resources (quotational rhizomes) enable semiosis via anticipation, expectation, and disruption because the 'found object' is always a recognizable unit, employed materially as a trace of the past via a circular teleology: an issue of recognition (depiction), semiosis (denotation), and technical fluency.[389] This uniform conceptual approach defines continuities between digital media, "found footage films," and other analogue productions as a specific genre with its own conventions and usages, as film historian Catherine Russell explains:

> The found image always points, however, obliquely, to an original production context, a culturally inscribed niche in the society of the spectacle, be it Hollywood, home movies, advertising or educational films. [...] Dialectical images create a "now" that is always transitory and momentary. The reference to the past in the form of an image produces a present as a moment in a historical continuum that is in perpetual change. The imagination of the future is thus grounded in the imagery of a past that cannot be salvaged but allegorically recalled.[390]

Russell's "dialectical image" evokes an encounter with its quotational contents via the *montage* or *collage* typical of "found footage" films.[391] But the capacity of generative media to reconfigure, recombine, and/or recreate earlier productions distinguishes the established traditions of *transformation/remix* and *appropriation/collage* from the innovations of *intervention/glitch*. Traditional 'found media' define their quotations through both a concern for the contents of the work, and via the role of *déjà*: intertextual knowledge frames the use of quotational rhizomes by linking the new role to its source within already existing media.[392] This pseudo-recognition is essential to their semiosis.

Déjà engagement with 'found objects' is utterly predictable, without being prescriptive—linking the transformative functions of *transformation/remix* and *appropriation/collage* to those of *intervention/glitch*. The technical fluency that identifies glitches, and the 'intentional function' that manages the transformations of diagnostic recognition into symbolic articulation renders the variations created by glitching as structural transformations which create entirely new materials that are nevertheless derivative of earlier productions. Assuming an *un*glitched 'canonical' source invents this intertextual relationship for media where it is not otherwise present. This tangential articulation distinguishes *intervention/glitch* as a unique category of quotational media that originates in their contingency and variability. However, technical fluency maintains a connection between 'canonical' source and glitched variant even if that source is unknown. Glitch Art offers a unique semiosis where the *déjà* self-quotation happens immediately, upon first encounter, rather than as a result of replays or other returns. The instrumental nature of digital code converges on the predictability of *déjà* encounters, obfuscating technical fluency, cultural knowledge and apperception to pose as a singular experience: the /glitch/.

6.3 Generative Quotations

The contemporary discursive aesthetic internalizes post-modern aesthetics that became increasingly common during the 1960s, 1970s, and 1980s in which artworks self-consciously reproduced earlier art.[393] The intertextuality invoked directly in Andy Warhol's use of familiar imagery in his paintings,[394] or Sherrie Levine's rephotography of earlier photographer's works,[395] and indirectly in paintings that transform earlier geometric abstraction into a codex of formative elements has an explicitly semiotic foundation according to painter Peter Halley:

> The Formalist project in geometry is discredited. [...] the crisis in geometry is a crisis of the signified. It no longer seems possible to accept geometric form as either transcendental order, detached signifier, or as the basic gestalt of visual perception (as did Arnheim). We are launched instead into s structuralist search for veiled signifieds that the geometric sign may yield. [...] Based on this analysis, we may come to see in the work of these geometric transcendentalists a classicizing mechanism at work in which the very object of discomfort, geometry, is transformed into an object of adulation.[396]

All relationships between immanent encounter and interpretation are historical products produced by *a priori* knowledge. Established iconography becomes a lexicon awaiting manipulation—apprehending geometry as a symbolic articulation requires an encultured given—the traditional lineage of uses he proposes becomes the only acknowledged framework for signification, placing the audience's past experiences at the center of semiosis, a process that "ceaselessly posits meaning ceaselessly to evaporate it, carrying out a systematic exemption of meaning."[397] What is at stake for the *poesis* of Glitch Art in this contemporary "era of repetition"[398] is the potential to express something that is neither clearly nor unquestionably assembled from preexisting parts, yet relies on the technical fluency which explains its generative basis to link the glitched media-object to an *un*glitched original: the 'iconography of error' belongs to the lineage of abstract art [Figure 6.3], bringing its articulation into dialogue with Halley's semic proposal.

The *déjà* exploited by Glitch Art depends on established fluencies and knowledge transforming historical visual art into a metaphoric lexicon; however, this process does not disrupt semiosis. Halley confuses pseudo-recognition with the serial variation that eliminates the unfamiliar and *Unheimlich* utterance by assimilating their discomfiting affects. Eco's "classicizing mechanism" is the recoding of existing signs essential to the faux-novelty of each intertextual utterance:

> What is more interesting is when the quotation is explicit and recognizable, as happens in post modern literature and art, which blatantly and ironically play on the intertextuality ... aware of the quotation, the spectator is brought to elaborate ironically on the nature of such a device and to acknowledge the fact that one has been invited to play upon one's encyclopedic knowledge. [399]

The *déjà* depends on the audience's encyclopedic fluency gleaned from past experience to recognize the work being transformed via its immanent use. Drawing attention to the specific quotation *and* to the ways that all duplications reflexively quote their sources is a reciprocal connection between immanence and remembrance where the audience actively attempts to resolve the indeterminate potentials within their apperceptions. Recognizing quotations exploits the audience's knowledge and past experience that anticipates and recognizes divergences from established norms—the same semic function that identifies the glitch. Each *déjà* encounter creates new, deeper, *different* meanings,[400] while also opening up the potential for radically divergent interpretations that theorist Jean-Francois Lyotard proposed in his book *The Postmodern Condition*:

> Paralogy must be distinguished from innovation: the latter is under the command of the system, or at the very least

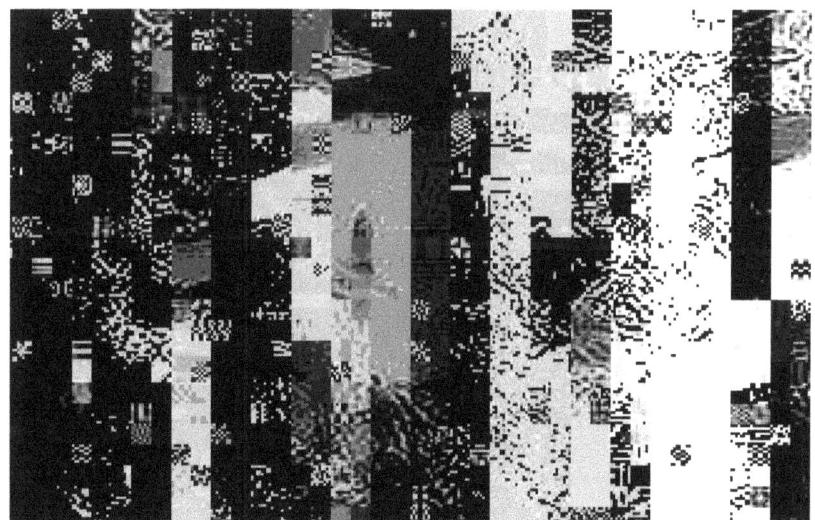

6.3   The lineage of twentieth century geometric abstraction is readily apparent in Glitch Art:

[TOP] An abstract painting by Ellsworth Kelly: *Seine* (1951), oil on wood, Philadelphia Museum of Art: Purchased with funds contributed in memory of Anne d'Harnoncourt and other Museum Funds, 2008, accession number 2008-228-1
DOI: https://philamuseum.org/collection/object/295031;

[BOTTOM] Michael Betancourt, an early example of Glitch Art produced by databending JPEGs: *#003* (1999) from the *In Codings* series. Copyright © 1999 by Michael Betancourt / courtesy Artists' Rights Society (ARS).

used by it to improve its efficiency; the former is a move (the importance of which is often not recognized until later) played in the pragmatics of knowledge. The fact that it is in reality frequently, but not necessarily, the case that one is transformed into the other presents no difficulties for this hypothesis.[401]

Paralogy emerges from interpretation, not as an innate feature of the work, but as a product of misalignments between signifying elements within that work (i.e. /glitch/). The consciousness of this construction is discursive, even if the quotations are submerged by transformative glitching, illuminating the performative aspects not only of apperception, but of the actions required to produce a coherent understanding of what is being encountered. The self-consciousness produced by the apparent digitality of media draws attention to the fragmentary nature of its nature as a quotational excerpt from an *a priori* source. The reversibility of /glitch/ acting between complicity and rupture—a superposition of mutually exclusive potential engagements—creates a potential for ambivalence that is reiterated by the instability of reference common to *intervention/glitch.* The critical potentials in Glitch Art derive from this capacity for paralogy to converge on the same critical potentials Russell identifies for found footage and the problematics of *déjà* described by Stiegler which create its criticality, but also undermine any "culturally inscribed niche in the society of the spectacle."

Digital media create new potentials for intertextual and quotational productions that parallel the alterations produced by glitch techniques to challenge the assumed stability of predetermined and fixed assets ('found objects') in historical "found footage" media. The *déjà* self-evident in the allusive "I've seen that before!" directly shapes the intertextual recognitions in Filmmaker Peggy Ahwesh's *She Puppet* (2001), an early example of the genre of "machinima"[402] that uses video games as quotational rhizomes to generate "found footage" that is a hybrid between the "found" film strip/video and the original, independent production.[403] It is not possible to re-render alternative versions of the shots quoted from traditional film or video, yet digital media, such as the video games used in "machinima," allows the artist to make multiple and alternate versions of the same elements. The quotational rhizome's generative capacity enables each of the shots in *She Puppet* to become a divergent quotation of itself. Early computer animator Kenneth Knowlton recognized this capacity for variation is foundational for digital media:

The speed, ease and economy of computer animation permits the movie-maker to take several tries at a scene— producing a whole family of film clips—from which

he chooses the most appealing result, a luxury never
before possible.[404]

Knowlton's experiments with the BEFLIX programming language
between 1964 and 1968 exploited the capacity of digital media to
create variations, and his analysis anticipates how Ahwesh uses
variations generated by the *Tomb Raider* video game (1996) to
collapse beliefs about the uniqueness and originality of the source.
The digital system produces variations around a fixed and already
known theme by re-rendering a limited set of assets that retain their
identity. Although *She Puppet* employs the conventions of montage
familiar from historical "found footage" filmmaking, recognizing
its generative source changes how technical fluency and 'historical
knowledge' inform its apprehension: what is being *found* in *She
Puppet* has a different character than film, or video, or any other
analog media-object.[405] The "uniqueness" of this generative media
is an artifice, contingent, and subject to transformation because the
interactive nature the video game source allows her material to exceed
the familiar conceptions of recombinant media. Even though the
shots are entirely new, original, and unique, they are also "fixed" and
"stable," allowing the recognitions of *déjà* to inform their *poesis* and
apprehension. Made from variations generated on demand, *She Puppet*
presents the audience with a series of alternative versions of the same
scene, sequence, or event.[406] Its articulation invites a meditation on
the significance of the repetitions and what they mean for ideas such
as originality, identity, and coherence. Recognizing this variability
inheres in the technical fluency that identifies the shots as products
of a video game, but is also immanent in watching the video. Using
a quotational rhizome expands the recombinant potentials of digital
media into novel territory where the historically fixed distinctions of
original::quotational become entangled.

Knowlton's role for variations/repetitions as an aesthetic tool
converges on the same question of *correspondence* that is central to
Stiegler's proposal of *déjà* and the peculiar experience of memory
and expectation that superposes the quotation in the experience of
saudade that informs the constancy of all technical media. Distinctions
between semblance and resemblance demonstrate Stiegler's "small
differences among small differences" that formerly accumulated
between different live performances are now replaced by differences
that correspond to the physicality of the 'canonical' recording, the
vagaries of its presentation, and the audience's familiarity with it.
The accumulation and appearance of different material markers
accentuated in/by glitched media that define the 'iconography
of error' become an inherent change to the expression, each new
glitch creating a variant of the 'canonical' digital source file. Thus

déjà for glitches is a doppelgänger—both a pseudo-diagnostic for
what it presents, and in reference to the (absent/hypothetical) work
it transforms. These features of Glitch Art are foregrounded by the
generative capacities of the quotational rhizome and its potentials
for paralogy.

6.4 A Transcendent Aesthetic

The discursive aesthetic offers transcendence as an interpretive
move for the audience in response to semantic cues literally physically
present to perception. This *telos* allows a semic shift which considers an
immaterial and invented alternative to perception, instrumentalizing
transcendence as a machinic operation. The empirical foundation of
this expression shapes semiosis in a denial of immediate experience
that prioritizes the audience's response—*glitched!*—to produce
the discursive aesthetic. This process is capricious, tethered to the
identification of glitches, but addressing them as signifiers for what
cannot otherwise be presented. Technical fluency is central to this
signification: the quotational association between human-readable
form and digital file does not begin with the execution of code,
but with the variability-in-display as an indication of an idealized,
'canonical' work that can never appear. The immanent digital display
is not 'the media,' but merely one instance of a vastly reproducible
and replicable work whose deferral to the *un*glitched established the
fantasy of digital perfection in an idealized the source file that is more
complete, more perfect, more reliable than any immanent presentation:
the erasure of immanent physicality that is the aura of the digital
produces transcendence as its vernacular significance.[407]

This intersection between cultural fluency, technical knowledge,
and pseudo-diagnostic recognition forces a reconsideration of glitch
interventions as a transcendent signifier entangled with the *déjà* of
past experience that shapes apprehension and enables the recovery of
glitched media as a quotation of itself. These integral affects impose
another level of articulation between the 'canonical' source ('found
object') and its transformation, resulting in a 'quotational-yet-novel
intertextuality' whose connection to its earlier source may not be
readily apparent. In *Dérive* (2020), Glitch Artist Kaspar Ravel [Figure
6.4] extends the use of quotational rhizomes begun by "machinima,"
but instead of a video game, they employed architectural GiS data
for the city of Paris to generate their footage. This recreation of actual
physical spaces allowed the manipulation and "fly through" to be
both a novel production and a semic product of a 'found object' that
is both the rendered *un*glitched video and the GiS data. Yet, unlike the
'canonical' source referenced through quotation and simultaneously
present as a material clip being shown again, the "past" denoted in

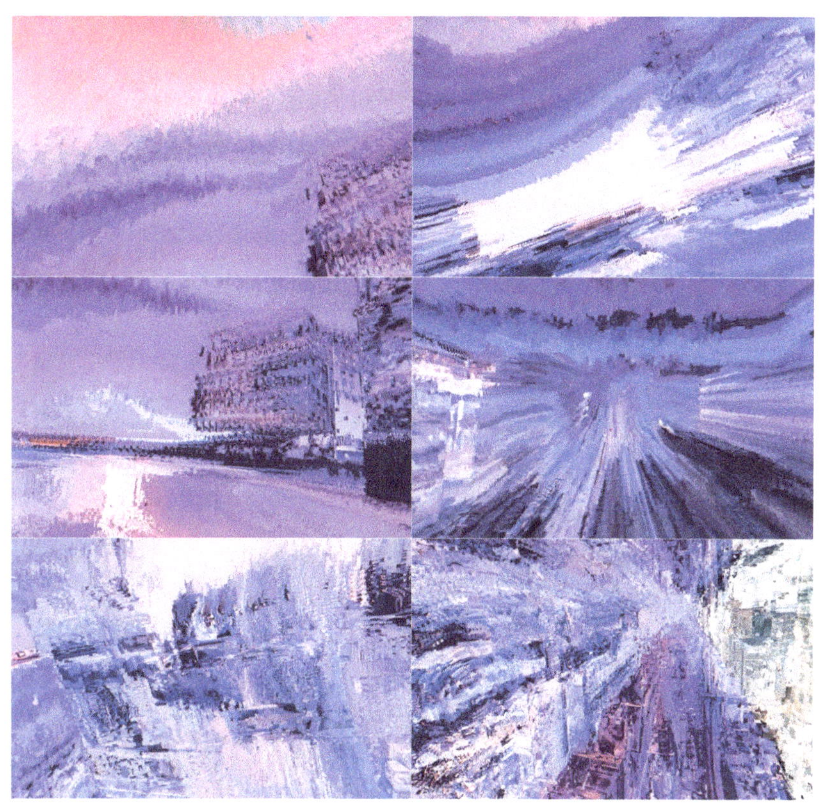

6.4   Kaspar Ravel, selected stills from the short video *Dérive* (2020), commissioned by the Société du Grand Paris, and implemented by the artistic and cultural department of the Grand Paris Express with the Centquatre-Paris as producer; used with permission of the artist.

glitches is never immanent, and its distinction from the 'canonical' media source is always hypothetical. This immersive, interactive VR presentation is an analogue to a cinematic long take, constant and unfolding,[408] but the novelty of this scene is countered by the datamoshing that obfuscates the separation between 'live action' and animation to invite understanding this video as 'real' rather than CGI.[409] Assumptions about 'reality' established by the history of cinema for movies to be made from views of the world called "shots" no longer describe the continuity of the long take.[410] Made for viewing as VR with a 'viewing scope' at the Paris metro, *Dérive* is literally a rapid, interactive flight through an urban environment whose varied ambiances create novel attractions that abstract the already abstracted terrain of the GiS data; the psychological disorientation of Situationalist Guy Debord's proposal becomes an experiential and visual disorientation.[411] The referential ambiguity created by the discursive relationship of glitched media and its 'source' renders these glitches as interventions in an existing work and as novel productions at the same time. This transformation of source files implies a 'canonical' source that the *déjà* entangles with the distinction between 'mere presentation' and 'ideal original,' thus allowing technical fluency to inform pseudo-recognition without the 'historical knowledge' of particular media works characteristic of intertextuality.

Glitch Art defers recognition.[412] Unlike the intertextual aesthetics of the twentieth century that invoke their sources,[413] these considerations of the interplay between *déjà, intertextuality,* and *technical fluency* reveal the unseen ideals of recognitions from "imagination and from fiction"[414] are discursive shifts in attention and consideration. Their semiosis estranges the apparent and assumed transformations enacted upon an idealized *un*glitched source from its correlates in actual, lived experience, or any familiarity enabling quotational intertextuality. How the audience engages this encounter via the instrumental relationship between data file and presentation internalizes the encyclopedic knowledge that is central to Eco's "post-modern aesthetic."

The automatic assumption of an absent, idealized, *un*glitched original is a discursive invention of the audience, mediated by the aura of the digital's denials of the physical presentation that are particular to digital media as a whole, a reflection of its generative basis. This *telos* challenges the immanent encounter: it can only become apparent through the potentially self-referential nature of limina, such as the glitch. When understood in these terms, the *poesis* suggested by Glitch Art appears to draw the aura of the digital into consciousness as a 'parting of the veil,'[415] enabling the fallacy that a glitch is an automatically political gesture.[416]

While the internal recognitions of glitches make note their presence, this identification is not necessarily critical—only a conscious choice by the audience, one that may be cued by the contextual use of a glitch, can become critical; however, the 'discursive aesthetic' renders what "remains" in the glitched image indicative of what is missing, replacing the *dé*jà that concerns Stiegler with a discursive engagement shaped by how the aura of the digital directs attention away from the glitch towards an absent and hypothetical ideal. The generative basis of digital media justifies this Platonic[417] understanding of the immanent work as a variation on the digital file, replacing the intertextuality of quotations and Stiegler's recognition that past experience shapes all apperception with a free floating *déjà* derived from technical fluency. The *intervention/glitch* and its discursive aesthetic is a distinct tendency within the familiar lineage of recombinant media and intertextual or quotational relationships because it eliminates the need to identify the new work through the recognition of specific earlier works.

Transcendent signification is not merely rhetorical, but a discursive shift in attention and semiosis dictated by empirical features of the work. This reasoning is evasive, indirect by nature. The hypothetical perfection made possible by the digital instrumentality contrasts directly with the actual products of its implementation—static or moving, visual or textual, audible or silent—have the same computational basis and thus all have a capacity for failure and breakdown that is never far from consciousness. The physical presentation thus recedes in significance, becoming only one instance (however flawed).[418] Dimensions of production and encounter for media always arise from expectations based on past experience. Because digital technology has made the distribution of media simple, inexpensive and readily accessible, the profusion of existing works, coupled with the capacities of computer technology to manipulate those works,[419] has amplified the creation of new media from fragments of old productions. The transparency posed by digital media precisely blocks this potential for self-consciousness, even in works cueing *poeisis*, because the critical apprehension of the discursive aesthetic requires more than just the formal appreciation of this iconography as expressive. Considerations of glitches reveal an engagement whose artistry lies in the apparent and assumed transformations enacted upon idealized sources: the error recognized establishes the glitched image into a "quotation" of its unbroken self, a flawed copy of a perfect original that may not actually exist. The distillate of history apparent in this displacement is at the same time neither an originary creation that refers to its own uniqueness, nor is it a self-consciously assembled variation on familiar tropes (*déjà*), but a mechanistic deviation (discursive) that may bring the audience's expectations for an absent-but-ideal original into consciousness, challenging that transcendence as a contingency.

6.5 Implicit Quotations

Transcendence directs consideration away from the immanent glitch to situate its production semiotically, as a Platonic aesthetic of digital perfection that informs the disjunction between encounter and expectation.[420] Interpreting the fragmentation of Figures 6.2 (Mae Murray) and 6.4 (Paris) as interventions in a source file distinguishes their recognizable imagery from the impacts of glitching, inviting a pseudo-diagnostic recognition of a 'canonical' source paralleling how the diagnostic role of glitch procedures invites an acknowledgment of digitally encoding via technical fluency. This affect that has nothing to do with the technical source of the glitches, but is instead predicated on a direct, coincident assumption that the "contents" of the media *being-glitched* will appear as such, thus entangling the symptomatic analysis of the glitch with a secondary diagnostic recognition of *what* has been glitched, and the pseudo-diagnostic that understands it as a quotational transformation of that *un*glitched source. These instant judgments and decisions create semiosis by dictating what are the expressive elements and which aspects are insignificant. However swift, this aesthetic reverie upon questions of what is broken and unbroken articulates the aura of the digital's refusal of physicality.

This affect of the aura of the digital "erases" glitches—an engagement that is apparent when comparing the recognizable imagery of Figures 6.2 and 6.4 to the entirely abstract Figure 6.5. Although all three works utilize the same technical fluency and iconography that enables recognizing them *as-glitched*,[421] the semic differences between all three are obvious: 6.5 does s not have the affect of a familiar image being disrupted. It does not produce the recognition of a transformed quotational source. Both 6.2 and 6.4 enable audiences to understand them as a flawed copy of a perfect original by invoking the diagnosis of glitches that understands them as *failure–as–failure*; this identification is absent from 6.5. The discursive aesthetic enabled by 6.2 and 6.4 is a tacit 'correction' to the vicissitudes and failings shown by the 'iconography of error.' Conceiving glitches as deviant variations of a 'canonical' source (i.e. invoking a quotational semiosis) informs the diagnosis of

6.5   Michael Betancourt, *2014_023 (0;01;07;15), July 18, 2014.png* (2014), a digitally rendered abstraction produced using both databending and datamoshing to eliminate all recognizable elements of its original imagery.
Copyright © 2014 by Michael Betancourt / courtesy Artists' Rights Society.

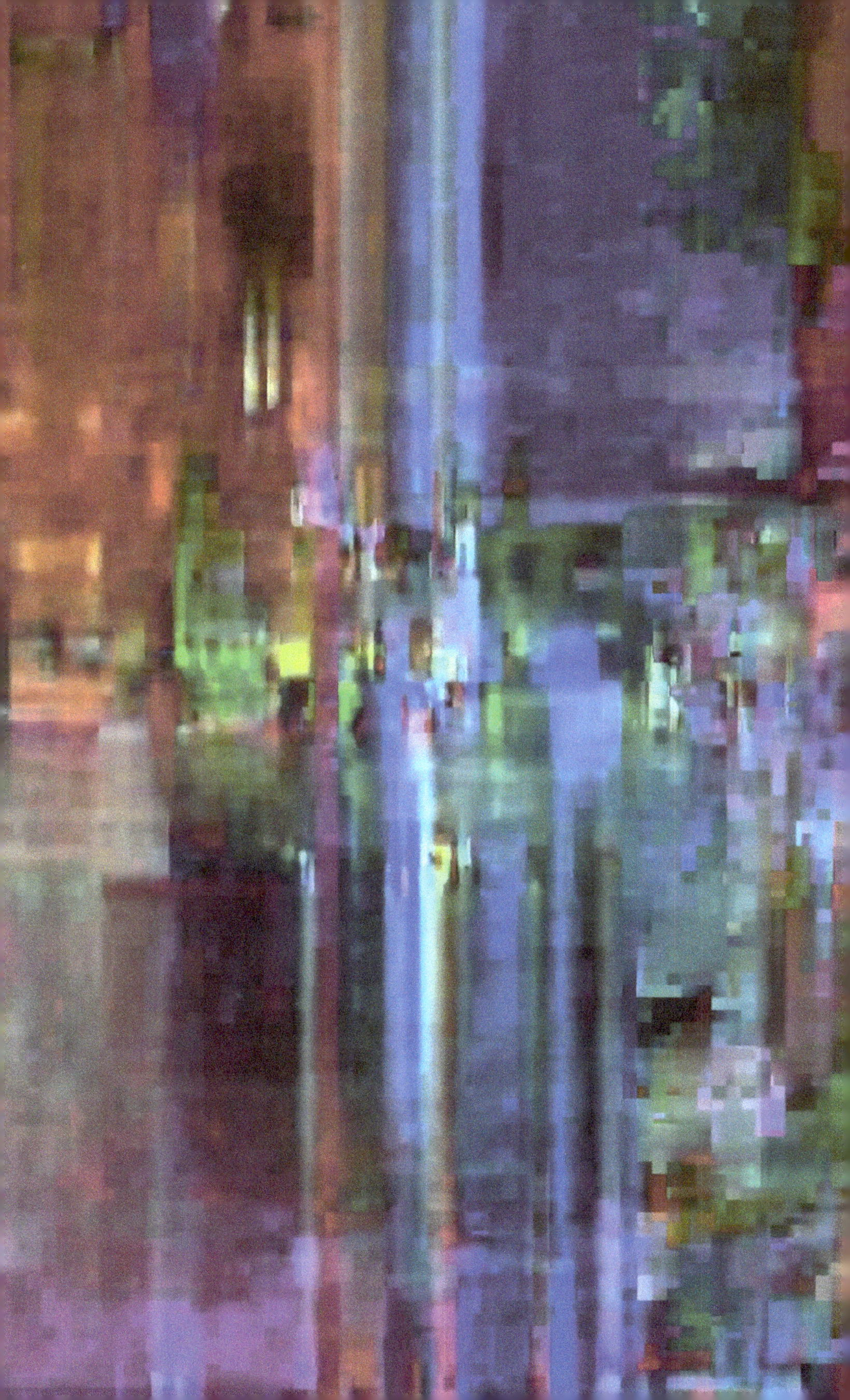

glitches as 'merely transitory,' thus linking both intentionally and unintentionally produced glitches to the same discursive reasoning that deploys technical fluency because when *mal*functions are engaged normatively as-failure it deflects and skirts semiosis 'around' the error by evacuating it of expressive meaning. The implicit transcendence of the digital generally, visualized through glitches, thus superposes their expressivity with their potential for *poeisis*. As the immanent encounter cedes significance to encultured knowledge the discursive aesthetic asserts itself, rendering all digital media as implicit quotations of the absent file, idealizing that data as an inviolate perfection that cannot be realized.

6.6 Discursive Transcendence

Recognizing a glitch is more than merely an identification of the 'iconography of error'—the act of encountering a glitch invites the audience to consider it as a transformation of a hypothetical and unseen original. Technical fluency understands any glitch as a potential variation: identifying it as an 'original that has *become* glitched' produces a *telos* whose transcendence functions instrumentally through the 'iconography of error.' This discursive justifies assumptions about the 'origin' or 'source' of the media object, while enabling a transcendent understanding that arises from its semiotics (demonstrating the encultured constraints on interpretation and their social foundations).[422] The "transcendence" offered by aesthetic works is an historical affect linked to the autonomy of art that emerged in Europe during the Renaissance, and assumed its contemporary configuration in the nineteenth century.[423] The metaphysical fantasies superimposed on the physical operations of digital technology distance this ideological belief from its immanent origins in specific cues and their semiotic elaboration. Glitching transforms these denials of materiality identified by the aura of the digital into an *aesthetic* consideration that makes this universal displacement of attention to a transcendent ideal apparent. All digital images produce the discursive response, but only in special circumstances does it become an aesthetic and reflexive dimension of their apprehension which leads to the acknowledgement of this transcendent signification by truncating the quotational dimensions of media recognition. Both the instrumentality of the computational operation and its source in the data file assert concerns with an absent-but-essential 'original' that guides engagement with *all* digital media, but how the aura of the digital virtualizes the "glitched" creates a necessarily *conscious* correlate in the hypothetical, "unbroken" original.[424] These recognitions that defer attention to another version of the same work are definitional for glitches. This ideology declares all physical manifestations and presentations on-screen imperfect replicas of a perfect (virtual) original, the data file becomes a 'transcendent value' ratified by its distinction from the glitch.[425]

These digital assertions of metaphysical significance—all transcendent meanings are metaphysical—displaces attention from the immanent encounter in an expression of the aura of the digital's negation of physical experience. The semiotic and cultural apparatuses that diagnose "glitches" also generate the transcendent by drawing the conceived ideal into the reverie precisely through its absence, thus creating the potential for that idealization to become a dimension of signification. Glitch Art has the potential to accentuate/emphasize this discursive aesthetic that is already present in all digital works; criticality is neither guaranteed, nor an essential feature of their apprehension. The shift in attention created by the "glitch aesthetic" is a product of ideological beliefs, expressions established through the continuity between contemporary and historical modes of articulation.[426] This foundation allows the absent ideal to mirror the demands for a unity of form and meaning, and thus assert an illusion of the essential convergence between what "remains" in the glitched image and what is missing. Transcendence is a product of skirting around the *mis*functions produced by 'errors' whose semiosis realizes the aura of the digital as an immanent feature of digital aesthetics.

Only abnormal circumstances draws these transcendent claims into consciousness, creating the fallacy that a glitch is a 'parting of the veil' on computational operations,[427] and thus an automatically 'political' gesture.[428] Factors of apprehension, articulation, and appraisal normally hidden by the everyday 'transparency' of digital media can rise into consciousness during these aesthetic reveries. Every audience can, by an autonomous choice, engage in critical signification—*paralogy*. This contingent product of interpretive engagement is a reflexive capacity that opens interpretations to contradictory and antithetical meanings. The *mis*functions in his works act semiotically as indications of the transitory nature of images, suggesting an allegorical encoding as a demand for political change rather than merely a decoration of the words shown.

Digital technology dominates contemporary society; the emergence of an aesthetic derived from technical fluency with that media is an instrumentalization of its immaterial ideology. The aura of the digital's shift from material concerns to the virtual realm of ideas is rendered immanent by the demonstrations[429] enabled by Glitch Art's discursive aesthetic that potentially challenges this idealization of the virtual against its physical presentation. These digital expressions skirt an unrealized and imaginary perfection—an essentially transcendent belief about data reflected in the aura of the digital. Glitch Art brings this instrumental attempt to render metaphysical values immanent via computational processing into consciousness as a specifically aesthetic experience, revealing transcendence as a discursive process that arises from how encultured and empirically present cues may direct engagement towards an unbounded reverie when accompanied by a desire for *poeisis*.

Interpreting glitches thus triggers an imaginary transcendence guided by the illusory perfection enveloping all digital media, and which highlights the gap between immaterial/ideal and physical/encounter. This discursive transcendence identifies the 'iconography of error' as semantic vehicles for interpretations that exceed or "transcend" their empirical subject. With Glitch Art specifically, audience identifications of glitches cues the shift to consider a hypothetically ideal *un*glitched source; semiosis ignores the physical encounter by leaping towards an imaginary–but–perfect "original." This refusal of the immanent encounter informs how the aura of the digital directs articulation beyond the tangible work: emergent from the interplay between perception, cultural knowledge, and contextual imagination in the construction of significance, it reveals how internalized ideologies of digital perfection equally manifest in creative practice and viewership as expressive leaps engaging with apperceptions of empirically intangible/hypothetical works that transform meaning, but which remain tied to physical cues to begin semiosis. The metaphysical is a derivative sign function arising from this intersection of ideology and enculturation transforming/discarding semio-perception, thus presenting itself as independent of the physicality that produces it.

CONCLUSIONS

Semiotics is not nor should it be considered a totalizing or complete systems theory for glitches and Glitch Art: its utility lies in the *general* model it offers for a wide range of phenomena addressed by perception and relying on cultural fluency and expertise; however, to consider the experientially-based expressions of technical media and art requires an acknowledgement that these works are neither lexical nor language-based, and depend instead on exploits of everyday phenomenal perception whose articulations happen invisibly, instantaneously, and unconsciously. Glitches and their role in Glitch Art offer opportunities to bring these hidden dimensions into consciousness, and that capacity lies at the foundation of their critical potentials. The interest of this study has been to explore these moments of instability and transition, and semiotics provides a readymade language for that transition between mute inarticulate matter and the structured order essential to expressive communication. Glitches complicate, obstruct, and confuse these tectonic shifts in semiosis, which is precisely why that theoretical model was of interest: it, too, is glitched when confronting glitches.

[1] The Utility of Liminal Phenomena

The interpretive model of semiotics does not merely concern languages and language-like utterances. Since the 1980s an approach to semiosis has emerged that understands it as the interpretation of ambiguous and ambivalent semantic cues recognized in perception, organized by past experience, and dependent upon established expertise. Abandoning the idea of fixed and immutable 'communication' has allowed the extension of semiotics to non-lexical forms (such as images and music); within this expansive approach to signs and meaning is the recognition that semiosis for media-objects differs from the 'double articulation' of language, which is governed by codes shared by author and audience equally—a codex of instructions that guides their application as an instrumentality for communication. In media these semic orders are propositional rather than prescriptive, resulting in ambiguities about their own validity and appropriateness. Often the *thingness* of media presentations's exploit of mundane perception obscures their encoded or expressive dimensions: the recognition of glitches provides an avenue for exploring these questions of sign formation and the foundations of the semic process in media.[430] Liminal and marginal phenomena are of particular interest to these examinations because they foreground the assumptions about semiotic order, demonstrating the instantaneous perceptual decisions that shape articulation. Glitch Art is an acute example of those liminalities where the relational desires of the audience for specific kinds of engagement determine *if* and *what* there is to consider, invisibly and autonomously shaping basic questions about interpretation, starting with category assignment. These ambiguous articulations force an acknowledgement that "errors" are neither self-evident, nor easily resolved by an imposition of /intent/ via the 'intentional function.' These emergent constraints on articulation elevate variation to become an organizational principle, first as the hidden and autonomous protocols of internal machine operations, then a second time in the audience's anticipation that evaluates that output using their past experience and fluency with the cultural codes of art and iconography.

Encultured beliefs about 'correct' operation determines what is and is not a glitch, and distinguishes the instrumental operations of the digital realm from the expectations that govern the human-readable rendering. For the machine, meta-stable responses that move within a range of potentials are impossible "unknowns" that cannot be executed, while their ambivalence is a valued aesthetic expression for human audiences. The "post-digital" aesthetics that define Glitch Art equally depend upon and exploit artifacts that have became commonplace features of human communication and art in the first two decades of the twenty-first century. The aesthetic problem of superposition shapes the *poeisis* of Glitch Art by centering an ambivalence that must be and is *always* resolved, even though it destabilizes this resolution as a momentary contingency subject to continuous revision and reconsideration; thus the critical and analytic interest of /glitch/ includes more than merely the structural alterations, aesthetics, and artifacts produced by Glitch Art.[431]

The diagnostic approach must begin by rhetorically connecting the glitch to the technical medium in what is always a fundamentally self-referential claim. Being the *thing–in–itself* precludes any other meaning—a designation of "glitch" or "technical failure" claims to be an indexical proof about an essential nature that reifies its relationship to 'the real' as an immanent demonstration of *causality*. The commonplace treatment of /glitch/ as an irrelevant and idiosyncratic rupture with the normative functioning of the machine reflects this mystification of digital technology as a magical realm beyond physical constraints and human control. These connections between indexicality and the encultured role of past experience in the identification of "noise" is an immanent aspiration to being a proof of 'the real.' The glitch is not just a *thing–in–itself*, it is also a specific artifact existing within the symbolic system of *representation*: 'errors' only become meaningful in those specific situations where they cannot otherwise be ignored as "noise" to correct.

Within this proximate enframing of experience, a technical failure is never "only" a product of symptomatic analysis: it also always a syntactic vehicle that *signifies* "technical failure." This convergence between the diagnostic mode and symbolic expression is the superposition posed by /glitch/: a stoppage where interpretation cannot continue without a human decision about engaging the glitch *as-normative* (representationally) or *as-glitched* (symptomatically). These peculiar dynamics conflates indexical claims, the indexical aspiration to demonstrative proof, and their structural role in how ideology normalizes disruptions through enculturation.

The ambivalence of glitches performs Lyotard's concept of "paralogy" through *how* these autonomous products of machines always invoke a residual encoding by virtue of being produced by and for a human audience/user. The protocols that alter data by introducing alternatives into the error-prone decoding process are an instability that exploits the precise instructions of computer programming. Thus /glitch/ may be valid to the machine, but the results are anomalous for the human audience, allowing the familiar opposition of *original::quotational* to break down because the generative basis of *intervention/glitch* demonstrates a series of paralogies that interrupt and alter the normally stable digital semiosis.[432] The instability of their semiosis corresponds to a precise uncertainty about when to engage *as-if* encoded: the 'intentional function' describes the *interpretive status* that allows the glitch to be engaged *as-if* it was an intended creation, but it remains an ambivalent and metastable *desire* for signification, one that is continuously subject to immediate revaluations and reassessments.

Considering a glitch symbolically understands its "error" as a 'material function' that transforms what might otherwise be disruptive "noise" into a component of 'transparent' articulation—thus becoming a sign. Unlike symptomatic analysis, which is a *causal* explanation that reflexively justifies treating glitches diagnostically as problems to eliminate. This separation highlights the elliptical role of the aura of the digital evident in how the "average reader" engages glitches only to eliminate them from consideration and consciousness. Relegation to the 'external realm' of non-signification (except as a technical problem to correct) means glitches cannot be anything other than "noise" that distorts and corrupts the "signal." Although this vernacular use does

not delve deeply into the problematics of Glitch Art, this familiarity
has produced the 'iconography of error' utilized by it. The 'material
function' encodes these artifacts as evidence for digital materiality, and
exploits their commonplace appearances to achieve a conventional
expression of "authenticity." The interlocking of the 'intentional
function' with the entangled dimensions of /glitch/—relationality,
indexicality, and autonomous generation—contain the flaws and
unexpected artifacts generated by digital machines and thus
neutralizes their disruptive potentials. These metastable semiotics
inform both their expressive, aesthetic contemplation and their
symptomatic analysis equally.

[2] Transcendent Instrumentalities

The reflexive awareness that defines the discursive aesthetic by
denying immanent perception is common to all glitches because
technical fluency assumes all glitched media are imaginary
"quotations" of an unbroken self, a flawed copy of a perfect original
that may not actually exist. When understood in these terms, Glitch
Art becomes a dimension of the same idealization of the source file
that defines the aura of the digital and shapes the apperception of all
digital media: "transcendence" precisely describes how this discursive
aesthetic continues the avant-garde lineage that used machinery to
express a primordial, metaphysical spirituality immanent in/as art—a
tendency in psychedelic film, video art, and digital media[433] has been
underway since the 1950s,[434] evident in historical attempts to use
media to evoke, induce, or accompany visionary experiences.[435] The
transcendence of Glitch Art arises from how 'the digital' is conceived in
immaterial terms: an ideological blindness to physicality and materiality
eliminates concerns with the physical basis of digital technology. These
elisions parallel those dimensions of digital culture—social, economic,
political—that also vanish from conscious consideration.[436] As an
aesthetic concept, this "aura of the digital" develops a transcendent
value implicit in identifying the immaterial digital file as the "true"
work via a discursive aesthetic: it identifies a distinction between
the immaterial file and its physical presentation that matches the
denial of the gallery exhibition context in Modernist aesthetics. This
action effaces the object encountered by substituting an idealized
imaginary work contained by the instrumental data file for the
"earlier productions" required by intertextuality, understanding each
immanent digital presentation (glitched or not) as an imperfect "copy"
of that absent original. Technical fluency thus idealizes the source file:
a direct consequence of the aura of the digital's refusal of materiality—
not only the capital, labor, and resources digital technology consumes,
but also in considering the immanent display on-screen of digital
files[437]—the discursive aesthetic develops as a potential response

to these everyday presentations, rather than being specifically or exclusively an aspect of Glitch Art.

At the same time, Glitch Art also reveals the dialectical claim of opposition between *glitched* and *un-glitched* to be an illusion created by assumptions about the nature of digitally encoded data. Only abnormal circumstances draws the artifacts produced by digital errors into consciousness, allowing them to appear to 'part the veil' on computational operations in a strictly conventional and artificial revelation of digital materiality. The generative "noise" of digital media understood *as-expressive* (via the 'material function') rather than *as-glitch* (symptom of breakdown) transforms *mal*functions into *mis*functions[438] to recapitulate the heritage of early twentieth century visual music,[439] abstract painting,[440] and avant-garde[441] or "absolute film."[442] This lineage attempts to render a metaphysical 'reality of the mind'[443] immanent: an avant-garde and Modernist, even Formalist,[444] heritage that assumed a dazzling universal presence as Glitch Art emerged during the first decades of the twenty-first century in a reflection of the dominance enjoyed by the aura of the digital during that same period.[445] These cultural (spiritual) beliefs about abstraction[446] become apparent in digital media as the transcendence of glitches.

Idealizing the data file is an escape from the limitations and flaws of its material presentation. This discursive aesthetic ramifies the apparently immanent identification of the digital file or datastream as the "true" work, thus declaring all presentations on-screen and all physical manifestations (such as printouts) imperfect replicas of a perfect (virtual) original, the data file in a denial of its physicality via the aura of the digital.[447] Attempts to create an autonomous, critical aesthetic form independent of human interpretations rely upon an implicit transcendence that ignores the actual work presented to consider an (absent) ideal. They reflect a cultural desire to replace human agency with autonomous processes.[448]

[3] The Meaning of Glitches and Glitch Art

Why—the assumptions/desires that predetermine and direct interpretations while imposing invisible and unacknowledged limits on semiosis and apperception equally invoke and emerge from the internalized ranges of potential that are the true foundations of meaning–knowledge. The proposal advanced throughout this book concerns an interpretive schema that is non-dialectical; it offers instead a dynamic range of infinite graduations whose general tendencies—signal::noise and symbolic::diagnostic—are not defined by oppositions, even if they are bounded by points of mutual incompatibility in extremis. It is precisely this tendency to simplify and polarize (i.e. dialectical thought) that /glitch/ specifically deranges;

the paradoxes that emerge only develop into fallacies when the reader or interpreter insists on one potential to the exclusion of the others. Unlike the fixed positions that are the essential premise of dialects (and their alchemical heritage), it is the oppositions themselves that are unstable, each fading into the next. Keeping this alterior mode of reasoning firmly fixed in one's mind brings these discarded, ignored, masked potentials into consciousness. They deny the dialectical its validity, thus offering the /glitch/ as a mode of/for a non-binary critical reckoning. Abandoning these fallacies of dialectical polarization enters into a superposed realm where incompleteness, contingency, and ambiguity are dominant rather than minimized, and the discursive skill of thought necessitates an empirical embrace of alterity, multiplicity, and transitoriness.

The dialectical struggles with the superposition of diagnostic and symbolic modes in addressing /glitch/. The alchemical process of combination and distillation fails when confronted by an unresolvable continuous spectrum, thus affirming the importance of /glitch/ as a descriptor of the metastable in/for analysis. In being a liminal moment for interpretation, poised at the transition, /glitch/ is instructive, granting access to these changes in state as inchoate matter becomes encoded expression. The dualities and binary oppositions that superficially define digital codes inherently include a third element, the interval marker, that unit of distinction that makes the parsing of the binary encoding of digital information possible. This separating mechanism, typically ignored and invisible within both computer code and dialectical thinking, is simultaneously instrumentalized by the digital system and represents a trap from which human cognition must escape. The media theorist Peter Lurie identified these limitations in his analysis of the recombination made possible by digital art processes:

> Our genetic and computer codes may be Manichean, but our thinking must not be. Dualism, which originated as a theory about the structure of the world, has calcified into an analytical set piece. We must find another model. We must bring a multivalent tool to bear on political, sociological, philosophical or economic issues. It would be rigorously open-minded, continuously recalibrated. It would cast dichotomies as guideposts rather than fenced-in camps. It would be vibrantly relational, a cross-pollinating perspective yielding imaginative solutions rather than deadening, zero-sum compromises.[449]

What Lurie demands in opposition to the dialectic is the ambivalent space described by superposition and its accompanying and logically necessary 'information space' that is a relational field where the polarized oppositions of dialectics serve as points of mutual exclusion in a much larger realm of graduated and mutually linked differences: /glitch/ describes these points of instability, moments within this space, but not the space itself. When confronting Glitch Art these metastable dynamics become immanent because there is no adjustment possible; there is nothing wrong with the "transmission." The superposed convergence of incompatible and mutually exclusive interpretations is an encoded expression that is simultaneously an uncoded *thing–in–itself*, contradicting the immediacy and transparency of the recognition *as-error* that paradoxically defines Glitch Art. These aesthetics are not just pretty patterns generated by a machine. They offer a protracted opportunity for meditation upon the technical interface of interpretation, expressed in/between the realm of digital operations, the encoding of technical media, and the desires for coherence by the human audience. Each of these factors deploys the same process of active engagement that semiotics theorizes to bring meaning to otherwise mute matter, but as /glitch/ does so, it also opens the potential for a reflexive response to this process: signification comes unstuck and reveals the secret of its multiple becoming.

The ambivalence that /glitch/ exploits is an implicit and internalized product of ideological beliefs as singular, a view of fixed and stable relationships that can only proceed relationships as dialectical oppositions. For this understanding anything challenging these absolutes is a critical challenge. However, this conception of the audience is passive, their own technical fluency with digital media about a *perfect* original—the datastream—serves to mystify their encounters and interpretations. The alternative that embraces ambivalence; Glitch Art belongs to this shifting and dynamic approach that creates a discursive aesthetic by the same operations that makes identifying /glitch/ possible. This contra-dialectic avoids the fallacies of dialectics that assume interpretations are absolute and fixed positions; Glitch Art necessarily creates/renders these fallacies immanent to analysis since actual breakdowns only result in a stoppage—when the machine simply "crashes" and stops working the symbolic considerations of glitches as-expressions become increasingly unlikely, even impossible: addressing /glitch/ via its impacts on the normative, 'transparent' engagement that is concerned with communication—it apprehends only how the signified is transformed in/by the presentation—creates the fallacy[450] that a glitch is an automatically 'political' (critical) utterance.[451] The problem for any attempt to propose Glitch Art as an *automatically* critical expression is not its capacity to interrupt the normative progression of interpretations, but the adaptability of the audience to that stoppage. The immanent digital display is not the 'digital object,' but an image-carrier showing what is merely one instance of a vastly reproducible and replicable work whose ideological association of *mis*functions with a transcendental signified derives from how the dual normalizations of glitches as-errors to ignore or as-materiality for the digital enables a shift in address from the immanent encounter to their consideration as evidence for an absent, *un*glitched (ideal) original. The technical fluency that enables this identification also precisely blocks its self-consciousness engagement, even in works cueing *poeisis* because the critical apprehension of Glitch Art requires more than just the formal appreciation of this iconography as expressive. This development exposes the idealization of the data file in technical fluency via how recognizing the discursive shift in address creates a concern for the absent-but-essential 'original' that is unglitched,[452] which ironically understands this source (data file) as the 'real' work apart from the errors themselves.[453]

'Transparent' media are transformed by circulation through a variety of displays and presentations, justifying the audience identifying these discursive aesthetics via their normative readings concerned with the "content," rather than as/in the expression. Thus the intransigence of /glitch/ is *not* a disruption and effacement of the idealized original, but is instead an illusion invoked by the interpretive rejection of material concerns (the aura of the digital). Understanding the physical presentation as only one, flawed instance of an ideal and virtual original is a product of how technical fluency defines digital images as expressions of the datastream, which is then identified as the 'true work.' The hypothetical *perfect reproduction* is reified as the 'norm' for digital reproduction[454]—identifying anything produced by the machine as "glitch" (as a 'failure') is *only* possible because its audience recognizes it differs from both the *anticipated* imperfections of the immanent work *and* what they expect the ideal form to be; what the discursive aesthetic brings into consciousness with the glitch is a specifically aesthetic reverie whose transparency denies critical engagement, even though it can act as a cue for one. In consequence, the "glitch aesthetic" often acts transparently, drawing attention not to a critical meaning, but to the transcendence instrumentally contained in/as the datastream—it is an ironic cypher for an impossible perfection and authenticity of expression. These significances neither challenge nor critique the transparent relationships they depend on, even if they make their articulation a self-conscious stylistic gesture. The alterity of discursive reason to the lineage and traditions of dialectical thought cannot be more explicit or immanent than in the superpositions created by /glitch/ and its ambivalence.

[4] Expressive Prospects: AImages and Generative Glitches

Celluloid motion pictures are an expression of the Newtonian clockwork universe of the nineteenth century: regular units of equal duration whose fixed contents resist easy manipulation; in contrast, the digital media of the present are contingent, metastable, and fluidly transformable at all levels, expressions of a culture that has embraced uncertainty, indeterminacy, and superposition. The rise of Glitch Art, with its ambivalent recognitions and ambiguous properties, is the appropriate response to these cultural transformations that increasingly center human consciousness and interpretation. But how it continues to develop, its destiny as an aesthetic form, depends on factors entirely independent from its aesthetics: either. Whether it is conceived as a "movement," or is simply one response to the emergent dominance of digital media that, like the nostalgic embrace of vinyl records, is a cultural working-through of the destabilizing of traditional categories and cultural values will shape its future; it is entirely possible that Glitch Art is less a movement than a collective enthusiasm mediated and produced by the network effects of digital media— which will ultimately prove to be immanently fashionable until it isn't, at which point it will simply vanish and some new expressive approach to media will take its place. Yet there are reasons to doubt this sudden vanishing act will happen: the lineage of materiality in media is partly responsible for the wide spread embrace of glitching as a demonstration of 'authenticity,' and has cast glitches in that role since the invention of video art in the early 1960s. This use is part of a deeper history of cultural concerns about machines and automation that began with debates over industrial production machinery (and photography as art) in the nineteenth century. The challenges that industrialization offers to the traditional signifiers of fine craftsmanship—perfect finish, sharp edges, no evidence of the human hand—resulted in a resentment of flaws and other errors in response to the easy perfection made possible by machines. Embracing the token evidence of human agency apparent in these mistakes elevates what was 'unskilled' production into a place of higher value (status), but nevertheless does not escape the 'social paradigm' of the industrial,[455] since without the automated machinery that obviated the need for human skill, these aesthetics of the flawed become incoherent. These values are evident in how AI generative systems displace human agency in the direct production of the image; however, the distinction between an AImage and other forms of CGI is a matter of degree: the displacement of human action and the operations of the device remain constant.

Distinguishing the glitches that define Glitch Art from other types of error and flaw becomes important when confronting the contemporary emergence of generative technical media such as machine learning (AI). A brief tangential consideration will clarify these differences and offer insights into the prospects for AImages as Glitch Art: AI can (and often does) produce unexpected outputs that violate the audience's expectations; however, these works are not necessarily examples of either glitches or Glitch Art—instead, they tend to converge on the uncanny and alienating affects of Surrealist aesthetics. These potentials were identified by media historians Jennifer O'Meara and Cáit Murphy via experiments with the *DALL-E* text–to–image system in 2022. Their work addresses the 'typical' distortions produced by machine learning technologies:

> Beyond DALL-E Mini's name invoking that of famed surrealist artist Salvador Dalí, the generator's blending of machine learning with familiar images from the human world often leads to nightmarish results that reflect a wider historical interest in surrealist art, including its links with the 'uncanny' ... The overlaps between DALL-E and surrealist creations are perhaps best described as versions of [the Exquisite Corpse] game, where visual and often chaotic presentations of the body emerge from dynamic exchanges between multiple participants (each relinquishing control), and including that of the AI generator itself.[456]

The adage that a "picture is worth 1,000 words" becomes an instrumentality with these machines that generate deformed bodies, inviting understanding their outputs via abjection,[457] instances of 'body horror,' where the human form is rendered monstrous and alien by the operations of a machine—precisely the interest of what Surrealist aesthetics termed the "marvelous."[458] However disquieting the dysmorphic AImages created by text–to–image generation may be [Figure 7.1], they are products of the machine operating properly, generating an image in response to the instruction; there is no "glitch" here in the sense of an operational breakdown. The human agency directing the image-object remains tangential to these autonomous operations, even as this guidance oversees and orchestrates their function. AImages create difficulties for their audiences, not because of the content of the work or problems with the operations performed by the machine learning system, but between the "keyboard and the chair"—the same dependence on human response that characterizes the "broken aesthetic" for the 'traditional' glitch technique of databending[459] also informs the recognition and response to the outputs of text–to–image systems. The decision to address any the contents of image-object as *potentially* signifying (i.e. its visible features are elements of an aesthetic expression) is the same issue as deciding that it is intentional, a creative action performed to

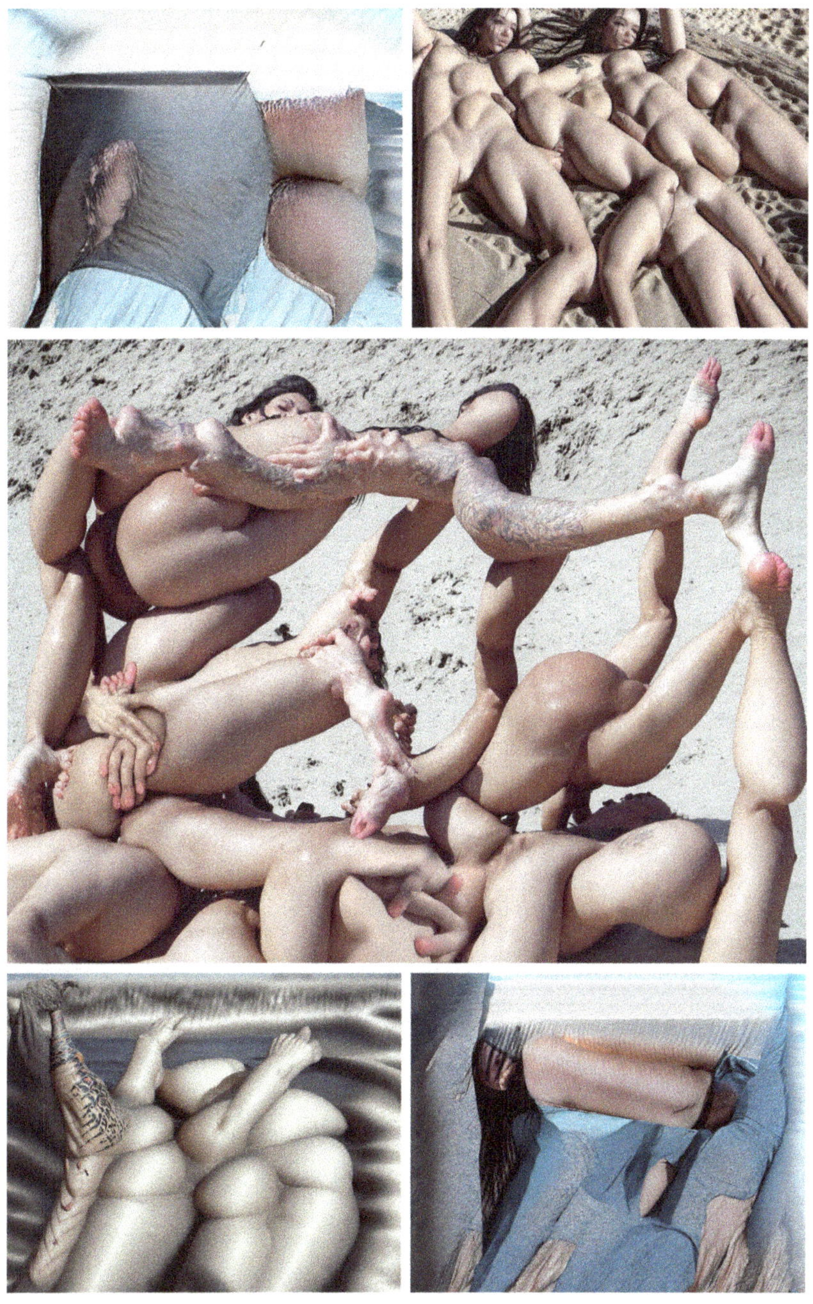

7.1   Michael Betancourt, a selection of dysmorphic AImages that suggest
       Surrealist aesthetics applied to figures and landscapes equally (2023).
       Courtesy Artists' Rights Society (ARS).

communicate something. The dysmorphic AImage is *not* a glitch, nor is it even an aberrant product of the system that produces it. On examination, these works are internally consistent and complete in the same ways that non-dysmorphic productions are. What has 'gone wrong' depends on the beholder, rather than the operations of the AI system. While these images may be undesirable, inappropriate, or even monstrous, they are not products of a the kinds of system failure evoked and exploited by Glitch Art.

The dysmorphic AImage and its Surrealist evocations center the human audience in the interpretive process, insisting on aesthetic reverie as a product of the audience's agency, thus centering the viewer, but without concern for the operations of the machine itself. This convergence of digital technology and Surrealist aesthetics has been a feature of popular engagements with computer generated imagery since the 1980s.[460] These images could be made by hand (as in the Surrealist paintings they recall) or generated autonomously; the distinction is moot.

Displacement causes the two bodies in Figure 7.2 to appear to be either turning away from, or towards the viewer. These distorted, misshapen bodies may produce an experience of 'painterly motion,' showing figures teasingly turn away from the viewer: this apparent motion emerges from how, as the eye moves across this image, the human mind fits the different positions of the body together to form a coherent whole. AImages can reproduce this effect [Figure 7.2, Left] because viewers, to make sense of the image as a whole body, must accommodate the distortions as 'caused' by movement—understanding it as a "good gestalt"[461]—thus audiences interpret these displacements or distortions as motion.[462] In the AImage, two radically mismatched views are joined above the waist, creating a dynamic twist that moves the upper body away from the viewer.

In traditional European painting, executing the 'painterly movement' effect was a complex technical process that emerged from life-drawing and work from living models; the AImage shows that what had to be planned can also be generated using local 'rules' for connecting different views of a body. A historical example of this technical effect appears in Baroque painter Peter Paul Rubens picture of his wife, Helene Fourment, wearing a fur wrap [Figure 7.2, Right]. The movements are interpreted from "signs" (the distortions) showing she has *moved* slightly while the spectator was looking. This technical effect must remain hidden, unnoticed by the viewer—to notice her hips (masked by the fur wrap) are rotationally mismatched breaks the illusion that the painting's presentation of a "tease" depends upon. The dynamic effect created in both pictures by using a contorting figure corresponds to historical painterly techniques

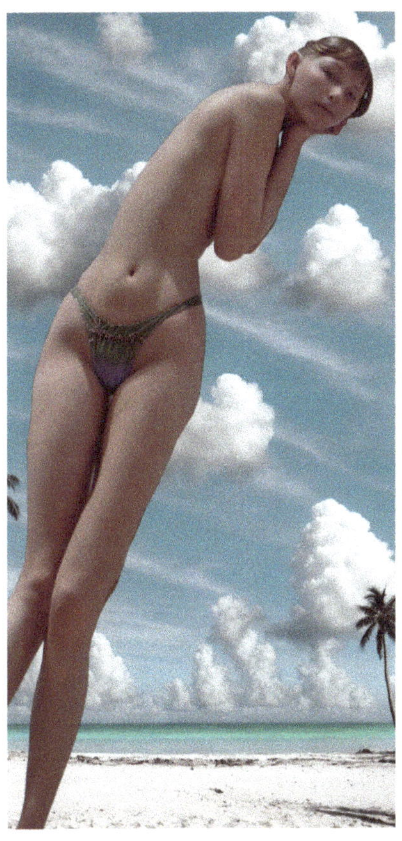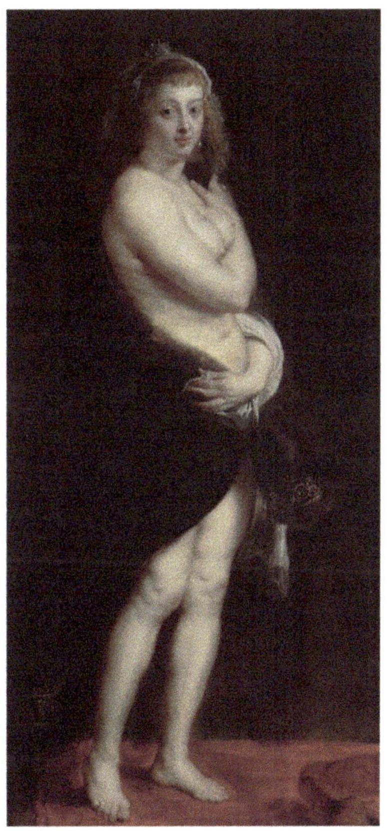

7.2   [LEFT] Michael Betancourt, an AImage of a posed 'body' that creates a
       motion affect due to its distortion (2023).
       Courtesy Artists' Rights Society (ARS).

       [RIGHT] Peter Paul Rubens, *Das Pelzchen* [*The Little Fur,* or
       Portrait of Helene Fourment in a Fur Wrap] (c. 1636–1638)
       Gemäldegalerie, 688, Kunsthistorisches Museum, Vienna.

for depicting motion. Recognizing the movements of these figures requires considering the distortions as a reflection of the 'intentional function,' a decision that justifies their understanding *as-expressive* rather than *as-error*.

Dysmorphic and distorted AImages, such as in Figure 7.1, thus potentially converge on earlier, painterly aesthetics precisely because they exploit the same capacity for unexpected, associative convergence[463] that is a feature of human cognition. The interpretive process is unstable, flexible, able to adapt to whatever phenomena it considers, a fluent adaptability that Surrealist painter Salvador Dalí exploited in his "paranoiac-critical method":

> Standing altogether apart from the influence of the sensory phenomena with which hallucination may be considered more or less concerned, the paranoiac activity always employs materials admitting of control and recognition. It is enough that the delirium of interpretation should have linked together the implications of the images of the different pictures covering a wall for the real existence of this link to be no longer deniable.[464]

The associative process that creates the metamorphic illusions in Dalí's Surrealist paintings exploit the same proximate junctures and low level convergences that are evident in AImages—connections made without concern for the "content" of the image, only its immanent form as a series of isolated and individuated details. The apparent automation of the "paranoiac-critical method" by AI still requires the audience to mentally engage these works through *automatisme*,[465] since the generative imagery only becomes coherent through the viewer's engagement with its dysmorphia as an expressive dimension of the articulation. This central role for the viewer in apprehending the AImage inevitably converges on the role of the viewer in Glitch Art, not because they are expressively similar, but because *all* expressions depend on their audience's choice to engage them; however, *unlike* Glitch Art, the ambivalences and uncertainties of the dysmorphic AImage do not make the operations of the system apparent, nor do they evoke the computational nature of digital media. This distinction is obvious when confronting examples of glitched AImages [Figure 7.3]—these works evoke the same sense of computational breakdown as in other, more traditional examples of Glitch Art. This distinction separates glitches from dysmorphia. They develop and belong to different lineages of aesthetic precedent. It is not the centering of the viewer that matters, but what is being brought to their attention and thus becoming central to the expression: for Glitch Art it is the computational

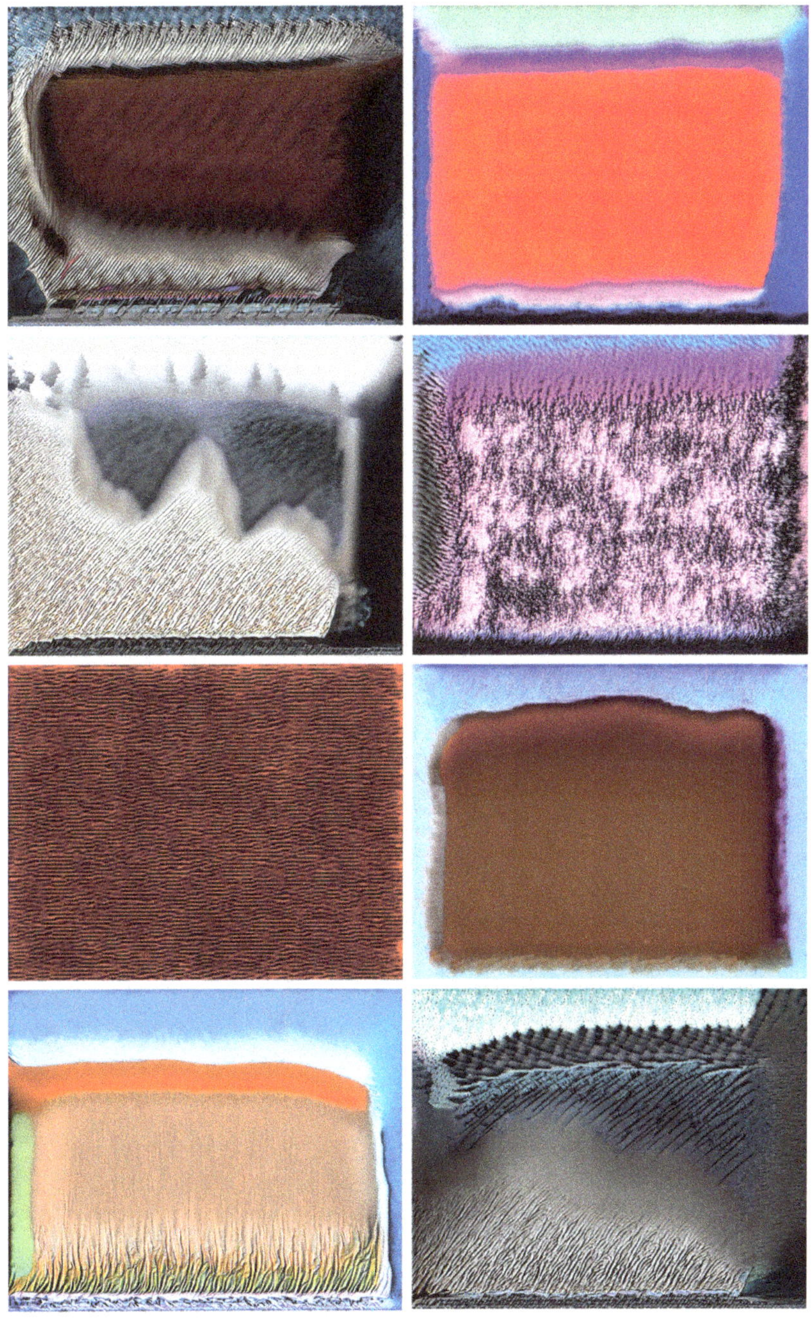

7.3 Examples of generative AImage glitches produced by LoRA models interacting to cancel each other's work, by Michael Betancourt (2023). Courtesy Artists' Rights Society (ARS).

141

operations, recognized by the audience through their technical fluency with computer technology.

Glitch Art's expressive errors emerge from artistic experiments with the autonomous aspects of technical media that are normally considered "fixed" or essential; its continuation into the realm of the AImage diverges from these distorted and Surrealist-inflected images precisely because, while the dysmorphic AImage may be unexpected, there is also no question that it is a product of typical and familiar generative functions. In fact, these images are so commonplace that their deviations from photographic reality often provide empirical features that AI has been able to simulate as iconographic features: there is no question that the machine is operating properly, even if its product is less than optimal. What distinguishes the glitched AImages from the dysmorphic AImage is that the glitched image does not merely challenge expectations, but also suggests the operations of the digital system responsible for that image. This secondary identification depends on the viewer's technical fluency that renders the resulting image via the 'material function' as a signifier for the autonomous processes that generate the output; it is not merely that they are unexpected, but that they can also suggest the protocols and technology responsible for the work. This self-referentiality remains constant in all expressive uses of glitches, apparent even in the analogue physicality of celluloid motion pictures, demonstrated by flickering and strobing images whose seething grain obscures and erases the content that would typically be the focus.

As the aesthetic potential of glitches is now no longer a marginal concern, but rather a commonplace element in the semiosis of media, the problematics of the /glitch/ have also begun to inflect the vernacular of technical media. No longer reflexively ignored, or spontaneously celebrated, glitches and the premise of Glitch Art, increasingly suggest an over-determined and artificial conception of digital materiality as a conventionalized Formalist gesture at expressing "authenticity" or "veracity" in an expression of a Contemporary moment that assumes the digital medium. These consolidations of the critical, interpretive, and heuristic lineage of avant-garde lineage to which Glitch Art belongs are neither surprising nor unexpected. The capacity of these approaches to technical media to be extended into the novel media being born with machine learning and AImages is both clear and an unknown territory. These instances of the aesthetic transformation Flusser described, where the "terror" of the *new* becomes the everyday, are now being supplanted by something else: *what comes next?*

Making predictions is hard, especially about the future:

[a] The continued creation of Glitch Art, expanding to address the operations and imperfections of AI systems which may offer new opportunities for critical reflection on the relationship between human society and the demands of digital capitalism.

[b] Glitch Art becoming an increasingly conventionalized and familiar visual style as the 'glitch aesthetic' is steadily automated (a trajectory that parallels Surrealism's popular embrace).

[c] The emergence of novel approaches that move beyond Glitch Art; however, the ways that artists have addressed technology may need to change as the use of errors as critical tools becomes increasingly naturalized as an uncritical *baroque* gesture.

[d] An aesthetic embracing new modes of human–AI collaboration and co-creativity that is less focused on exploits, and instead searches out new potentials would likely require abandoning the protocols of Glitch Art.

What will probably continue is the lineage of human gestures as expressions of authenticity, and the interplay between avant-garde disruptions, vernacular, and commercial embrace even as technological change demands the invention of new modes for critical engagement.

APPENDIX

There are three closely related terms in this discursive analysis that should be kept distinct in mind while reading it since their presentation within this text is similar:

> **/glitch/** designates the liminal moment of interface between mutually incompatible modes of recognition-interpretation, held in superposition, and whose resolution remains unstable.

> **Glitch Art** identifies those aesthetic works produced which invite and invoke a recognition of glitches, but which the audience simultaneously engages as aesthetic objects being presented for reflective apprehension (*poeisis*).

> **glitches** are any products of machine operations that their human audience diagnostically identifies as an error, failure, and/or breakdown, whether products of actual technical failures or not. They resemble the "errors" produced by either hardware failures or problems with the datastream,[466] as described by Figure 1.4:

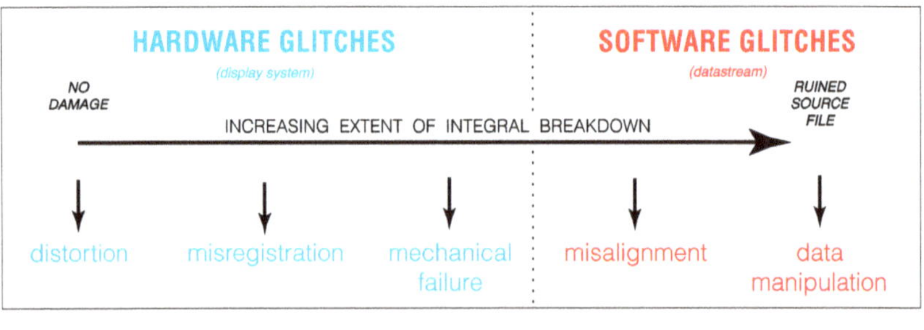

1.4   The empirical referents for the 'material function' in Glitch Art derive from glitches' capability to serve as diagnostics for technical breakdowns. These 'material markers' provide observable cues whose articulation reveals their diagnostic recognition (and any indexical claim about technology *as-broken*) also depends on the same encultured knowledge that defines technical expertise itself.

Hardware Glitches
(1) *Distortion*

Physical malfunctions of / in the presentation—problems with video screens, optical misalignments and electronic failures in video projectors for example are all physical failures that manifest as a distortion of the resulting presentation without altering or impacting the data. These mechanical faults and failings are the most common, and at the same time, the most transient. They reside in the particular device rather than being a feature of the data displayed. The earliest varieties of glitch belong to this category of failure: the RCA repair manuals published in the 1950s are concerned with the correction and identification of these physical failures in the display.

(2) *Misregistration*

The "noise" of historically analog recording technologies—the dirt, scratches, smudges and markings that can distort physical media also impact the playback of digital recordings on media such as CDs and DVDs where the data is accessed physically rather than electronically. The same physical interruptions that impact analog recordings can also distort and interrupt digital recordings that are physically stored. Most familiar from electronic music at the start of the twenty-first century, this approach to glitching engages the interface between the physical storage of the data and the data. The 'material markers' of celluloid film that feature prominently in structural and materialist films of the 1960s–1970s involve the inclusion of this "noise" in the presentation.

(3) *Mechanical Failure*

Familiar from electronic music, the most famous type of hardware failure is "circuit bending," the creation of short circuits and physical "failures" in the hardware that renders electronic signals for a human audience. These physical failures in the technology (as distinct from software) produce glitches and aberrant results without necessarily altering the digital files being presented. The protocol used in the production of Fenton's *Digital TV Dinner,* where the glitches result from striking the game console to cause the cartridge to pop "out" is an example of this physical engagement with technology that induces a glitch.

Software Glitches
(4) *Misalignment*

Misalignment between a digital file and the software that renders that file has two mirror-like variants: the first produces errors through the inappropriate application of decompression by decoding a compressed file using an incorrect codec, resulting in a transformation of the encoded data without damaging the file; the second involves the induced opening/reading of a file using an incorrect software application. For example, opening a motion encoded video file as audio, manipulating the audio version of the dataset, then engaging the results either as audio, or returning it to be video again. Both approaches involve mismatches between encoded data and its decoding, resulting in aberrant results when rendered for a human audience. These superficially structural affects are simultaneously integral, repeatable, and transitory since they impact the display of a digital file rather than its encoded data.

(5) *Data Manipulation*

Data manipulation covers a range of approaches and protocols, all of which are focused on the transformation and alteration of the digital file: its dataset is changed to induce aberrant results when "played" normally on a computer. These varieties of glitching are the most immediately recognized as being *glitch,* and are readily apparent as specific, named protocols such as "data moshing" in which a video file compressed using MPEG-1 has crucial image data removed (the I-frames), resulting in a cascading failure as the motion data is not refreshed with corresponding image data; Takeshi Murata's *Monster Movie* (2005) employed this technique to produce its distinctive effects. Other variants of data manipulation, such as "data bending" involve the introduction of transient errors into the datastream that also produce cascading failures. The occasional "drop-outs" in digital video feeds (commonly seen during bad weather) are common examples of these transformations. Directly changing data introduces errors and overflows when the file is rendered for a human audience that overlap with transformations of the data using incorrect and inappropriate software, resulting in convergent results when encountered in human readable form.

REFERENCES

1   Polan, D. *The Political Language of Film and the Avant-Garde* (Ann Arbor: UMI Research Press, 1985) pp. 36-40.

2   Tarasti, E. "The semiotics of A. J. Greimas: A European intellectual heritage seen from the inside and the outside" *Sign Systems Studies* vol. 45, no. 1/2 (2017) pp. 33-53.

3   Betancourt, M. *The Critique of Digital Capitalism* (Brooklyn: Punctum Books, 2016) pp. 153-190.

4   Eco, U. *A Theory of Semiotics* (Bloomington: Indiana University Press, 1979) p. 233.

5   Deleuze, G. *Cinema 2: The Time-Image* (Minneapolis: The University of Minnesota Press, 1989) pp. 25-26.

6   Piaget, J. *La psychologie de l'intelligence* (Paris: A. Cohn, 1947).

7   Bogdan, C. *The Semiotics of Visual Languages* (Boulder: East European Monographs, 2002) pp. 10-12.

8   Ziehen, T. *Lehrbuch der Logik auf positivistischer Grundlage mit Berücksichtigung der Geschichte der Logik* (Bonn: A. Marcus & E. Webere Verlag, 1920).

9   Eco, U. *A Theory of Semiotics* (Bloomington: Indiana University Press, 1979) pp. 232-233.

10   Betancourt, M. "The 'Intentional Function' in Still and Moving Photographic Images" *Semiotica: Journal of the International Association for Semiotic Studies*, vol. 246 (2022); DOI: https://doi.org/10.1515/sem-2020-0065

11   Eco, U. *A Theory of Semiotics* (Bloomington: Indiana University Press, 1979) pp. 232-233.

12   Eco, U. *A Theory of Semiotics* (Bloomington: Indiana University Press, 1979) p. 216.

13   The term "Glitch Art" was invented by the artist Ant Scott, who used it on his website www.beflix.com starting in 2001.
This term comes into common usage by 2005 to principally identify glitches employed in digital images and video.

14   Paul, C. and Levy, M. "Genealogies of the New Aesthetic" *Postdigital Aesthetics: Art, Computation and Design* ed. David M. Berry and Michael Dieter (New York: Palgrave Macmillan, 2015) p 31.

15   Flusser, V. *Into the Universe of Technical Images* trans. Nancy Ann Roth (Minneapolis: University of Minnesota Press, 2011).

16   Eco, U. *Interpretation and Overinterpretation* ed. Stefan Collini (Cambridge: Cambridge University Press, 1992).

17   Danto, A. *After the End of Art* (Princeton: Princeton University Press, 1997).

18   Scott, F. "Networks and Apparatuses, circa 1971: Or, Hippies Meet Computers" *Hippie Modernism: The Struggle for Utopia* ed. Andrew Blauvelt (Minneapolis: Walker Art Center, 2015) pp. 103-105.

19   Manon, H. and Temkin, D. "Notes on Glitch" *World Picture 6: WRONG* (2011); DOI: http://worldpicturejournal.com/WP_6/Manon.html, par. 5.

20   Manon, H. and Temkin, D. "Notes on Glitch" *World Picture 6: WRONG* (2011); DOI: http://worldpicturejournal.com/WP_6/Manon.html, par. 29.

21   Cloninger, C. "GltchLnguistx: The Machine in the Ghosts / Static Trapped in the Mouths" *Glitch reader(ror)* ed. Nick Briz, Evan Meaney, Rosa Menkman, William Robertson, Jon Satrom, Jessica Westbrook (Unsorted Books: 2011) p. 33.

22   Cascone, K. "The Aesthetics of Failure: 'Post-Digital' Tendencies in Contemporary Computer Music" *Computer Music Journal* vol. 24, no. 4 (Winter, 2000) pp. 12-18.

23   Applegate, M. "Glitched in Translation" *Amodern* no. 6 (July, 2016); DOI: http://amodern.net/article/glitched-in-translation/

24   Popper, F. *Art of the Electronic Age* (New York: Abrams, 1993) pp. 179-181.

25   Ernst, W. "There is no 'Error' in Techno-logistics" *Miscommunications: Errors, Mistakes, Media* ed. Maria Korolkova and Timothy Barker (London: Bloomsbury, 2021) pp. 79-92.

26   This expanded scope is apparent from studies of "glitch" such as Legacy Russell's *Glitch Feminism: A Manifesto* (Verso, 2020) or Nathan Allen Jones' *Glitch Poetics* (Open Humanities Press, 2022).

27   Briz, N. *Thoughts on Glitch Art 2.0* (December 20, 2015) https://nickbriz. com/thoughtsonglitchart/

28   O'Doherty, B. *Inside the White Cube: The Ideology of the Gallery Space, Expanded Edition* (Berkeley: University of California Press, 1986).

29   Manon, H. and Temkin, D. "Notes on Glitch" *World Picture 6: WRONG* (2011); DOI: http://worldpicturejournal.com/WP_6/Manon.html, par. 29.

30   Warde B. *The Crystal Goblet, Sixteen Essays on Typography* (London: Sylvan Press, 1955).

31   Barker, T. "Aesthetics of Error: Media Art, the Machine, the Unforeseen, and the Errant" *Error: Glitch, Noise, and Jam in New Media Cultures* ed. Mark Nunes (New York: Continuum, 2011) p. 52.

32   Menkman, R. *Network Notebooks 4: The Glitch Moment(um)* (Amsterdam: Institute of Network Cultures, 2011) p. 38.

33   Tanaka, J. and Taylor, M.E. "Object categories and expertise: Is the basic level in the eye of the beholder?" *Cognitive Psychology* 23 (1991) pp. 121-149.

34   Betancourt, M. *Glitch Art in Theory and Practice: Critical Failures and Post-Digital Aesthetics* (New York: Routledge, 2016) p. 130.

35   Le Grice, M. *Experimental Cinema in the Digital Age* (London: BFI Publishing, 2006) pp. 275.

36   Fried, M. "Art and Objecthood" *Minimal Art* ed. Gregory Battcock (Berkeley: University of California Press, 1995) pp. 116-147.

37   Gidal, P. *Materialist Film* (London: Routledge, 1989) pp. 15-16.

38   Burger, P. *Theory of the Avant-Garde* (Minneapolis: University of Minnesota Press, 1984) p.11.

39   Genette, G. *Paratexts: Thresholds of Interpretation* (New York: Cambridge University Press, 1987) pp. 10-11.

40   Flusser, V. *Into the Universe of Technical Images (Electronic Mediations)* trans. Nancy Ann Roth (Minneapolis: University of Minnesota Press, 2011) pp. 46-48.

41   Betancourt, M. *The Critique of Digital Capitalism* (Brooklyn: Punctum Books, 2016).

42   Reichardt, J. *Cybernetic Serendipity: the computer and the arts* (New York: Praeger, 1969).

43   Popper, F. *Art of the Electronic Age* (New York: Abrams, 1993) pp. 179-181.

44   Derrida, J. "Différance" *Margins of Philosophy* trans. Alan Bass (Chicago: Chicago University Press, 1982) pp. 1-29.

45   Ballard, S. "Information, noise and et al" *M/C Journal* vol. 10 no. 5 (2007) pp. 1-8.

46   Brown, S. "Introduction" *Synthesis: Processing and Collaboration* (San Diego: The Gallery@Calit2, 2011) p. 5.

47   Marzec, A. "Postdigital aesthetics – an art of imperfection, disturbances and disintegration" *Unframing Archives: Essays on Cinema and Visual Arts* ed. Eugénia Vilela, Filipe Martins and Né Barros (Porto: Universidade de Porto, 2017) pp. 31-42.

48   Larkin, B. "Degraded Images, Distorted Sounds: Nigerian Video and the Infrastructure of Piracy" *Public Culture* vol. 16, no. 2 (2004) p. 292.

49   Temkin, D. "Glitch && Human-Computer Interaction" *Non-Object Oriented Art*, Vol. 1, no. 1, January 2014; DOI: http://nooart.org/post/73353953758/temkin-glitchhumancomputerinteraction

50   Zinman, G. "Getting Messy: Chance and Glitch in Contemporary Video Art" *Abstract Video: The Moving Image in Contemporary Art* ed. Gabrielle Jennings (Oakland: University of California Press, 2015) p. 107.

51   Cascone, K. "The Aesthetics of Failure: 'Post-Digital' Tendencies in Contemporary Computer Music" *Computer Music Journal* vol. 24, no. 4 (Winter, 2000) pp. 12-18.

52   Tarasti, E. *Theory of Musical Semiotics* (Bloomington: Indiana University Press, 1994) pp. 73-76.

53   Chapman, S. "Guerrilla Television in the Digital Age" *Journal of Film and Video* vol. 64, nos. 1-2 (Spring/Summer 2012) p. 46.

54   Larkin, B. "Degraded Images, Distorted Sounds: Nigerian Video and the Infrastructure of Piracy" *Public Culture* vol. 16, no. 2 (2004) p. 291.

55   Kahn, D. *Noise, Water, Meat* (Cambridge: The MIT Press, 1999) p.25.

56   Attali, J. *Noise: The Political Economy of Music* (Minneapolis: University of Minnesota Press, 1985) p. 6.

57   Cascone, K. "The Aesthetics of Failure: 'Post-Digital' Tendencies in Contemporary Computer Music" *Computer Music Journal*, vol. 24, no. 4 (Winter, 2000) p. 3.

58   Paul, C. and Levy, M. "Genealogies of the New Aesthetic" *Postdigital Aesthetics: Art, Computation and Design* ed. David M. Berry and Michael Dieter (New York: Palgrave Macmillan, 2015) p 31.

59   Harris, R. "The Integrational Conception of the Sign" *Integrationist Notes and Papers 2006–2008* (Gamlingay: Bright Pen, 2009).

60   Eco, U. *Kant and the Platypus* (New York: Harvest Books, 2000) pp. 125-126.

61   Betancourt, M. *The Critique of Digital Capitalism* (Brooklyn: Punctum Books, 2016) pp. 153-190.

62   Peirce, C. S. *The Writings of Charles S. Peirce: A Chronological Edition, Volume 2: 1867-1871* (Bloomington: Indiana University Press, 1982) p. 56.

63   Betancourt, M. *Ideologies of the Real in Title Sequence, Motion Graphics and Cinema* (New York: Routledge, 2020) pp. 177-204

64   Betancourt, M. *The Critique of Digital Capitalism* (Brooklyn: Punctum Books, 2016) pp. 37-49.

65   Eco, U. *A Theory of Semiotics* (Bloomington: Indiana University Press, 1979) p. 221.

66   Betancourt, M. *Cinematic Articulation in Motion Graphics* (New York: Routledge, 2022) pp. 134-138.

67   Fineman, M. *Faking It: Manipulated Photography Before Photoshop* (New Haven: Metropolitan Museum of Art, 2012) pp. 128-129.

68   Menkman, Rosa. *Network Notebooks 4: The Glitch Moment(um)* (Amsterdam: Institute of Network Cultures, 2011) pp. 35-36.

69   Betancourt, M. *Glitch Art in Theory and Practice: Critical Failures and Post-Digital Aesthetics* (New York: Routledge, 2016) pp. 49-76.

70   Betancourt, M. "Critical Glitches and Glitch Art" *Hz*, no. 19 (July, 2014) np.

71   Brown, S. "Introduction" *Synthesis: Processing and Collaboration* (San Diego: The Gallery@Calit2, 2011) p. 5.

72   Meagher, J. *RCA Television Pict-O-Guide: An Aid to TV Troubleshooting, Volume 1* (Harrison, NJ: Radio Corporation of America, Tube Department, 1949).

73   Brown, S. "Introduction" *Synthesis: Processing and Collaboration* (San Diego: The Gallery@Calit2, 2011) p. 5.

74   Fielding, R. *The Technique of Special Effects Cinematography* (Oxford: Focal Press, 1984) pp. 405-406.

75   Sherman, T. "Vernacular Video" *INC Reader #4: Video Vortex Reader— Responses to YouTube* ed. Geert Lovink and Sabine Niederer (Amsterdam: Institute of Network Cultures, 2008) p. 162.

76   Bazin, A. *What is Cinema?* trans. Timothy Barnard (Montreal: Caboose, 2009) pp. 8-9.

77   Sontag, S. *On Photography* (New York: Anchor Books, 1977) p. 5.

78   Manseau, P. *The Apparitionists: A Tale of Phantoms, Fraud, Photography, and the Man who Captured Lincoln's Ghost* (New York: Houghton Mifflin, 2017) pp. 93-100.

79   Vanhanen, J. "a099: Loving the Ghost in the Machine," *CTheory* (November 26, 2001); DOI: https://www.ctheory.net/articles.aspx?id=312

80   Owens, S. *The Ghost: A Cultural History* (London: Tate Publishing, 2017) pp. 202-209.

81   Kaplan, L. *The Strange Case of William Mumler, Spirit Photographer* (Minneapolis: University of Minnesota Press, 2008) pp. 169-179.

82   Roh, F. "Introduction" *Abstract Pictures on Film: The Technique of Making Light Graphics* (New York: Viking Press, 1964).

83   Betancourt, M. *Cinematic Articulation in Motion Graphics, Routledge Studies in Media Theory and Practice* (Routledge, 2021) p. 30.

84   Cloninger, Curt. "GltchLnguistx: The Machine in the Ghosts / Static Trapped in the Mouths" in *Glitch reader(ror)* ed. Nick Briz, Evan Meaney, Rosa Menkman, William Robertson, Jon Satrom, Jessica Westbrook (Unsorted Books: 2011) p. 35.

85   Betancourt, M. "The 'Material Function' in Cinema: Resolving the Paradox of the Glitch" *Semiotica: Journal of the International Association for Semiotic Studies*, no. 236-237, 2020, pp. 251-273; DOI: https://doi.org/10.1515/sem-2019-0006

86   Grundell, V. *Flow and Friction: On the Tactical Potential of Interfacing with Glitch Art* (Stockholm: Art and Theory, 2016) pp. 28-30.

87   Betancourt, M. *Glitch Art in Theory and Practice: Critical Failures and Post-Digital Aesthetics* (New York: Routledge, 2016) pp. 86-100.

88   Merrell, F. "Toward a concept of pluralistic, inter-relational semiosis" *Σημειωτκή - Sign Systems Studies*, vol. 35 no. 1-2 (2007) p. 17.

89   Betancourt, M. "The 'intentional function' in still and moving photographic images" *Semiotica: Journal of the International Association for Semiotic Studies*, 2022; DOI: https://doi.org/10.1515/sem-2020-0065

90   Cloninger, C. "GltchLnguistx: The Machine in the Ghosts / Static Trapped in the Mouths" in *Glitch reader(ror)* ed. Nick Briz, Evan Meaney, Rosa Menkman, William Robertson, Jon Satrom, Jessica Westbrook (Unsorted Books: 2011) p. 33.

91   Meagher, J. *RCA Television Pict-O-Guide: An Aid to TV Troubleshooting, Volume 1* (Harrison, NJ: Radio Corporation of America, Tube Department, 1949).

92   Wiesing, L. *Artificial Presence: Philosophical Studies in Image Theory* trans. Nils F. Schott (Stanford: Stanford University Press, 2010) pp. 18-23.

93   Zinman, G. "Getting Messy: Chance and Glitch in Contemporary Video Art" *Abstract Video: The Moving Image in Contemporary Art* ed. Gabrielle Jennings (Oakland: University of California Press, 2015) pp. 98-115.

94   Poggioli, R. *The Theory of the Avant-Garde* (Cambridge: Harvard University Press, 1968) p. 125.

95   Betancourt, M. "Critical Glitches and Glitch Art" *Hz*, no. 19 (July, 2014) np.

96   Betancourt, M. "The 'Material Function' in Cinema: Resolving the Paradox of the Glitch" *Semiotica: Journal of the International Association for Semiotic Studies*, no. 236-237 (2020) pp. 251-273; DOI: https://doi.org/10.1515/sem-2019-0006

97   Foster, H. *The Return of the Real* (Cambridge: The MIT Press, 1996) p. 40.

98   Betancourt, M. *The Critique of Digital Capitalism* (Brooklyn: Punctum Books, 2016) pp. 37-49.

99   Betancourt, M. "The 'intentional function' in still and moving photographic images" *Semiotica: Journal of the International Association for Semiotic Studies*, 2022; DOI: https://doi.org/10.1515/sem-2020-0065

100 Eco, U. *A Theory of Semiotics* (Bloomington: Indiana University Press, 1979) p. 216.

101 Bogdan, C. *The Semiotics of Visual Languages* (Boulder: East European Monographs, 2002).

102 Barker, T. "Aesthetics of the Error: Media Art, the Machine, the Unforeseen, and the Errant" *Error: Glitch Noise and Jam in New Media Cultures*, ed. Mark Nunes (New York: Bloomsbury, 2011) pp. 46-48.

103 Eco, U. *A Theory of Semiotics* (Bloomington: Indiana University Press, 1979) p. 216.

104 Betancourt, M. *Glitch Art in Theory and Practice: Critical Failures and Post-Digital Aesthetics* (New York: Routledge, 2016) pp. 21-48.

105 Wittgenstein, L. *Philosophical Investigations* (Oxford: Blackwell Publishers, 2000) p. 198.

106 Deleuze, G. *Cinema 2: The Time-Image* (Minneapolis: The University of Minnesota Press, 1989) pp. 25-26.

107 Flusser, V. *Schriften, vol. 4: Kommunikologie* eds. Stefan Bollmann and Edith Flusser (Frankfurt: Suhrkamp, 1996) p. 150.

108 Eco, U. *A Theory of Semiotics* (Bloomington: Indiana University Press, 1979) pp. 208-217.

109 Eco, U. *A Theory of Semiotics* (Bloomington: Indiana University Press, 1979) pp. 256-258; 275-276.

110   Knapp, S. and Michaels, W.B. "Against Theory" *Critical Inquiry* vol. 8, no. 4 (Summer, 1982) pp. 717-728.

111   Eco, U. *A Theory of Semiotics* (Bloomington: Indiana University Press, 1979) pp. 135-136.

112 Shannon, C.E. "The Mathematical Theory of Communication" *The Mathematical Theory of Communication* eds. C.E. Shannon and W. Weaver (Chicago: University of Chicago Press, 1963) pp. 29-125.

113 Dann, K. *Bright Colors Falsely Seen* (New Haven: Yale, 1998) pp. 17-45.

114 Jakobson, R. *Selected writings III: poetry of grammar and grammar of poetry* (New York: Mouton Publishers, 1981) pp. 22-26.

115 Federici, F. *Biophysique Asémique (French edition)* (Amazon.fr, 2021) np.

116 Gaze, T. *Glyphs of uncertain meaning.* (Minneapolis: Post-Asemic Press, 2021) p. vi.

117 Touchon, C. *Listening with the eye: selected drawings.* (*Asemics.org*, 2022).

118 Foucault, M. *The archaeology of knowledge.* (New York: Pantheon, 1972) p. 88.

119 Golden, W. *The visual craft of William Golden.* (New York: George Braziller, 1962) p. 21.

120 Jakobson, R. *Selected Writings III: Poetry of Grammar and Grammar of Poetry.* (New York: Mouton Publishers, 1981) p. 25.

121 Spencer, H. *The Visible Word* (London: Lund Humphfies, 1969) p. 20.

122 Tarasti, E. *Existential Semiotics* (Bloomington: University of Indiana Press, 2000).

123 Eco, U. "The Poetics of the Open Work" *The Role of the Reader: Explorations in the Semiotics of Texts* (Bloomington: Indiana University Press, 1979) pp. 47-60.

124 Livingstone, P. "Intentionalism in aesthetics" *New Literary History* vol. 29, no. 4 (Autumn, 1998) pp. 831-846.

125 Eco, U. "The Poetics of the Open Work" *Participation* ed. Claire Bishop (New Haven: The MIT Press, 2006) p. 22.

126 Livingstone, P. "Intentionalism in Aesthetics" *New Literary History* vol. 29, no. 4 (Autumn, 1998) pp. 831-833.

127 Haley, P. *Peter Haley* (Paris: Musée D'Art Contemporain, 1992).

128 Greenberg, C. "Modernist Painting" *Clement Greenberg: The Collected Essays and Criticism, Volume 4* ed. John O'Brian (Chicago: University of Chicago Press, 1995) pp. 85-93.

129 There is an extensive literature on this proposal; see for example, Roland Barthes, "The Death of the Author" *Aspen* no. 5–6 (1967).

130 Eco, U. "The Poetics of the Open Work" *Participation: Documents of Contemporary Art* ed. Claire Bishop (Cambridge: MIT Press, 2006) pp. 20-40.

131 Barthes, R. "The Death of the Author" *Participation: Documents of Contemporary Art* ed. Claire Bishop (Cambridge: MIT Press, 2006) pp. 41-45.

132 Foucault, M. "The Author Function" from "What is an Author?" trans. D.F. Bouchard and S. Simon, *Language, Counter-Memory, Practice* (Ithaca: Cornell University Press, 1977) pp. 124-127.

133 Wimsatt, W. K., Jr. and Beardsley, M. C. "The Intentional Fallacy" *Essays in Modern Literary Criticism* ed. Ray B. West, Jr. (New York: Holt, Reinhart and Winston, 1962).

134 Carroll, L. *Alice's Adventures in Wonderland and Through the Looking Glass* (New York: Bantam, 1981) pp. 177-178.

135 Livingstone, P. "Intentionalism in aesthetics" *New Literary History* vol. 29, no. 4 (Autumn, 1998) pp. 831-846.

136 Jakobson, R. *Selected Writings III: Poetry of Grammar and Grammar of Poetry.* (New York: Mouton Publishers, 1981) pp. 22-26.

137 Jakobson, R. *Selected Writings III: Poetry of Grammar and Grammar of Poetry* (New York: Mouton Publishers, 1981) pp. 18-21.

138 Betancourt, M. *The Critique of Digital Capitalism* (Brooklyn: Punctum Books, 2016) pp. 148-151.

139 Borges, J. "From Allegory to Novel" *Other Inquisitions* (Austin: University of Texas Press, 1975) p. 155.

140 Foucault, M. *The Archaeology of Knowledge* (New York: Pantheon, 1972).

141 Jakobson, R. *Selected Writings III: Poetry of Grammar and Grammar of Poetry* (New York: Mouton Publishers, 1981) pp. 21-24.

142 Livingstone. "Intentionalism in aesthetics" *New Literary History* vol. 29, no. 4 (Autumn, 1998) pp. 831-833.

143 Jakobson, R. *Selected Writings III: Poetry of Grammar and Grammar of Poetry* (New York: Mouton Publishers, 1981) pp. 18-19.

144 Wittgenstein, L. *Philosophical Investigations* (Oxford: Blackwell Publishers, 2000) p. 198.

145 Montañés, J. *Titivillus: Il Demone dei refusi* (Perugia: Graphe.it Edizione, 2018).

146 Livingstone, P. "Intentionalism in Aesthetics" *New Literary History* vol. 29, no. 4 (Autumn, 1998) pp. 831-846.

147 Borges, J. "Pierre Menard, Author of the Quixote" *Ficciones* (New York: Grove Press, 1994).

148 Danto, A. *The Transfiguration of the Commonplace* (Cambridge: Harvard University Press, 1981) pp. 121-123.

149 Marks, L. "A Noisy Brush With the Infinite: Noise in Infolding-Unfolding Aesthetics" *The Oxford Handbook of Sound and Image in Digital Media* eds. C. Vernallis, A. Herzog, and J. Richardson (New York: Oxford University Press, 2015) pp. 101-114.

150 Goehr, L. *Red Sea, Red Square, Red Thread: A Philosophical Detective Story* (New York: Oxford University Press, 2022) pp. 15-17.

151 Goehr, L. *Red Sea, Red Square, Red Thread: A Philosophical Detective Story* (New York: Oxford University Press, 2022) pp. 15-17.

152 Herzogenrath, W. "Der Fernseher als Objekt: Videokunst und Videoskulptur in vier Jahrzehnten" *TV-Kultur: Das Fernsehen in der Kunst seit 1879* eds. W. Herzogenrath and W. Gaethgens (Dresden: Verlag der Kunst, 1997) pp. 110-123.

153 Eco, U. *The Limits of Interpretation* (Bloomington: Indiana University Press, 1994) p. 113.

154 Danto, A. *Transfiguration of the Commonplace* (Cambridge: Harvard, 1981) p. 81.

155 Williams, C. *Realism and the Cinema: A Reader* (London: Routledge, 1980) p. 36.

156 Betancourt, M. *The Critique of Digital Capitalism* (Brooklyn: Punctum Books, 2016) pp. 58-60.

157 *Latin–English English–Latin Dictionary* (Philadelphia: David McKay Company, 1947) p. 36

158 Temkin, D. "Glitch && Human-Computer Interaction" *Non-Object Oriented Art*, Vol. 1, no. 1, January 2014; DOI: http://nooart.org/post/73353953758/temkin-glitchhumancomputerinteraction

159 Manon, H. and Temkin, D. "Notes on Glitch" *World Picture 6, WRONG* 2011; DOI: http://worldpicturejournal.com/WP_6/Manon.html, par. 29.

160 Goodman, C. *Digital Visions: Computers and Art* (New York: Abrams, 1987) pp. 24-25.

161 Preston, S. "Reputations Made and in the Making" *The New York Times* 18 April, 1965.

162 Lippard, L. *Six Years: The Dematerialization of the Art Object* (Berkeley: The University of California Press, 1997).

163 Betancourt, M. "Intellectual Process, Visceral Result: Human Agency and the Production of Artworks via Automated Technology" *Journal of Visual Arts Practice*, vol. 7, no. 1 (June, 2008) pp. 11–18; DOI: https://doi.org/10.1386/jvap.7.1.11_1

164 Abbott, B. "Photography at the Crossroads" *Photographers on Photography* ed. Nathan Lyons (Englewood Cliffs: Prentice Hall, 1966).

165 Livingstone, P. "Intentionalism in aesthetics" *New Literary History* vol. 29, no. 4 (Autumn, 1998) pp. 831-846.

166 Eco, U. *The Limits of Interpretation* (Bloomington: Indiana University Press, 1994) p. 113.

167 Steyerl, H. *The Wretched of the Screen* (Berlin: Sternberg Press, 2012) p. 32.

168 Betancourt, M. *Cinematic Articulation in Motion Graphics, Routledge Studies in Media Theory and Practice* (Routledge, 2021).

169 Hochberg, J. and V. Brooks. "Movies in the Mind's Eye" *Post Theory* ed. David Bordwell and Noel Carroll (Madison: University of Wisconsin Press, 1996) pp. 368-369.

170 McEvilley, T. *Art and Discontent* (New York: Documentext, 1993) p. 29.

171 O'Doherty, B. *Inside the White Cube: The Ideology of the Gallery Space, Expanded Edition* (Berkeley: University of California Press, 1986) p. 52.

172 Cavell, S. *The World Viewed: Reflections on the Ontology of Film (Enlarged Edition)* (Cambridge: Harvard University Press, 1979).

173 Manon, H. and Temkin, D. "Notes on Glitch" *World Picture 6: WRONG* (2011); DOI: http://worldpicturejournal.com/WP_6/Manon.html, par. 25.

174 Williams, C. *Realism and the Cinema: A Reader* (London: Routledge, 1980) p. 36.

175 Metz, C. *Film Language* (New York: Oxford University Press, 1974) p. 98.

176 Rushton, R. *The Reality of Film: Theories of Filmic Reality* (Manchester: University of Manchester Press, 2011) pp. 44-47.

177 Dosi, G. "Technological paradigms and technological trajectories: a suggested interpretation of the determinants and directions of technical change" *Research Policy* vol. 11no. 3 (1982) pp. 151-153.

178 Betancourt, M. "Disruptive Technology: The Avant–Gardness of Avant-Garde Art" Article: a107 *CTheory* (May 1, 2002).

179 Derrida, J. *Of Grammatology* trans. Gayatri Chakravorty Spivak (Baltimore: The Johns Hopkins University Press, 1977).

180 Maltby, R. "A Brief Romantic Interlude: Dick and Jane go to 3 1/2 Seconds of the Classical Hollywood Cinema" *Post-Theory: Reconstructing Film Studies* ed. David Bordwell and Noel Carroll (Madison: University of Wisconsin Press, 1996) p. 435.

181 Brown, S. "Introduction" in *Synthesis: Processing and Collaboration* (San Diego: The Gallery@Calit2, 2011) p. 5.

182 Sitney, P. *Visionary Film: The American Avant-Garde 1943 – 1978 (Second Edition)* (New York: Oxford University Press, 1979) p. 370.

183 Paul, C. and Levy, M. "Genealogies of the New Aesthetic" *Postdigital Aesthetics: Art, Computation and Design* ed. David M. Berry and Michael Dieter (New York: Palgrave Macmillan, 2015) p 31.

184 Popper, F. *Art of the Electronic Age* (New York: Abrams, 1993).

185 Lyotard, J. *The Postmodern Condition: A Report on Knowledge* (Minneapolis: University of Minnesota Press, 1993) p. 61.

186 Menkman, R. *Network Notebooks 4: The Glitch Moment(um)* (Amsterdam: Institute of Network Cultures, 2011) p. 35.

187 Manon, H. and Temkin, D. "Notes on Glitch" *World Picture 6: WRONG* (2011); DOI: http://worldpicturejournal.com/WP_6/Manon.html, par. 25..

188 Temkin, D. "Glitch && Human-Computer Interaction" *Non-Object Oriented Art*, Vol. 1, no. 1, January 2014; DOI: http://nooart.org/post/73353953758/temkin-glitchhumancomputerinteraction

189 Cascone, K. "The Aesthetics of Failure: 'Post-Digital' Tendencies in Contemporary Computer Music" *Computer Music Journal* vol. 24, no. 4 (Winter, 2000) p. 13.

190 Betancourt, M. "Postcinema, Motion Perception and Glitch Movies" *AM Journal of Art and Media Studies* no. 15 (2018); DOI: 10.25038/am.v0i15.242

191 Larkin, B. "Degraded Images, Distorted Sounds: Nigerian Video and the Infrastructure of Piracy," *Public Culture* vol. 16 no. 2 (2004) p 291.

192 Temkin, D. "Glitch && Human-Computer Interaction" *Non-Object Oriented Art*, Vol. 1, no. 1, January 2014; DOI: http://nooart.org/post/73353953758/temkin-glitchhumancomputerinteraction

193 Kelly, C. *Cracked Media: the sound of Malfunction* (New Haven: MIT Press, 2009) pp. 59-60.

194 Larkin, B. "Degraded Images, Distorted Sounds: Nigerian Video and the Infrastructure of Piracy," *Public Culture* vol. 16 no. 2 (2004) p. 292.

195 Bogdan, C. *The Semiotics of Visual Languages* (Boulder: East European Monographs, 2002) pp. 10-12.

196 Greenberg, C. "Modernist Painting" *Clement Greenberg: The Collected Essays and Criticism, Volume 4* ed. John O'Brian (Chicago: University of Chicago Press, 1995) p. 86.

197 Hatfield, J. "Expanded Cinema and Narrative" *Millennium Film Journal* nos. 39–40, "Hidden Currents" (Winter, 2003) pp. 63–64.

198 Gitelman, L. "'Materiality Has Always Been in Play': An Interview with N. Katherine Hayles" *Iowa Journal of Cultural Studies* no. 2 (Fall 2002) p. 9.

199 Mitry, J. *Semiotics and the Analysis of Film* trans. Christopher King (Bloomington: University of Indiana Press, 2000) pp. 24-26.

200 Betancourt, M. *Cinematic Articulation in Motion Graphics, Routledge Studies in Media Theory and Practice* (Routledge, 2021) pp. 54-57.

201 Menkman, R. *Network Notebooks 4: The Glitch Moment(um)* (Amsterdam: Institute of Network Cultures, 2011) p. 35.

202 Betancourt, M. "Critical Glitches and Glitch Art" *Hz*, no. 19 (July, 2014) np.

203 Harris, R. "The Integrational Conception of the Sign" *Integrationist Notes and Papers 2006–2008* (Gamlingay: Bright Pen, 2009).

204 Harris, R. *Signs, Language, and Communication* (New York: Routledge, 1996) p. 12.

205 Betancourt, M. *Cinematic Articulation in Motion Graphics, Routledge Studies in Media Theory and Practice* (Routledge, 2021) pp. 163-175.

206 Eco, U. *Kant and the Platypus* (New York: Harvest Books, 2000) pp. 125-126.

207 Betancourt, M. *The Critique of Digital Capitalism* (Brooklyn: Punctum Books, 2016) pp. 61-74.

208 Clark, T.J. "Clement Greenberg's Theory of Art" *Critical Inquiry* vol. 9, no. 1 (September, 1982) pp. 139-156.

209 Betancourt, M. "Critical Glitches and Glitch Art" *Hz*, no. 19 (July, 2014) np.

210 Fer, B. *On Abstract Art* (New Haven: Yale University Press, 1997).

211 Greenberg, C. "Newer Laocoon" *Clement Greenberg: The Collected Essays and Criticism, Volume 4* ed. John O'Brian (Chicago: University of Chicago Press, 1995) p. 305.

212 Drucker, J. *Theorizing Modernism: Visual Art and the Critical Tradition* (New York: Columbia University Press, 1994) pp. 63-69.

213 Clark, T. J. "Clement Greenberg's Theory of Art" *Critical Inquiry* vol. 9, no. 1 (September, 1982) pp. 139-156.

214 Crimp, D. *On The Museum's Ruins* (Cambridge: The MIT Press, 1993).

215 Betancourt, M. *Art, AI and Culture* (Savannah: I'm Press'd, 2022) pp. 73-75.

216 Kant, I. "Section 1: Pure Reason in its Dogmatic Use" *The Critique of Pure Reason*, trans. Werner Pluhar (Indianapolis: Hackett Publishing Company, 1996) p. 675.

217 Greenberg, C. "Newer Laocoon" *Clement Greenberg: The Collected Essays and Criticism, Volume 4* ed. John O'Brian (Chicago: University of Chicago Press, 1995) p. 305.

218 Crimp, D. "On The Museum's Ruins" *The Anti-Aesthetic* ed. Hal Foster (Seattle: Bay Press, 1983) pp.43-56.

219 Morgan, R. *The End of the Art World* (New York: Allworth Press, 1998) p. 13.

220 Foster, H. *The Return of the Real* (Cambridge: The MIT Press, 1996) p. 99.

221 Harman, G. *Object-Oriented Ontology* (New York: Pelican, 2018).

222 Kuspit, D. "The *Ars Morendi* according to Robert Morris" *Robert Morris: Works of the Eighties* (Chicago: Museum of Contemporary Art, 1986) p. 17.

223 Kraus, R. "Sense and Sensibility—Reflections on Post-60s Sculpture" *Artforum* (November 1973).

224 Danto, A. *The Transfiguration of the Commonplace* (Cambridge: Harvard University Press, 1981) pp. 4-8.

225 Wollheim, R. *The Institutional Theory of Art* (Cambridge: Cambridge University Press, 2015).

226 Ziehen, T. *Lehrbuch der Logik auf positivistischer Grundlage mit Berücksichtigung der Geschichte der Logik* (Bonn: A. Marcus & E. Webere Verlag, 1920).

227 Eco, U. *The Limits of Interpretation* (Bloomington: University of Indiana Press, 1994). p. 92

228 Austin, J. L. *Philosophical Papers* ed. J. O. Urmson and G. J. Warnock (Oxford: Oxford University Press, 1970) p. 55.

229 Muliaee, M. and Mehrvarz, M. "Fai(lure): Encounter with the Unstable Medium in the Work of Art" *Miscommunications: Errors, Mistakes, Media* ed. Korolkova, M. and Barker, T. (London: Bloomsbury, 2021) p. 157.

230 Wittgenstein, L. *Philosophical Investigations* (Oxford: Blackwell Publishers, 2000) p. 198.

231 Shannon, C. E. "A mathematical theory of communication" *ACM SIGMOBILE Mobile Computing and Communications Review* vol. 5, no. 1 (January 2001) pp. 3–55; DOI: https://doi.org/10.1145/584091.584093

232 Weaver, W. "Recent Contributions to the Mathematical Theory of Communication" *The Mathematical Theory of Communication* ed. C.E. Shannon and W. Weaver (Chicago: University of Illinois Press, 1963) p. 9.

233 Meagher, J. *RCA Television Pict-O-Guide: An Aid to TV Troubleshooting, Volume 1* (Harrison, NJ: Radio Corporation of America, Tube Department, 1949).

234 Barnett, D. *Movement as Meaning in Experimental Film* (New York: Rodopi, 2008) pp. 16-17.

235 Betancourt, M. *Cinematic Articulation in Motion Graphics, Routledge Studies in Media Theory and Practice* (Routledge, 2021).

236 Lotringer, S. and Virilio, P. *The Accident of Art* (New York: Semiotext(e), 2005) p. 74.

237 Keedy, J. "Zombie Modernism" *Texts on Type* ed. Steven Heller and Philip B. Meggs (New York: Allworth Press, 2001) pp. 159-169.

238 Menkman, R. *Lexicon of Glitch Affect* (2019) DOI: https://beyondresolution.info/Lexicon-of-Glitch-Affect

239 Betancourt, M. *Art, AI and Culture* (Savannah: I'mPress'd, 2022).

240 Foucault, M. *This Is Not A Pipe* Berkeley: University of California Press, 1982) p. 44.

241 O'Doherty, B. *Inside the White Cube: The Ideology of the Gallery Space, Revised Edition* (Berkeley: The University of California Press, 2000).

242 Kosuth, J. "Art After Philosophy" *Conceptual Art* ed. Ursula Meyer (New York: Dutton, 1972) pp. 152-171.

243 In this regard, the static image must be acknowledged has having different contextual problems than the motion image: *duration* alters the consideration of the 'intentional function' in evaluating the cued construction and organization of media because the structured time of motion images alters the calculus of encoding in ways that are inaccessible to static images.

244 Tanaka, J., Curran, T. and Sheinberg, D.L. "The Training and Transfer of Real-World Perceptual Expertise" *Psychological Science* vol. 16, no. 2 (2005) pp. 145-151.

245 Danto, A. *Transfiguration of the Commonplace* (Cambridge: Harvard, 1981) p. 115.

246 Deleuze, G. *Cinema 2: The Time-Image* (Minneapolis: The University of Minnesota Press, 1989) pp. 25-26.

247 Eco, U. *A Theory of Semiotics* (Bloomington: Indiana University Press, 1979) p. 216.

248 Phillips, C. *Photography in the Modern Era: European Documents and Critical Writing, 1913-1940* (New York: Aperture, 1989) p. 110.

249 Robinson, H. "Paradoxes of Art, Science and Photography (1892)" *Photographers on Photog- raphy: Foundations of Modern Photography Series* ed. Nathan Lyons (Englewood Cliffs: Pren-tice- Hall, 1966) p. 86.

250 Noll, A. M. "Human or Machine: A subjective comparison of Piet Mondrian's *Composition With Lines* (1917) and a Computer-Generated Picture" *Psychological Record* vol. 16, no. 1 (1966) pp. 1-10.

251 Flusser, V. "Habit: The True Aesthetic Criterion" *Vilém Flusser: Writings* ed. Andreas Ströhl; trans. Erik Eisel (Minneapolis: University of Minneapolis Press, 2002) p. 53.

252 Meyer, U. "Introduction" *Conceptual Art* (New York: Dutton, 1970) p. x.

253 Breton, A. *Manifestoes of Surrealism* trans. Richard Seaver and Helen R. Lane (Ann Arbor: University of Michigan Press, 1972).

254 Poggioli, R. *The Theory of the Avant-Garde* (Cambridge: Harvard University Press, 1968).

255 Morgan, R. *The End of the Art World* (New York: Allworth Press, 1998) pp. 35-38.

256 Greenberg, C. *Clement Greenberg: The Collected Essays and Criticism, Volume 1* ed. John O'Brian (Chicago: University of Chicago Press, 1986) pp. 5-11.

257 Greenberg, C. *Clement Greenberg: The Collected Essays and Criticism, Volume 1* ed. John O'Brian (Chicago: University of Chicago Press, 1986) p. 32.

258 Sontag, S. "Notes on Camp" *Against Interpretation* (New York: Delta, 1966) pp. 275-292.

259 Greenberg, C. *Clement Greenberg: The Collected Essays and Criticism, Volume 1* ed. John O'Brian (Chicago: University of Chicago Press, 1986) pp. 5-11.

260 Flusser, V. "Habit: The True Aesthetic Criterion" *Vilém Flusser: Writings* ed. Andreas Ströhl; trans. Erik Eisel (Minneapolis: University of Minnesota Press, 2002). p. 51.

261 Flusser, V. "Habit: The True Aesthetic Criterion" *Vilém Flusser: Writings* ed. Andreas Ströhl; trans. Erik Eisel (Minneapolis: University of Minneapolis Press, 2002) pp. 51-57.

262 Crimp, D. *On The Museum's Ruins* (Cambridge: The MIT Press, 1993) p. 150.

263 Flusser, V. "Habit" *Vilém Flusser: writings* ed. Andreas Ströhl; trans. Erik Eisel (Minneapolis: University of Minnesota Press, 2002). p. 54-55.

264 Flusser, V. "Habit: The True Aesthetic Criterion" *Vilém Flusser: Writings* ed. Andreas Ströhl; trans. Erik Eisel (Minneapolis: University of Minneapolis Press, 2002) p. 52.

265 Freud, S. *"The Uncanny* (1919)" trans. Alix Strachey, accessed online, February 2, 2018; DOI: http://web.mit.edu/allanmc/www/freud1.pdf

266 Foster, H. *The Return of the Real* (Cambridge: The MIT Press, 1996) pp. 205-206.

267 Poggioli, R. *The Theory of the Avant-Garde* (Cambridge: Harvard University Press, 1968) p. 82.

268 Brecht, B. "Alienation Effects in Chinese Acting" *Brecht on Theater: The Development of an Aesthetic* ed. and trans. J. Willet (New York: Hill and Wang, 1992) p. 92.

269 Jentsch, E. *"On the Psychology of the Uncanny* (1906)" trans. Roy Sellars, *Angelaki* 2.1 (1995) pp. 7-16.

270 Betancourt, M. "Critical Glitches and Glitch Art" *Harmonia: Glitch, Movies and Visual Music* (Rockport: Wildside Press, 2018) pp. 149-172.

271 Irei, N. "'Abolishing Aesthetics': *Gestus* in Brecht's *Arturo Ui*" *Rocky Mountain Review,* vol. 70, no. 2 (Fall 2016) p. 150.

272 Robinson. D. *Estrangement and the Somatics of Literature* (Baltimore: Johns Hopkins University Press, 2008) p. 199.

273 Brecht, B. "The Popular and the Realistic" *Brecht on Theater: The Development of an Aesthetic* ed. and trans. J. Willet (New York: Hill and Wang, 1992) p. 108-109.

274 Piaget, J. *La psychologie de l'intelligence* (Paris: A. Cohn, 1947).

275 Eco, U. *A Theory of Semiotics* (Bloomington: Indiana University Press, 1979) pp. 232-233.

276 Foucault, M. *The Archaeology of Knowledge* (New York: Pantheon, 1972) p. 90.

277 Weyler, K. "Seriality and Susanna Rowson's *Sincerity*" *Legacy: A Journal of American Women Writers* vol. 34, no. 1 (2017) p. 169.

278 Robinson. D. *Estrangement and the Somatics of Literature* (Baltimore: Johns Hopkins University Press, 2008) pp. 198-200.

279 Eco, U. *The Limits of Interpretation* (Bloomington: Indiana University Press, 1990) p. 92.

280 Larkin, B. "Degraded Images, Distorted Sounds: Nigerian Video and the Infrastructure of Piracy," *Public Culture* 16(2): 2004, p 291.

281 Tuchman, M. "Hidden Meanings in Abstract Art" *The Spiritual in Art: Abstract Painting, 1890–1985* (New York: Abbeville, 1985) pp. 17-62.

282 Malina, F. *Kinetic Art* (New York: Dover, 1974).

283 Schnapp, J. "Bad Dada (Evola)" *The Dada Seminars*, ed. Leah Dickerman with Matthew S. Witkowski (Washington, DC: National Gallery of Art/ DAP, 2005) pp. 50-51.

284 Marks, L. "On Colored-hearing Synaesthesia: Cross-modal Translations of Sensory Dimensions" *Synaesthesia: Classic and Contemporary Readings* ed. Simon Baron-Cohen and John E. Harrison (Cambridge: Blackwell, 1997) pp. 49-98.

285 Galeyev, B. "Open Letter on Synaesthesia" *Leonardo*, vol. 34, no. 4 (2001) pp. 362-363.

286 Wright, W.H. *The Future of Painting* (New York: B. W. Huebsch, Inc., 1923) pp. 47-50.

287 Moritz, W. "Visual Music and Film-as-an-Art Before 1950" *On the Edge of America: California Modernist Art, 1900-1950,* Paul J. Karlstrom, ed. (Berkeley: University of California Press, 1996) p. 224.

288 Greenberg, C. "After Abstract Expressionism" *Clement Greenberg: The Collected Essays and Criticism, Volume 4* ed. John O'Brian (Chicago: University of Chicago Press, 1995) p. 131.

289 Dann, K. *Bright Colors Falsely Seen* (New Haven: Yale, 1998) pp. 94-95.

290 Schnapp, J. "Bad Dada (Evola)" *The Dada Seminars*, ed. Leah Dickerman with Matthew S. Witkowski (Washington DC: National Gallery of Art/ DAP: 2005) pp. 50-51.

291 Kandinsky, V. *Concerning the Spiritual in Art* (New York: Dover, 1977) p. 31.

292 Brakhage, S. *Metaphors on Vision* ed. P. Adams Sitney (Anthology Film Archives/Light Industry, New York, 2017).

293 Althaus, K.; Mühling, M.; Schneider, S. *World Receivers: Georgiana Houghton — Hilma af Klint — Emma Kunz* (Munich: Hirmer Publishers, 2021).

294 Bashkoff, T. *Hilma af Klint: Paintings for the Future* (New York: Guggenheim Museum Publications, 2018).

295 Wees, W.C. *Light Moving in Time: Studies in the Visual Aesthetics of Avant-Garde Film* (Berkeley: University of California Press, 1992) pp. 137-146.

296 Betancourt, M. "A Taxonomy of Abstract Form Using Studies of Synaesthesia and Hallucinations" *Leonardo*, vol. 40, no. 1 (2007) pp. 59-65.

297 Vergo, P. *The Music of Painting* (London: Phaidon, 2010) pp. 254-309.

298 Moritz, W. "Visual Music and Film-as-an-Art Before 1950" *On the Edge of America: California Modernist Art, 1900-1950,* ed. Paul J. Karlstrom (Berkeley: University of California Press, 1996).

299 Wees, W.C. *Light Moving in Time: Studies in the Visual Aesthetics of Avant-Garde Film* (Berkeley: University of California Press, 1992).

300 Schwartz, L. *The Computer Artist's Handbook* (New York: Norton, 1992) pp. 151-152.

301 Ringbom, S. "Transcending the Visible: The Generation of the Abstract Pioneers" *The Spiritual in Art: Abstract Painting, 1890-1985,* ed. M. Tuchman (New York: Abbeville Press, 1985).

302 Ione, A. and Tyler, C. "Is F-Sharp Colored Violet?" *Journal of the History of the Neuroscience,* vol. 13, no. 1 (2004) pp. 62-64.

303 Fry, R. "The French Post-Impressionists (preface to catalog for the Second Post-Impressionist exhibition, 1912)" *Vision and Design* (London: Pelican Books, 1937) pp. 195-196.

304 Levi-Strauss, C. *The Raw and the Cooked* (Chicago: University of Chicago Press, 1983) p. 22.

305 Eco, U. *The Limits of Interpretation* (Bloomington: University of Indiana Press 1994) pp. 83-100.

306 Railing, P. *Malevich on Suprematism—Six Essays: 1915 to 1926* (Iowa City: University of Iowa Museum of Art, 1999).

307 McEvilley, T. *Art and Discontent* (New York: Documentext, 1993) pp. 29-35.

308 Goodman, C. *Digital Visions: Computers and Art* (New York: Abrams, 1987) pp. 156-158.

309 Klüver, H. *Mescal and Mechanisms of Hallucinations* (Chicago: University of Chicago Press, 1966) p. 66.

310 Kandinsky, V. *Concerning the Spiritual in Art* (New York: Dover, 1977) p. 31.

311 Railing, P. *Malevich on Suprematism—Six Essays: 1915 to 1926* (Iowa City: University of Iowa Museum of Art, 1999).

312 Werner, G. and Edlund, B. *Viking Eggeling Diagonalsymfonin: Spjutspets I Återvändsgränd* (Lund: Novapress, 1997); see also Werner, G. "Spearhead in a Blind Alley: Viking Eggeling's *Diagonal Symphony*" *Nordic Explorations: Film Before 1930* (Sydney: John Libbey & Co, 1999) pp. 232-235.

313 McEvilley, T. *Art and Discontent* (New York: Documentext, 1993) pp. 29-35.

314 Betancourt, M. "Visual Music and Abstraction: From Avant-Garde Synaesthesia to Digital Technesthesia" *Iconology of Abstraction: Non-Figurative Images and the Modern World (Advances in Art and Visual Studies)* ed. Krešimir Purgar (Routledge, 2020) pp. 143-159.

315 Betancourt, M. "A Taxonomy of Abstract Form Using Studies of Synaesthesia and Hallucinations" *Leonardo*, vol. 40, no. 1 (2007) pp. 59-65.

316 Klüver, H. *Mescal and Mechanisms of Hallucinations* (Chicago: University of Chicago Press, 1966) p. 66.

317 van Campen, C. "Synesthesia and Artistic Experimentation," *Psyche*, vol. 3, no. 6 (November, 1997) np.

318 Eco, U. "Interpreting Serials" *The Limits of Interpretation* (Bloomington: Indiana University Press, 1994) pp. 98-100.

319 Goodman, C. *Digital Visions: Computers and Art* (New York: Abrams, 1987) pp. 156-158.

320 Norden, M.F. "The Avant-Garde Cinema of the 1920s: Connections to Futurism, Precisionism and Suprematism" *Leonardo*, vol. 17, no. 2 (1984) p. 112.

321 Selfridge-Field, E. "The invention of the fortepiano as intellectual history" *Early Music*, vol. 33, no. 1 (February 2005) pp. 81-94.

322 Kircher, A. "Liber III, Caput XIII, SII: De Genere Chromatico" *Musurgia Universalis (Facsimile Edition)* (New York: George Olms Verlag, 1970) p. 240.

323 Hankins, T. "The Ocular Harpsichord of Louis-Bertrand Castel; or, The Instrument That Wasn't" *Osiris*, No. 9, 1994, pp. 141-151.

324 Moritz, W. "Visual Music and Film-as-an-Art Before 1950" *On the Edge of America: California Modernist Art, 1900-1950,* Paul J. Karlstrom, ed. (Berkeley: University of California Press, 1996).

325 Corra, B. "Abstract Cinema – Chromatic Music" *Futurist manifestos* (New York: Art Works, 2001) pp. 66-69.

326 Hankins, T. "The Ocular Harpsichord of Louis–Bertrand Castel; or, The Instrument That Wasn't" *Osiris*, no. 9 (1994) pp. 141–151.

327 Corra, B. "Abstract Cinema – Chromatic Music" *Futurist Manifestos* (New York: Art Works, 2001) pp. 66-68.

328 Lawder, S. *The Cubist Cinema* (New York: Anthology Film Archives, 1980).

329 Alderton, Z. "Colour, Shape, and Music: The Presence of Thought Forms in Abstract Art" *Literature & Aesthetics*, vol. 21, no. 1 (June, 2011) pp. 236-258.

330 Hanson, V. *H. P. Blavatsky and the Secret Doctrine* (London: Theosophical Publishing, 1971).

331 Galeyev, B. "Open Letter on Synaesthesia" *Leonardo*, vol. 34, no. 4 (2001) pp. 362-363.

332 The designation of the German abstract and visual music animations as "absolute films" began with the filmmakers themselves. The Novembergruppe exhibition of May 3, 1925 (a program which included Ruttmann, Richter, and Eggeling's films) was titled *"Der Absolute Film."*

333 de Haas, P. "Cinema: The Manipulation of Materials" *Dada-Constructivism* exhibition catalog (London: Annely Juda Fine Art, 1984) np.

334 Ruttmann, W. "Painting with the Medium of Light" *The German Avant-Garde Film of the 1920s*, ed. Angelika Leitner and Uwe Nitschke (Munich: Goethe Institute, 1989) p.104.

335 Werner, G. and Edlund, B. *Viking Eggeling Diagonalsymfonin: Spjutspets I Återvändsgränd* (Lund: Novapress, 1997). See also Gösta Werner, "Spearhead in a Blind Alley: Viking Eggeling's *Diagonal Symphony*" *Nordic Explorations: Film Before 1930* (Sydney: John Libbey & Co, 1999) pp. 232-235.

336 Richter, H. "My Experience with Movement in Painting and in Film" *The Nature and Art of Motion*, ed. György Kepes (New York: George Brazillier, 1965) p. 144.

337 Moritz, W. *Optical Poetry: The Life and Work of Oscar Fischinger* (Eastleigh: John Libbey Publishing, 2004).

338 Le Grice, M. *Abstract Film and Beyond* (Cambridge: MIT Press, 1981) pp. 19-31. See also Schobert, W. *The German Avant-Garde Film of the 1920s* (Munich: Deutsches Filmmuseum, 1989).

339 Mollaghan, A. *The Visual Music Film* (New York: Palgrave, 2015) pp. 97-139.

340 Hegel, G.F.W. *The Phenomenology of Mind* trans. J. B. Baillie (New York: MacMillan, 1910) p. 340.

341 Harris, W.T. *Hegel's Logic* (Chicago: Griggs and Company, 1890) p. 120.

342 Poggioli, R. *The Theory of the Avant-Garde* (Cambridge: Harvard University Press, 1968).

343 Foucault, M. *The Birth of the Clinic* (New York: Routledge, 1976) p. xiii.

344 Klüver, H. *Mescal and Mechanisms of Hallucinations* (Chicago: University of Chicago Press, 1966) p. 93.

345 Hoffman, H. "The Search for 'the real' in the Visual Arts" *Search for 'The Real'* ed. Sara T. Weeks and Bartlet H. Hayes, Jr. (Cambridge: MIT Press, 1967) p. 40.

346 Ades, D. *Dalí's Optical Illusions* (Hartford: Yale University Press, 2000) p. 12.

347 Dann, K. *Bright Colors Falsely Seen* (New Haven: Yale, 1998) p. 91.

348 Noll, A.M. "Human or Machine: A subjective comparison of Piet
Mondrian's *Composition With Lines* (1917) and a Computer-Generated
Picture" *Psychological Record*, vol. 16, no. 1 (January, 1966) pp. 1-10.

349 Noll, A.M. 'The Digital Computer as a Creative Medium,' *IEEE Spectrum*,
vol. 4, no 10 (1967) pp. 89-95.

350 Reichardt, J. *The Computer in Art* (New York: Van Norstrand Reinhold,
1971) pp. 77-78.

351 Halley, P. 'The Crisis in Geometry,' *Peter Halley: Collected Essays, 1981-87*
(Sonnabend Gallery, New York, 1991) pp. 75-105.

352 Betancourt, M. "The Invention of Glitch Video: *Digital TV Dinner* (1978)"
Millennium Film Journal, no. 65 (Spring, 2017) pp. 54-63.

353 "Jamie Fenton," biography webpage on personal website;
DOI: http://www.fentonia.com/bio accessed, February 4, 2014.
An expanded quote was provided in a private email, February 7, 2015:
"I was the lead software engineer on the *Arcade* project. I had 2 engineers
helping me. Part of my role was to make sure that the hardware guys
created a good design. Jeff Frederiksen was the lead hardware guy—he
was and is brilliant (and a little difficult to work with, since he could
change a design on a moments notice). Right now Jeff is working at Apple
on the *iPhone*. All this means I can point-out where in the code things
went wrong."

354 Jakobson, R. *Selected Writings III: Poetry of Grammar and Grammar of Poetry*
(New York: Mouton Publishers, 1981) pp 22-26.

355 Garrison, M. "The Poetics of Ambivalence" *Archetypal Psychiatry* (Spring,
1982) p. 227.

356 Bleuler, E. *Dementia Praecox, or the Group of Schizophrenias* (New York:
International Universities Press, 1950) pp. 271–286.

357 Harris, R. *Integrating Reality* (London: New Generation Publishing, 2012).

358 Betancourt, M. *Ideologies of the Real in Title Sequence, Motion Graphics and
Cinema* (New York: Routledge, 2020) p. 178.

359 Hanhardt, J. "The Medium Viewed: The American Avant-Garde Film"
A History of the American Avant-Garde Cinema (New York: The American
Federation of the Arts, 1976) p. 22.

360 Hatfield, J. "Expanded Cinema and Narrative" *Millennium Film Journal*,
nos. 39–40 (Winter, 2003) pp. 63–64.

361 Donguy, J. "Machine Head: Raoul Hausmann and the Optophone"
Leonardo, vol. 34, no. 3 (2001) pp. 217–220.

362 Nochlin, L. *Realism* (New York: Penguin Books, 1975) pp. 13-23.

363 Betancourt, M. "Technesthesia and Synaesthesia" *Harmonia: Glitch, Movies and Visual Art* (Cabin John: Wildside Press, 2018) pp. 145-148.

364 Colpitt, F. " Systems of Opinion: Abstract Painting Since 1959" *Abstract Art in the Late Twentieth Century* ed. Francis Colpitt (New York: Cambridge University Press, 2002) pp. 153-203.

365 Eco, U. "Interpreting Serials" *The Limits of Interpretation* (Bloomington: University of Indiana Press, 1994) pp. 83-100.

366 Tarasti, E. *Theory of Musical Semiotics* (Bloomington: Indiana University Press, 1994) pp. 73-76.

367 Betancourt, M. *Glitch Art in Theory and Practice: Critical Failures and Post-Digital Aesthetics* (New York: Routledge, 2016) pp. 21-22.

368 Betancourt, M. "Glitched Media as Found/Transformed Footage: Post-Digitality in Takeshi Murata's *Monster Movie* (2005)" *Found Footage Magazine*, no. 3, 2017 pp. 48-57.

369 Löwith, K. *Meaning in History* (University of Chicago Press, 1949) p. 54.

370 Navas, E. *Remix-Theory: The Aesthetics of Sampling* (New York: Springer, 2012) pp. 22-27.

371 Barthes, R. "The Death of the Author" *Image—Music—Text* trans. Stephen Heath (New York: Hill and Wang, 1977) p. 146.

372 Eco, Umberto. *The Limits of Interpretation* (Bloomington: Indiana University Press, 1990) p. 92.

373 Russell, C. *Experimental Ethnography: The Work of Film in the Age of Video* (Durham: Duke University Press, 1999) pp. 238-239.

374 Eco, U. *The Limits of Interpretation* (Bloomington: University of Indiana Press, 1994) p. 92.

375 Stiegler, B. *Technics and Time, 3: Cinematic Time and the Question of Malaise* trans. Stephen Barker (Stanford: Stanford University Press, 2011) pp. 17-19.

376 Jakobovits, L. "Semantic Satiation and Cognitive Dynamics" (Washington: U.S. Department of Education, 1966); see also Das, J.P. *Verbal Conditioning and Behavior* (Oxford: Pergamon Press, 2014) p. 92.

377 Betancourt, M. *Glitch Art in Theory and Practice: Critical Failures and Post-Digital Aesthetics* (New York: Routledge, 2016) pp. 49-72.

378 Nitsche, M., Mazalek, A., and Clifton, P. "Moving Digital Puppets" *Understanding Machinima*, ed. Jenna Ng (London: Bloomsbury, 2013) pp. 63-84.

379 Navas, Eduardo. *Remix-Theory: The Aesthetics of Sampling* (New York: Springer, 2012) pp. 22-27.

380 Wees, W. C. *Recycled Images* (New York: Anthology Film Archives, 1993) pp. 52-53.

381 Betancourt, M. "Postcinema, Motion Perception and Glitch Movies" *AM Journal of Art and Media Studies* no. 15 (2018).

382 Betancourt, M. *The Critique of Digital Capitalism* (Brooklyn: Punctum Books, 2016) pp. 37-60.

383 O'Doherty, B. *Inside the White Cube: The Ideology of the Gallery Space, Revised Edition* (Berkeley: The University of California Press, 2000) pp. 51-55.

384 Kahn, D. *Noise, Water, Meat* (Cambridge: The MIT Press, 1999).

385 Navas, E. *Remix Theory: The Aesthetics of Sampling* (New York: Springer, 2012) p. 154.

386 Betancourt, M. "Found Objects, Generative Footage, and Machinima: Peggy Ahwesh's *She Puppet* (2001)" *Found Footage Magazine*, no. 6 (2020) pp. 76-83.

387 Viegl, T. "Machinima: On the Invention and Innovation of a New Media Technology" *Imagery in the 21st Century* ed. Oliver Grau and Thomas Viegl (Cambridge: The MIT Press, 2011) pp. 81-96.

388 Foucault, M. *This is Not a Pipe* (Berkeley: University of California Press, 1982) p. 44.

389 Eco, U. *The Limits of Interpretation* (Bloomington: University of Indiana Press, 1994) pp. 84-85.

390 Russell, C. *Experimental Ethnography* (Durham: Duke University Press, 1999) pp. 238-253.

391 Wees, W. C. *Recycled Images* (New York: Anthology Film Archives, 1993) pp. 52-53.

392 Lapedis, H. "Popping the Question: The Function and Effect of Popular Music in Cinema." Popular Music, Vol. 18, No. 3 (Oct., 1999) pp. 375-6.

393 Foster, H. *The Return of the Real* (Cambridge: The MIT Press, 1996) pp. 99-124; 218-222.

394 Smith, P. *And Warhol's Art and Films* (Ann Arbor: UMI Research Press, 1986) pp. 105-117.

395 Crimp, D. *On The Museum's Ruins* (Cambridge: The MIT Press, 1993) pp. 129-134.

396 Halley, P. "The Crisis in Geometry" *Collected Essays 1981-1987* (New York: Bischofberger/Sonnabend, 1988) pp. 75-80.

397 Barthes, R. "The Death of the Author" *Image—Music—Text* trans. Stephen Heath (New York: Hill and Wang, 1977) p. 147.

398 Eco, U. *The Limits of Interpretation* (Bloomington: University of Indiana Press, 1994) p. 84.

399 Eco, U. *The Limits of Interpretation* (Bloomington: University of Indiana Press, 1994) pp. 88-89.

400 Eco, U. *The Limits of Interpretation* (Bloomington: University of Indiana Press, 1994) p. 87.

401 Lyotard, J. *The Postmodern Condition: A Report on Knowledge* (Minneapolis: University of Minnesota Press, 1993) p. 61.

402 Mapes-Frances, A. "A Strange Exiled Body: Gamespace and (Anti-) Algorithmic Choreographies" *Journal of Art Criticism* (Spring 2016) posted May 5, 2016; DOI: https://journalofartcriticism.wordpress.com/2016/05/05/a-strange-exiled-body-gamespace-and-anti-algorithmic-choreographies/

403 Gidal, P. *Materialist Film* (London: Routledge, 1989) pp. 15-16.

404 Knowlton, K. "Computer Animated Movies" *Cybernetic Serendipity* (London: Studio International, 1968) p. 67.

405 Salen, K. and Zimmerman, E. *Rules of Play: Game Design Fundamentals* (Cambridge: The MIT Press, 2004) p. 539.

406 Brown, S. "Be(ing)dazzled: Living in Machinima" *Understanding Machinima*, ed. Jenna Ng (London: Bloomsbury, 2013) p. 44-45.

407 Lotringer, S. and Virilio, P. *The Accident of Art* (New York: Semiotext(e), 2005) p. 74.

408 Betancourt, M. "Glitch Art and the Cinematic Articulation of the 'Shot': The Convergence of Datamoshing with the Long Take" *Journal of Visual Arts Practice*, vol. 21, no 1 (2022) pp. 41-71; DOI: https://doi.org/10.1080/14702029.2021.2020592

409 Cavell, S. *The World Viewed: Reflections on the Ontology of Film (Enlarged Edition)* (Cambridge: Harvard University Press, 1979).

410 Bazin, A. *What is Cinema?* trans. Timothy Barnard (Montreal: Caboose, 2009) pp. 8-9.

411 Debord, G. "Theory of the Dérive" *Les Lèvres Nues* no. 9 (November 1956).

412 Menkman, R. *Network Notebooks 4: The Glitch Moment(um)* (Amsterdam: Institute of Network Cultures, 2011) p. 35.

413 Russell, C. *Experimental Ethnography: The Work of Film in the Age of Video* (Durham: Duke University Press, 1999) pp. 238-239.

414 Stiegler, B. *Technics and Time, 3: Cinematic Time and the Question of Malaise* trans. Stephen Barker (Stanford: Stanford University Press, 2011) pp. 17-19.

415 Adorno, T. *Aesthetic Theory* (Minneapolis: University of Minnesota Press, 1998) pp. 246-248.

416 Betancourt, M. "Critical Glitches and Glitch Art" *Hz*, no. 19 (July, 2014) np.

417 Plato. "The Allegory of the Cave" *The Republic* trans. Thomas Sheehan sec. 514 a, 2 to 517 a, 7;
DOI: https://web.stanford.edu/class/ihum40/cave.pdf

418 Amerika, M. *The Museum of Glitch Aesthetics: featuring the work of The Artist 2.0* (London: 2012).

419 Wees, W. C. *Recycled Images* (New York: Anthology Film Archives, 1993) pp. 52-53.

420 Fer, B. *Abstract Art* (New Haven: Yale University Press, 1997) p. 149.

421 Moradi, I. "Introduction" *Glitch: Designing Imperfection* ed. Iman Moradi, Ant Scott, Joe Gilmore and Christopher Murphy (New York: Mark Batty, 2009) pp. 8-9.

422 Acha, J. *Arte y sociedad*; Adolfo Sánchez Vásquez, *Las ideas estéticas de Marx* (Siglo XXI, 2005); and Mijail Mitrovic, "Robinsonadas: Adolfo Sánchez Vásquez, Juan Acha y el problema del arte como categoría histórica," *Antagonismos*, no. 3 (2021).

423 Perniola, M. "El arte como categoría histórica," *Hueso Húmero*, no. 11 (October–December 1981).

424 Attali, J. *Noise: The Political Economy of Music* (Minneapolis: University of Minnesota Press, 1985) p. 6.

425 Wees, W.C. *Light Moving in Time: Studies in the Visual Aesthetics of Avant-Garde Film* (Berkeley: University of California Press, 1992) pp. 137-146.

426 Bartra, R. "Sobre la articulación de modos de producción en América Latina" *Modos de producción en América Latina* (Delva Editores, 1976).

427 Betancourt, M. "Critical Glitches and Glitch Art" *Hz*, no. 19 (July, 2014) np.

428 Adorno, T. *Aesthetic Theory* (Minneapolis: University of Minnesota Press, 1998) pp. 246-248.

429 Foucault, M. *The Birth of the Clinic* (New York: Routledge, 1976) p. xiii.

430 Dedić, N. "Avant-Garde Transformation of Artistic Labor: The Productivist View of Boris Arvatov" *AM Journal of Art and Media* no. 28 (2022) pp. 133-134.

431 Youngblood, G. "A Medium Matures: Video and the Cinematic Enterprise" *Ars Electronica: Facing the Future* ed. Timothy Druckrey (New Haven: The MIT Press, 1999) pp. 45-46.

432 Lyotard, J. *The Postmodern Condition: A Report on Knowledge* (Minneapolis: University of Minnesota Press, 1993) p. 61.

433 Scott, F. "Networks and Apparatuses, circa 1971: Or, Hippies Meet Computers" *Hippie Modernism: The Struggle for Utopia* ed. Andrew Blauvelt (Minneapolis: Walker Art Center, 2015) pp. 103-105.

434 Youngblood, G. *Expanded Cinema* (New York: Dutton, 1970) pp. 185-193.

435 Carroll, N. "The Essence of Cinema" *Philosophical Studies* vol. 89, no. 2/3 (March, 1988) pp. 324-325.

436 Betancourt, M. *The Critique of Digital Capitalism* (Brooklyn: Punctum Books, 2016) pp. 58-60.

437 Betancourt, M. *The Critique of Digital Capitalism* (Brooklyn: Punctum Books, 2016) pp. 56-60.

438 Betancourt, M. *Glitch Art in Theory and Practice: Critical Failures and Post-Digital Aesthetics* (New York: Routledge, 2016) pp. 17-18.

439 de Haas, P. *Cinema Absolu: Avant-Garde 1920-1930* (Valreas: Mettray editions, 2018); see also, Daniels, D. and Naumann, S. *See This Sound: Audiovisuology, a reader* (Köln: Walter König, 2015).

440 Wright, W.H. *The Future of Painting* (New York: B. W. Huebsch, Inc., 1923) pp. 47-50.

441 Lawder, S. *The Cubist Cinema* (New York: Anthology Film Archives, 1980).

442 Moritz, W. "Visual Music and Film-as-an-Art Before 1950" *On the Edge of America: California Modernist Art, 1900-1950*, Paul J. Karlstrom, ed. (Berkeley: University of California Press, 1996) p. 224.

443 Hegel, G.F.W. *The Phenomenology of Mind* trans. J. B. Baillie (New York: MacMillan, 1910) p. 340.

444 Goodman, C. *Digital Visions: Computers and Art* (New York: Abrams, 1987) pp. 156-158.

445 Betancourt, M. *The Critique of Digital Capitalism* (Brooklyn: Punctum Books, 2016) pp. 56-60.

446 Brougher, K. *Visual Music: Art and Film Since 1900* (New York: Thames and Hudson, 2005).

447 Betancourt, M. *The Critique of Digital Capitalism* (Brooklyn: Punctum Books, 2016) pp. 61-74.

448 Betancourt, M. *Art, AI and Culture* (Savannah: I'm Press'd, 2022).

449 Lurie, P. "The Rush to Judgment: Binary Thinking in a Digital Age" CTheory, posted March 30, 2004; DOI: https://journals.uvic.ca/index.php/ctheory/article/view/14562/5408

450 Betancourt, M. "Critical Glitches and Glitch Art" *Hz*, no. 19 (July, 2014) np.

451 Adorno, T. *Aesthetic Theory* (Minneapolis: University of Minnesota Press, 1998) pp. 246-248.

452 Attali, J. *Noise: The Political Economy of Music* (Minneapolis: University of Minnesota Press, 1985) p. 6.

453 Cloninger, C. "GltchLnguistx: The Machine in the Ghosts / Static Trapped in the Mouths" *Glitch reader(ror)* ed. Nick Briz, Evan Meaney, Rosa Menkman, William Robertson, Jon Satrom, Jessica Westbrook (Unsorted Books: 2011) p. 33.

454 Betancourt, M. *The Critique of Digital Capitalism* (Brooklyn: Punctum, 2016) pp. 61-74.

455 Dosi, G. "Technological paradigms and technological trajectories: a suggested interpretation of the determinants and directions of technical change" *Research Policy* vol. 11 no. 3 (1982) pp. 151-153.

456 O'Meara, J. and Murphy, C. "Aberrant AI creations: co-creating surrealist body horror using the DALL-E Mini text–to–image generator" *Convergence: The International Journal of Research into New Media Technologies* vol. 0 no. 0 (2023) pp. 1–27; DOI: https://doi.org/10.1177/13548565231185865

457 Kristeva, J. *Powers of Horror: An Essay on Abjection* (New York: Columbia University Press, 1982).

458 Breton, A. *Manifestos of Surrealism* (The University of Michigan Press, Ann Arbor, 1972).

459 Temkin, D. "Glitch && Human-Computer Interaction" *Non-Object Oriented Art*, Vol. 1, no. 1, January 2014; DOI: http://nooart.org/post/73353953758/temkin-glitchhumancomputerinteraction

460 Popper, F. *Art of the Electronic Age.* (New York, Abrams: 1993).

461 Hochberg, J. and Brooks, V. "Movies in the Mind's Eye" *Post Theory* ed. David Bordwell and Noel Carroll (Madison: University of Wisconsin Press, 1996) pp. 368-369.

462 Betancourt, M. "Motion Perception in Movies and Paintings: Towards a New Kinetic Art" *CTheory* (2002); DOI: https://www.ctheory.net/articles.aspx?id=349

463 Caws, M. *The Surrealist Painters and Poets: An Anthology* (Cambridge: The MIT Press: 2001).

464 Dalí, S. *Oui* (Boston: Exact Change, 1998) p. 179.

465 Breton, A. *Manifestos of Surrealism* (The University of Michigan Press, Ann Arbor, 1972).

466 These five categories of technical failure were originally included as the "Glossary" in *Glitch Art in Theory and Practice: Critical Failures and Post-Digital Aesthetics* (Routledge, 2016) pp. 133-136; DOI: https://doi.org/10.4324/9781315414812

INDEX

www.ingramcontent.com/pod-product-compliance
Lightning Source LLC
Chambersburg PA
CBHW052359030726
47599CB00014B/1138